The American Gardener's World of Bulbs

The American Gardener's World of Bulbs

BULBS FOR FORMAL AND INFORMAL GARDENS

JUDY GLATTSTEIN

With a Foreword by Rob Proctor

LITTLE, BROWN AND COMPANY

Boston New York Toronto London

FIRST EDITION

Line drawings by Patricia M. Kay. Unless otherwise indicated, all photographs are by Judy Glattstein.

LIBRARY OF CONGRESS CATALOGING-IN-PUBLICATION DATA
Glattstein, Judy.
The American gardener's world of bulbs : bulbs for formal and informal gardens / by Judy Glattstein. — 1st ed.
p. cm.
Includes index.
ISBN 0-316-31593-1
1. Bulbs—United States. 2. Bulbs—Canada. I. Title.
II. Title: World of bulbs.
SB425.G58 1994
635.9′44′097—dc20 93-38714

10 9 8 7 6 5 4 3 2 1

NIL

Designed by Barbara Werden

Published simultaneously in Canada by Little, Brown & Company (Canada) Limited

PRINTED IN THE UNITED STATES OF AMERICA

Contents

Foreword *Rob Proctor* vi

Introduction viii

Interlude: Definitions xiii

1 First Spring 3

2 Second Spring 22

3 Daffodils, Hyacinths, and Tulips: The Big Three of Spring 35

4 Offbeat Bulbs: The Neglected Natives 56

5 Hardy Summer Bulbs 74

6 Tender Bulbs for Summer Color 90

7 Unfamiliar Tender Bulbs for the Summer Garden 110

8 Bulbs for Autumn Interest 128

Appendix 1: Planting, Cultivation, and Propagation Techniques 148

Appendix 2: Sources 154

Index 157

Foreword

AUTUMN is a hectic time for bulb fanciers. I burrow into the cooling soil with the burning fever of anticipation. My patio is littered with netted bags, labels, and hastily sketched plans of where groups of bulbs should be planted. Hardened from a summer in the garden, my muscles have nevertheless begun to ache from the intensity of the work. I glance at the cardboard boxes of bulbs yet to be planted and wonder if I've overestimated my stamina and, indeed, the size of my garden. I fret over the forecast of snow.

In the midst of my bulb planting arrives the manuscript for the book. I glare at it on the kitchen counter for a few days. I finally move it to my office, where I pretend not to notice it for a few more days. My enthusiasm for bulbs has all but faded; the last thing I want to think about this evening is more damn bulbs.

I turn the pages, and suddenly spring arrives. I can visualize the first snowdrops and aconites, and remember the scent of grape hyacinths. I begin to wonder where I can get my hands on bulbs of *Fritillaria michailovskyi*. I regret that I forgot to transplant my *Brimeura* from my old garden when I moved, and I make a note to order some.

By the time I get to the daffodils, I forget that my arm aches. Not only did I not order enough bulbs, but I am missing some wonderful combinations. I scribble notes to myself and wish I'd had this book a few months earlier. I read on, and smugly realize I'll be ahead of the game next spring, as I plant both tender and hardy summer-blooming bulbs. I'll place my order early for fall colchicum, cyclamen, and a host of autumn-flowering crocus I can barely wait to try.

Gardening books written by real gardeners are invaluable. This is such a book. Judy Glattstein takes us by the hand and guides us through the seasons, stopping occasionally to tell a choice historical anecdote or offer a critical piece of advice. The words ring true, based on experience that can only be gained on one's hands and knees in the garden.

It is unfortunate that too many of us pay attention only to spring-flowering bulbs. Glorious as they are — tulips, daffodils, and so forth — they are truly just the beginning. For some gardeners in the South and West, they're not even practical. Fortunately, Judy travels widely and has a firm understanding of regional gardening outside her own lovely garden. The enormous diversity of South African and Central and South American bulbs is a boon to gardeners in warm and mild climates.Those of us in the temperate part of the nation may also enjoy gorgeous Peruvian daffodils, harlequin flowers, and pineapple lilies as "annuals." And our beautiful native woodlanders — jack-in-the-pulpit, Dutchman's breeches, and trout lilies — vital for shade gardeners, get a thorough treatment.

Judy has a keen eye not only for detail and description but for classic plant combinations for the garden. She is adventurous as well, seeking out the unusual and rare. It is surprising when a book can satisfy the "what-where-when" questions of novice gardeners and tantalize the old hands as well. I hope beginners will be able to glean the essential information they need initially, and then "grow up" with the help of this book. The appendix on planting, cultivation, and propagation may become one of the most-thumbed sections. I am delighted that this volume also sorts out some taxonomic problems in its course, making sense out of some recent name changes.

Equally valuable is information about the country of origin and native habitat of many species, always an aid in simulating conditions in the garden where a plant will have the best chance to thrive. I also appreciate frank appraisals of the odds on growing a rare or difficult bulb, although I am not easily dissuaded from trying something even if the odds may be against me. I'll be back in the garden tomorrow morning, again planting with the determination of a wild creature preparing for winter. My mission, however, is not one of survival, but of beauty and discovery. In *The American Gardener's World of Bulbs* I have a trustworthy manual to help guide me.

ROB PROCTOR
1 November 1993
Denver, Colorado

Introduction

EACH AUTUMN, blazoned across every nursery and garden center in the United States and Canada, the banners announcing "Holland Bulbs Are Here" are as certain a sign of the season as the first robin is of spring. These dormant lumpy brown objects, so modest themselves yet enticing as displayed in bins and boxes, become every gardener's focus for this season, tokens of our expectation of winter's passage and spring's return. The slogan is deceptive, in that only a scattering (if any) ever originated in Holland, and not all of them are technically bulbs. Commonly we associate the term "bulb" with Dutch imports, plants that originally grew in Europe, Asia, the Middle East. Native North American plants have also developed the same method of getting through hard times: *Sanguinaria canadensis,* bloodroot; *Trillium* spp.; *Arisaema triphyllum,* jack-in-the-pulpit; *Dicentra cucullaria,* Dutchman's breeches. These "bulbous plants" may be true bulbs, corms, or tubers (see Interlude: Definitions, in the following pages). Recently the term "geophyte" has been used to refer collectively to herbaceous perennials with fleshy underground structures whose primary function is to store food and moisture. I find this noun less cumbersome than "bulbous plant," and will use it throughout this book.

In spring the first snowdrops pierce the icy soil with dainty white flowers wrapped in protective membranes. They are more charming in combination with the first flowers on hellebores than isolated in lonely splendor. In summer, lilies, no matter how regal, are finer when woven through a tapestry of other flowers. It is the harmonious use of plants in combination that creates a garden rather than a mere collection. The world of geophytes can provide the gardener with simple or lavish, subtle or gaudy flowers for the sunny or shady garden in spring, summer, autumn.

Planting time is here; the bulbs have arrived from Holland. (ILLUSTRATION COURTESY OF THE NETHERLANDS FLOWER BULB INFORMATION CENTER)

The rosy flowers of Persian violets, *Cyclamen coum,* peek jauntily through a fluffy covering of snow.

Barely stretching through the icy crust, frost-proof golden flowers of winter aconite, *Eranthis hiemalis,* reward the discerning gardener.

Gardeners delight in perennial pleasures, herbaceous plants that return year after year and enchant us with their charms. We tend to reserve the term "perennial" for herbaceous plants with fibrous roots, forgetting that "geophytes" are obviously of perennial inclination. They store food reserves in anticipation of the next season's growth and can better cope with the rigors of soillessness, storage, and shipment than perennials with fibrous roots, unsuited to spending time out of the earth. Geophytes, whether adapted to winter dormancy (hibernation) or summer dormancy (aestivation), survived the rigors of a long, slow ocean voyage in the days of sailing ships, when herbaceous plants languished while awaiting the 1836 invention of the Wardian case, a nearly airtight container with glass sides and top used for transporting growing plants. Thus as gardeners we think nothing of the routine availability of tulips from the steppes of central Asia, lilies from China and Japan, crocus and daffodils from Europe, gladiolus from South Africa, dahlias from Mexico, amaryllis from South America. Scrutiny of the history of plant introduction provides a fascinating mirror to historical voyages of discovery. The introduction of geophytes into cultivation was a byproduct of exploration motivated by economic interests. When the sun never set on the British empire, plants from these far-flung regions were brought back to England along with silks and spices. Ensuing colonization, especially by the British and Dutch, provided the impetus for the introduction of new plants. Small wonder that the Italians named so many plants *indicus,* the French *canadensis,* the Dutch *japonicus,* and the British *virginianus* — these particular regions of the world were their commercial territories, their domains.

Gardeners today select the geophytes they cultivate based on leaf and flower, their appearance during the growing season. Our criteria depend on aesthetics — the size, color, and shape of the flowers, how freely they are produced, the season in which they appear, how easy they are to grow. This is the opposite of the earliest human interest, which basically focused on the underground portion of the plant and whether it was edible. Nomadic societies of hunters and food gatherers were not concerned with geophytes for aesthetic reasons but as a source of food. When agrarian societies arose, the same period that saw the selection and development of grains — wheat, barley, and rice — also introduced to cultivation various onions and onion relatives: leeks, scallions, chives, garlic. Potatoes from the Andes could thrive where other crops could not, and the name became a generic term for any underground tuber or root. Small wonder that common names European explorers gave to North American geophytes included Eskimo potato (*Fritillaria camschatcensis*) and Indian potato (*Apios americana*), evidence of their use as a foodstuff by the indigenous people. When food supplies became more secure, when societies developed to the point where there was leisure, then growing plants just for their looks became a possibility.

And what diversity of beautiful flowers and foliage is available for gardens across the country. There are geophytes that flower in the cold climates of Maine and Minnesota, others suited to balmy Maryland and Georgia, others for the moist subtropical conditions in Florida, and still others for the warm, dry climate of California. Unfortunately, most gardeners are only familiar with daffodils, tulips, and crocus, so that is what they grow, regardless of their location. For many gardeners ignorance of the wide array of geophytes limits their options to a scant familiar few. There are geophytes for sun and shade, for spring, summer, or autumn interest. And when they become an element in the garden, are integrated with other, fibrous-rooted perennials, annuals, and shrubs, geophytes become a source of magic.

Some cold-hardy geophytes are adaptable enough to flower wherever they are planted across the country. *Crocus vernus* (a parent of the Dutch hybrid crocus) can be observed working its way north with the spring, as it flowers in late February in San Francisco and Baton Rouge; early March in Athens, Georgia, and Hope, Arkansas; late March around Fayetteville, Arkansas, and Washington, D.C.; late

With lambent purity, white bells of the common snowdrop, *Galanthus nivalis,* are among the first flowers to greet the new year.

You need not turn your back on winter. With a little planning, when snow comes, the snowdrops are not far behind.

March to early April in East Lansing, Michigan, and Ithaca, New York; and late April in Ottawa and Nova Scotia. Not all geophytes, not even all crocus, are as adaptable. *Crocus flavus* and *C. sieberi,* for example, simply will not grow in warm-winter climates. Conversely, geophytes from mild climates, such as *Ixia,* from southern Africa, are excellent for southern California and would not be suitable in Chicago, Denver, or Canada. There are ways to maneuver around these restrictions, however. Tender geophytes can be cosseted in cold climates and lifted and stored in protected quarters over the winter. Cold-climate bulbs may be handled as annuals and precooled before planting to delude them into the belief that winter has occurred.

In our own gardens, first observation of a hitherto unknown, never-before-grown plant captures our imagination. Each of us becomes an explorer, even if our sources are nurseries and catalogs rather than expeditions into remote regions. My investigations into the wonderful diversity of geophytes is founded on the paths of those who went before me. My research was made easier by them, and I must especially thank those librarians whose repositories hold this information. Their preservation of historical volumes and contemporary texts provided the chain of continuity that is the foundation for this modest endeavor. My gratitude to Bernadette Callery of the New York Botanical Garden, who let me plug in, turn on, and spend day after day drifting through the stacks making serendipitous discoveries and transcribing them to diskette; Marie Long of the same institution, who unfailingly provided requested journals, bulletins, vertical files; Mr. C. W. J. Lut of the Research Institution Rijksherbarium/Hortus Botanicus of the Rijksuniversiteit Leiden, for permitting me access to the institution's rare books collection; Marijn van Hoorn of the bibliotheek Teylers Museum, in Haarlem, where I spent a sunny morning traveling in time as I examined Bessler's *Hortus Eystettenis,* with faded annotations added by the quill pen of a previous researcher ages ago; and Dr. Johan van Scheepern, taxonomist at the Royal Dutch Bulbgrowers Association, in Hillegom, for his help with current nomenclature and access to old catalogs. These Dutch appointments were arranged with the kind assistance of Carla Teune, curator of the Leiden Botanic Garden, who, additionally, took me to nurseries and gardens and displayed extraordinary patience with my ofttimes intemperate enthusiasm. Her thorough knowledge of the bulb trade corrected errors on my part. Any that remain are certainly my own. B. F. Bruinsma was the most patient and pleasant of chauffeurs. His assistance in obtaining information about tulip consumption during World War II authenticated stories that would otherwise be classified as hearsay. Staff at The Netherlands Flowerbulb Research Institute were most helpful, both at their headquarters in Hillegom, and in their Brooklyn, New York, office, where Sally Ferguson provided her able assistance. The staff of my local library in Wilton, Connecticut, whose good-tempered patience with absurd-sounding questions that really had some connection with this book made many days seem brighter. David Ostergren, Peg Rogers, and Beth Mason of the Wilton Answers desk always knew where to find the answer.

When we lived in Holland in 1973 my Dutch friends could not understand my American pronunciation of Latin names, nor I theirs. But when we wrote them out, all was clear, for Linnaean classification provides us with uniform names for plants and animals. However, taxonomy is in constant flux, as new discoveries, a better understanding of familial relationships, and examination of historical sources rearranges familiar nomenclature. Particular thanks are due Dr. Peter Goldblatt of the Missouri Botanic Garden, in St. Louis, whose knowledge of the taxonomy of South African iridaceous geophytes was most helpful.

Above all, special thanks go to my husband, Paul. His interest in gardening is minimal, but his support of me and of this project was great. This book could not have been written without his ability to retrieve lost files and unscramble computer glitches created by my ignorance.

It is early March as I write this. The first snowdrops, Persian violets, winter aconites, the first crocus are all in bloom. The dance begins anew.

Interlude

DEFINITIONS

Arrayed on a 1-inch grid, this assortment of bulbs, corms, and tubers (anemones, daffodil, tulips, crocus, and hyacinths) is only a fraction of the diversity available.

IF YOU are botanically knowledgeable, or easily intimidated by technical matters, skip over the rest of this section. If, on the other hand, you are curious as to just what makes a bulb a bulb, rather than a corm or tuber, or where taxonomists are cataloging various bulbous plants at the moment, read on.

A bulb, corm, or tuber is a plant's means of getting through hard times. This can be winter cold or summer heat and drought. The geophyte's neat and tidy underground storage of food reserves indicates its perennial nature, for an annual would not survive to the next year. Technically speaking, not all of what we call "bulbs" are bulbs. More correctly called bulbous or bulb-like plants, these plant packages include true BULBS, TUBERS, and CORMS. And the distinctions among them do make some difference to the gardener.

The most familiar of true BULBS is, unquestionably, the onion. Placed along with such other kitchen lilies as shallots, garlic, leeks, and chives in the genus *Allium*, there are ornamental species for the garden as well. Envision an onion. It has a papery golden-brown, white, or reddish skin, which is called a TUNIC. Often at the bottom of the bulb are a few dried remnants of the roots. These arise from a BASAL PLATE. When an onion is cut apart (perhaps to get a slice for your hamburger), there is a definite internal structure of concentric rings. These modified leaves are called SCALES, and they store the food reserves. If you leave the onion in the vegetable drawer too long it will begin to sprout. The green leaves arise from the center of the bulb. So true bulbs have a distinct internal structure made up of scales, a vertical orientation, a basal plate, and sometimes (but not always) a tunic. Small, nonflowering offsets form underground from lateral buds at the base of the bulb. This is common in such familiar bulbs as daffodils, hyacinths, and tulips. Eventually they mature and reach flowering size. A few bulbs reproduce by means of BULBILS, which are small bulb-like structures borne on the stem in the leaf axil. Perhaps the most familiar example of this is the black-spotted, orange-flowered *Lilium lancifolium,* tiger lily. This naturalized bulb is found along roadsides from New England to South Dakota, and south to Virginia. It is sterile, produces no seed, and reproduces by means of these aerial bulbils. Other lilies often produce BULBLETS on the underground portion of the stem. Unlike allium, lilies do not have a tunic. Fritillaria also lack a tunic. Bulbs without a tunic can dry out more quickly than those that have such a protective covering, and should be planted promptly.

In addition to onions, such familiar garden flowers as snowdrops and lilies are true bulbs. *Amaryllis belladonna* has the simplest type of bulb, with the flower bud appearing from the side between old scales, rather than between the current year's youngest leaves, as in *Narcissus.* It is generally a good idea to plant bulbs right-side up, but the plants are better at this than some novice gardeners. A friend once told me how he had planted 50 tulips, being careful to see that the pointy end where the roots come out was oriented down. Well, that meant that the basal plate was uppermost. The following spring the shoots went up, the roots grew down, and his tulips flowered, although a couple of weeks later than I would expect of that particular variety. Over time, disoriented bulbs will right themselves.

CORMS are formed from modified stem tissue and the food-storage portion consists of solid, undifferentiated tissue. The corm is replaced every year, and often the old remnant clings to the base of the new one, as is commonly seen in gladiolus. There is a tunic, which can be of two types: papery, with a ringed appearance, called ANNULATE, or fibrous, with a mesh-like structure, called RETICULATE. Corms have a basal plate from which the roots emerge. These roots are contractile; they pull the new corm down and thus prevent their eventual surfacing. There is a vertical orientation, and shoots arise either clustered at the top, as in crocus, or from the top or side, as in montbretia. Small offsets, or cormels, are formed from lateral buds at the base of the current year's corm. In addition to gladiolus, crocus are a familiar and popular corm.

TUBERS usually originate from modified stem tissue, and, like corms, the food-storage portion consists of solid, undifferentiated tissue. Unlike corms, tubers have no basal plate. There are different types of tubers arising from modified stem tissue. *Anemone blanda,* windflower, is an example of a RHIZOME TUBER, and all species of *Cyclamen* are TUBER-CORMS. Some tubers are derived from root tissue. *Dahlia* is one example, and its underground storage structure is called a ROOT TUBER. Tubers have a very different appearance from bulbs. There is a gradation between the types, but in general these bulbous plants have a relatively unspecialized, simple structure. Rhizome tubers produce shoots from the upper surface and roots from the lower surface, while tuber-corms are disc shaped, producing shoots on the upper surface and root from either the upper or lower surface. Unlike corms, these are perennial structures and do not produce offsets, only increasing in size as they age. (There is a marvelous apocryphal story about an Englishman who bought a house because of the size of the cyclamen tubers in the garden.)

Think of the potato, a root tuber. There are growing points scattered over the surface. A familiar garden flower with tuberous roots that are also edible like the potato is the dahlia, although reportedly they have a bitter taste.

Tubers can dry out more quickly than bulbs, especially tunicate bulbs, which are somewhat protected by their protective membrane. Tubers like the dahlia that are lifted for winter storage need to be packed in some material to prevent their desiccation. Small tubers such as *Anemone blanda,* windflower, and *Eranthis hiemalis,* winter aconite, should be given planting priority over small tunicate bulbs such as *Galanthus nivalis,* snowdrops.

It is somewhat tiresome to say "bulb, corm, and tuber" or "bulbous plant." More important, it is incorrect to refer to all these lumpy underground structures as bulbs.

The term "geophyte" has recently begun to come into use as a useful descriptive term, much as annual, tree, or shrub. Unfamiliar, it may seem pretentious. With time, its usefulness will be even more apparent.

Many different plant families have found these underground reserves of food to be a useful strategy for survival. Cyclamen are in the family *Primulaceae,* dahlia in *Compositae,* arisaema in *Araceae,* while anemones and winter aconites are placed in the *Ranunculaceae.* However, three families in particular contain the majority of the world's geophytes and have been named for their outstanding genera. They are *Iridaceae,* of which *Iris, Crocus,* and *Gladiolus* are members; *Amaryllidaceae,* which contains *Amaryllis, Narcissus, Hippeastrum,* and *Galanthus* among others; and *Liliaceae.* Of the three families, *Liliaceae, Iridaceae,* and *Amaryllidaceae,* the latter two are the most distinct. *Amaryllidaceae* has been somewhat cleaned up since George Bentham and Joseph Dalton Hooker formulated it in 1883. Certain groups — *Hypoxidaceae* (*Hypoxis, Rhodohypoxis*), *Agavaceae* (*Agave, Polianthes*), and *Alstroemeriaceae* — have been detached from it into separate families. *Allium* is a problem in that it has six stamens and a superior ovary, qualifying the genus for inclusion in *Liliaceae,* which is where Bentham and Hooker placed it. However, the flowers are carried in umbels, which is the characteristic inflorescence for *Amaryllidaceae,* and some authors have incorporated it into this family. One authority, J. G. Agardh, took the view that *Allium* should be placed in a separate family, the *Alliaceae,* and this opinion has currently found favor.

Historically, *Liliaceae,* or the lily family, contained 240 genera with approximately 3,600 species found around the world, most abundantly in temperate and subtropical areas. Bulbs are common, with corms and tubers occurring less often. The leaves arise from the base or attached to the stem, usually alternate, sometimes whorled, rarely opposite. The classic genus is *Lilium,* and the family also includes *Colchicum, Erythronium, Fritillaria, Hyacinthus, Muscari, Scilla, Trillium,* and *Tulipa.*

In a September 1989 article in *The Plantsman,* noted geophyte expert Brian Mathew discussed taxonomic revisions suggested for this plant family. The herbarium at Kew Gardens in London has, based in large part on the work of the Danish botanist Rolf Dahlgren — author, with H. Trevor Clifford, of *The Monocotyledons* (1982), and, with H. Trevor Clifford and P. F. Yeo, of *The Families of the Monocotyledons* (1985) — recognized many "new" families. Not that the majority of these plant families are newly established. Rather, they have been resurrected based on current research. The new system would divide *Liliaceae* into over 20 smaller and more uniform family units, not all of which contain genera with bulbous underground portions.

In its revised, narrowed sense the modified *Liliaceae* now consists of a few horticulturally very important genera including *Lilium, Calochortus, Cardocrinum, Erythronium, Fritillaria, Nomocharis,* and *Tulipa.* They are bulbous plants, mostly with large showy flowers, whose leaves are carried on the flower stems. Where they appear to be basal, as in some dwarf *Tulipa* species and *Erythronium,* they are in fact carried on the stem below ground level. The fruits are dry capsules. Distribution is almost entirely within the northern hemisphere, and its members are widespread on all the continents.

Hyacinthaceae is one of the larger, horticulturally more important groups for gardeners in temperate climates, as it contains the genera *Hyacinthus, Camassia, Chionodoxa, Galtonia, Hyacinthella, Lachenalia, Muscari, Ornithogallum, Puschkinia, Scilla,* and *Veltheimia.* They are bulbous plants with true basal leaves and leafless flower stems, usually with a raceme of smallish flowers. The fruits are usually dry capsules. Their distribution is very wide, but predominantly in the temperate regions of the Old World.

Alliaceae contains the genera *Allium, Agapanthus, Brodiaea, Ipheion, Nothoscordum,* and *Tulbaghia.* The flowers are borne in umbels; the fruiting stage consists of dry capsules. The family has a very wide distribution in the Americas and in the Old World.

Colchicaceae includes the genera *Colchicum, Bulbocodium, Gloriosa,* and *Merendera,* all with similar rootstocks, all containing poisonous alkaloids (colchicine and related compounds). The underground part consists of a distinctive corm that produces a growing point from the lowermost extremity each year. The fruits usually consist of dry capsules.

Trilliaceae contains the genera *Trillium, Paris,* and *Scoliopus.* These are rhizomatous herbs typically found in temperate-zone woodland habitats of the northern hemisphere. The leaves are carried on the stem, usually in a whorl of three or more. Though they have the typical parallel veins of monocotyledons, they often have distinct secondary veins also. The flowers are solitary, borne at the apex of the stem, and are followed by berries or fleshy capsules.

Convallariaceae includes the genera *Convallaria, Aspidistra, Clintonia, Disporum, Liriope, Maianthemum (Smilacina), Medeola, Ophiopogon, Polygonatum, Reineckia, Streptopus, Tricyrtus,* and *Uvularia,* which are predominantly woodland dwellers with branching rhizomes and leafy stems. The fruits are usually colored berries. They are widely distributed, but mainly in northern temperate zones.

Hemerocallidaceae contains but a single genus, *Hemerocallis,* as does *Hostaceae,* which contains the genus *Hosta.*

The other two plant families prominent for the number of geophytes they contain are also monocots, germinating with a single-seed leaf and with leaves having parallel veination. They are *Amaryllidaceae,* the amaryllis family, and *Iridaceae,* the iris family. *Amaryllidaceae* contains approximately 90 genera with about 1,200 species distributed in South America, South Africa, and the Mediterranean region. These are tunicate bulbs or corms, with rhizomes occurring rarely. Leaves are generally few, basal, and rarely on the scape. They differ from the old *Liliaceae* in having umbellate inflorescence (where all the pedicels are the same length and arise from the same point, like a dandelion) with a spathaceous bract (a single leaf-like structure that encloses the immature flower buds), and differ from *Iridaceae* in having six stamens. The model genus is *Amaryllis,* and the family also includes not only *Galanthus, Hippeastrum,* and *Narcissus* but *Allium, Clivia, Leucojum, Lycoris,* and *Nerine.*

Iridaceae contains about 60 genera with approximately 800 or so species. The storage portion can be bulbous, cormous, or rhizomatous. The leaves are mostly basal, usually double-ranked, and linear to sword-like. The flowers can be solitary, in clusters, or in racemes or panicles. They have six perianth segments (petals), which can be separate or united at the base into a long or short tube. There are three stamens. In addition to *Crocus, Gladiolus,* and *Iris,* genera *Acidanthera, Crocosmia,* and *Freesia* are also placed in this family.

The American Gardener's World of Bulbs

1

First Spring

Galanthus, Leucojum, Eranthis, Cyclamen, Crocus, Scilla, Chionodoxa

With elegant flowers, *Galanthus* 'Magnet' is one of the less-common snowdrops worth adding to your garden.

IN LATE winter the trees of the deciduous woodland are bare of leaves, yet the forest is not a barren place. Grays and browns of tree bark and twigs command attention against the simplified landscape. Since autumn a few evergreen herbaceous perennials such as the bear's foot hellebore, *Helleborus foetidus;* Christmas rose, *H. niger;* Christmas fern, *Polystichum achrostichoides;* and familiar ground covers like myrtle, *Vinca minor,* have been standing assurance amid the subdued tans and browns of last year's fallen leaves. The days are still brief, the ground frozen, yet there is promise of the seasonal turn, the endless dance of the planet around the sun that warms and leads to growth. These are the opening moments of the first spring. It is not tied to an arbitrary calendar date but is instead a variable, dependent on the depth and duration of winter's cold, modified by any lasting snow cover that ameliorated the worst of conditions.

Even in winter the interlaced bare branches of the canopy and understory trees provide a modicum of shelter from frost. They slow radiant heat loss to the sky on still, clear, cold nights. The yearly leaf drop in autumn provides a protective mulch, and gradually decays into humus, returning organic matter to the soil. The critical factor for growth and bloom of woodland plants is the yearly cycle from bare branch to leafy cover. The plants' requirement for sunlight as an energy source, and increasing shade reducing its late-spring/summer availability in the forest, lead to earliest growth in the herbaceous plants.

Many geophytes are ideally adapted to these conditions, generally beginning their growth before the woody plants leaf out. Often they complete their cycle and go dormant as maximum shade develops. Their very nature as geophytes permits the use of stored, reserve nutrients before the soil is warmed. The first blooms of the new year will come from some of the geophytes, small plants with frost-proof constitutions.

My gardens were and are in southern Connecticut, first in Norwalk, and then in Wilton. The two sites are about ten miles and half a hardiness zone apart. Norwalk, on Long Island Sound, is coastal while Wilton is just those few critical miles inland and behind a ridge that halts some of the moderating effects found near a large body of water. The Norwalk garden consistently had species crocus such as *Crocus laevigatus fontenayi* and *C. sieberi* 'Hubert Edelstein' flowering in January. By late February my colder Wilton garden usually has snowdrops, *Galanthus nivalis,* snowflakes, *Leucojum vernum;* Persian violets, *Cyclamen coum;* and winter aconites, *Eranthis hiemalis,* in bloom. My friend Edith Eddleman, a garden designer and writer in North Carolina, has had bulbs in bloom for six weeks by this time, and C. Coleston Burrell, garden designer, writer, and photographer in Minnesota, is still deep in snow. But for each of us, rather than an arbitrary marking of the vernal equinox in March and despite the varied dates, these first flowers signal spring's arrival.

Snowdrops and Snowflakes

To many gardeners the most familiar of the small geophytes of spring is the snowdrop, generally the common snowdrop, *Galanthus nivalis.* As it emerges in the late winter, the flower bud is sheathed between a pair of narrow grayish-green leaves wrapped in a membrane that helps in pushing through the frozen soil. The solitary white flower is pendant on a leafless stem 5 inches tall, with three large, oval, outer segments flared outward, and three small inner petals forming a notched tube, which has a green marking near the opening. As it has been cultivated for so many centuries, the common snowdrop grows wild outside its origins in Europe from Spain easterly to Russia. It was the Romans who brought it to Britain, where it is naturalized.

The English garden writer Edward Augustus Bowles (1865–1954) wrote early in this century, "The French name of Perce-Neige may seem rather fanciful, but a few years ago a very late fall of snow persisted long enough for the sprouting snowdrops to melt a passage through the crust. . . . The charming sight of snowdrop flowers rising above the dingy surface of the melting snow and appearing whiter than the snow itself in the low rays of the afternoon sun justified the pretty French name." This passage serves to emphasize the difference between one garden and another, for in my Connecticut location the juxtaposition of snowdrops and snow is a familiar sight.

In a mild winter *Galanthus nivalis* will open its flowers in late February or early March to make one of the first displays of spring. It often blooms in tandem with the yellow buttercup-like blooms of winter aconite, *Eranthis hiemalis.* Since bees will fly on mild days and snowdrops are the only game in town this early in the year, the insects break a long winter fast with this welcome nectar. On a sunny day in March their attentions provide a hum of activity. Obligingly, snowdrops remain in bloom for several weeks, loitering in the chilly weather of first spring. I've seen their stems frozen solid, so that they snap when picked. The stalk leans over toward the ground, then reerects itself when conditions moderate. After several repetitions of this cycle they acquire a slight list, but the flowers remain jaunty throughout.

The snowdrop's bulb is small, covered with a brown skin. The price is also small, which helps encourage mass planting. As with other bulbs, the soil should be loosened first, and some fertilizer with a good proportion of phosphorus and potash added. These two nutrients are the second and third numbers in the analysis on a fertilizer bag. Do not overfeed. A tablespoon of fertilizer for a half-dozen bulbs is adequate. Mix well with the soil at the bottom of the planting hole, and add some unamended soil. Then place the bulbs, making sure they are approximately twice as deep as they are big; that is, place a 1-inch bulb 2 inches below the soil surface. Plant more deeply in sandy soils, more shallowly in clay soils. Snowdrops dislike drying out and should be one of the first bulbs to be planted in autumn. As bulbs make root growth at this time, be sure to irrigate if natural rainfall is lacking.

Bonemeal is an old standby for bulbs. Slow acting, its nutrients are not available until spring; meanwhile it will attract every skunk in the neighborhood searching for bones, who will dig up (but not eat) the bulbs. As with daffodils and some other *Amaryllidaceae,* the sticky juice in the bulb is full of needle-shaped crystals of silica, called raphides, which render the bulbs unpalatable.

Many English gardening books recommend planting snowdrops "in the green." This means moving them in the spring after flowering, but while the leaves are still on the bulb. While some British vendors supply bulbs in spring as growing plants, in the United States they are not available at that time. The hint can be taken, however, and separation of one's own bulbs or their transfer from one friend's garden to another can be a springtime task. If they are to be moved in the spring, lift them with as little damage to the roots as possible, separate the clumps, and replant promptly, keeping the bulbs watered and leaves in healthy growth as long as possible. As with other small bulbs, more is better. Twenty-five is a reasonable starting quantity and 100 or more is better. Snowdrops are delightful clustered at the base of a majestic oak, or in among shrubs. To lift your spirits on a drear gray day, plant some where they can be observed from a window.

A 1973 wholesale bulb catalog from van Tubergen in Holland lists a dozen varieties of galanthus. About the only varieties or cultivars readily available today are the familiar single-flowered *Galanthus nivalis* and its double-flowered counterpart, *G. nivalis* 'Flore Pleno'. Occasionally you will have a pleasant surprise, as happened when I planted a hundred of the common snowdrop. Next spring one bulb flowered with the outer wing-like petals tipped in green. This, I learned, is the variety *G. nivalis* 'Viridapicis'.

It is important to inquire about the origin of purchased bulbs. Currently *Galanthus,* along with all species of *Cyclamen* and *Sternbergia,* are under the protection of CITES (Conventions on International Trade of Endangered Species) Appendix II, which requires an export certificate from the country of origin (seeds are exempt). These regulations seek to slow and bring to a halt the widespread collection of these bulbs from the wild, especially in Turkey, as overcollection has decimated natural populations. When purchasing bulbs it is reasonable and ethical to choose a vendor offering propagated rather than collected bulbs. The phrase "nursery grown" or "nursery cultivated" says nothing about the method of propagation of the material.

Beverly Nichols, the English garden writer, divided his friends into the category of shrinker and nonshrinker, with the former able to imagine themselves small enough to look up into the bell of a snowdrop. When I cut some to enjoy indoors (where their honey-like fragrance can also be better appreciated) I like to follow his suggestion and stand the small vase on a mirror to better appreciate the heart of the flower.

Remember that the common snowdrop is in growth only early in the season; it will go dormant soon after. The two points to consider when planning your garden are: first, it will leave a gap when dormant in summer, and second, it is sensible to combine it with other plants of interest at this early time of year. While the snowdrop looks wonderful with *Eranthis hiemalis,* the winter aconite, just as both are in bloom at the same time, they also go dormant together. Think beyond the moment of bloom. Simplest is a combination of snowdrops with an evergreen ground cover. Pachysandra will not do, as it is too vigorous to permit the normal growth of the snowdrops. A better choice would be *Vinca minor,* myrtle, whose glossy evergreen leaves will look tidy beneath the white flowers of the snowdrop and provide a simple carpet afterward. I've seen a sweep of snowdrops looking like the Milky Way in such a combination. Or consider *Phlox stolonifera,* the evergreen woodland phlox, which flowers in Connecticut in early May, long after the snowdrop. Another choice would be evergreen Christmas fern, *Polystichum achrostichoides,* but be careful to site the snowdrops at the edge of the fern clump, where they will not be hidden by the drooping fronds. Yet another option is to combine these little bulbs with other plants such as hosta, which begin their growth as the bulbs cease theirs. This will also address the question of bare space, without disturbing the relatively shallow bulbs as the planting of annuals might. Space a group of bulbs between the hosta, or in front of them, but not with the hosta directly on top of the bulbs.

Besides the familiar, modest, common snowdrop there are variations. One frequently available form is the double common snowdrop, *Galanthus nivalis* 'Flore Pleno' (also called *plenus*), which is not to everyone's taste, especially those who appreciate the chaste simplicity of the type. There are actually several double forms, some with a more neatly, tightly doubled center. None produce seed, and hence are vegetatively very prolific. A few produce pollen, and this was used by Mr. H. A. Greatorex of Norwich, England, to fertilize *Galanthus plicatus.* Approximately a dozen seedlings were selected, which have inherited the large and shapely outer petals of the seed parents, and have very symmetrical, compact rosettes, boldly marked with green for their centers. These named forms include 'Ophelia', 'Desdemona', 'Dionysus', and 'Cordelia'.

Another quite lovely variation is the green-tipped snowdrop, *G. nivalis* 'Viridapicis', which has a strong green marking at the tip of the outer petals. Originally found in the early 1900s growing near an old farmhouse by Mynheer Johannes M. C. Hoog, it was introduced by C. G. van Tubergen. This is a vigorous form that multiplies well by offsets. I enjoy combining it with green-flowered hellebores such as *Helleborus foetidus,* with its dark, blackish-green, neatly incised foliage and 18-inch-high stalks with clustered small apple-green flowers on top; or *H. viride,* with singly held pale green flowers. Either of these with snowdrops and winter aconites creates a charming scene. Additionally, the green-tipped snowdrop is pleasing with *Pachysandra terminalis* 'White Edge', less vigorous in growth than the plain green form and with a simple white edge to the leaves, which makes an agreeable association.

One variety that is neither common nor cheap is *Galanthus nivalis regina-olgae.* I have no idea who Queen Olga was, but her snowdrop flowers in October without leaves, which appear the following spring. I have tried this twice, with poor success on both occasions.

Following are brief descriptions of some less frequently available cultivars that are worth seeking out to add to your garden.

Originally introduced as *Galanthus imperati,* 'Atkinsii' is named for James Atkins, a nurseryman of Painswick, Gloucestershire, who received it from a friend in the 1860s. This hybrid of *G. nivalis* x *G. plicatus* is one of the tallest snowdrops, with 6- to 10-inch stems that make it very suitable for cutting. It reproduces rapidly by offsets. The flowers are longish and charming.

In 'Magnet', raised by James Allen of Shepton Mallet, Somerset, noted for his work with snowdrops in the late nineteenth century, the flower is held out and away from the stem on a long pedicel, which allows it to sway in a light breeze. Two hybrids of his are 'Merlin' and 'Robin Hood', with large handsome flowers whose inner petals are entirely green. These are the result of crosses between *G. plicatus* and *G. elwesii.*

'Sam Arnott' is also a robust variety, with large, sweetly honey-scented roundish flowers (as the outer petals are broad and quite short). There is a very broad, heart-shaped green marking around the opening of the inner petals. It is named for Samuel Arnott, Provost of Dumfries, in whose garden it appeared. He sent it to Henry J. Elwes of Colesbourne, Gloucestershire, who introduced it to cultivation.

'Straffan' was brought to the garden of that name in County Kildare by Lord Clarina upon his return from the Crimean War. This is an Irish variety that, when well grown, will produce a second, later-appearing flower, thus greatly extending the period of bloom.

Any of these selections are going to be difficult to find, and expensive. Try to buy three or five (I think they like their own company), cosset them, and plan on dividing

The giant snowdrop, *Galanthus elwesii,* is an elegant, sturdy bulb, seen here thriving in a Colorado buffalo grass lawn. (SANDY SNYDER)

Eminently suitable in woodland, snowdrops cluster at the base of an oak in the author's garden.

them as they increase by offsets. Naturally such elite acquisitions need a choice setting, and should be planted separately from the common snowdrop, in a setting where they can readily be observed and appreciated.

There are still other species, also rare and highly desirable. One of my especial favorites is the giant snowdrop, *Galanthus elwesii.* This is in the series Latifolii, those snowdrops whose leaves wrap around each other at the base at maturity, rather than being pressed flat against each other as in the common snowdrop, which is in the series Nivales. It is puzzling as to why this is not the most eagerly sought-after species, as it is larger in stature and flower as well as two weeks earlier in bloom than the common snowdrop, being in full flower at Wave Hill in the Riverdale section of the Bronx, New York, as early as January 8. In cultivation for over a century, it was first collected by the French botanical explorer and botanist Benedict Balansa in 1854 and introduced twenty years later by H. J. Elwes. It has in the past been imported by the thousands from western Turkey. However, it multiplies well by offsets and there is no reason why small stocks could not rapidly be built up into good quantity. The leaves are a glaucous gray-green, much broader than those of *G. nivalis,* as much as 1½ inches wide. There is also a well-defined ridge on the back of the lower half of the leaves. This is, as a species, variable, but the forms generally offered (scarce though they are) are robust, from 8 to 12 inches tall. The globose flowers have cupped outer petals, and are distinguished by a second green marking on the inner tube at its base, rather than only one at the sinus, as in *G. nivalis.* This will sometimes extend and fuse with the marks at the opening of the tube, staining it green throughout its length. This species will accept somewhat drier conditions than the common snowdrop, but cannot be considered drought tolerant.

Scarce in cultivation, *Galanthus ikariae,* also in the series Latifolii, is a snowdrop that has been through several name changes, having been formerly known as *G. latifolius, G. ikariae* ssp. *latifolius,* and *G. platyphyllus.* It is readily distinguished from the other species because, unlike them, it has 1½-inch-wide bright green leaves, recurved at the ends, without any glaucous bloom on the surface. The flowers, one to a stem as with all snowdrops, have a green marking only at the opening of the inner petals, which can be quite wide, extending as much as half the length of the tube. In the wild it is found in Turkey, the Caucasus, northwestern Iran, and westward into Greece. It, too, will accept drier conditions than the common snowdrop.

Galanthus caucasicus is quite variable. There is a form known as *G. caucasicus* var. *hiemalis* that precociously flowers in late autumn to midwinter. In 1993 it flowered in my garden on Thanksgiving Day. There are some select forms that flower in December, although February/March is more typical. The leaves are folded one around the other in the sheath, which is helpful in recognizing this species, as leaf width, overall size, and flowering time can differ so much from plant to plant.

Galanthus plicatus is in the series Plicati, those species with the leaves flat against each other in bud and the margins of the leaves somewhat rolled or folded back. Bulbs of this species were also brought back to Straffan by Lord Clarina. In appearance the flowers are similar to those of the common snowdrop, but appear later, in late March or even April.

As well as snowdrops in the spring garden there can be snowflakes. Up until the mid-fifteenth century, snowflakes and snowdrops were often lumped together. It was in Rembert Dodoens's *Florum et coronariarum odoratarumque nomullarum herbarum historia* of 1568, under the heading 'De Leucoio bulboso', that the snowdrop was first described. Although 'Leucojum' was used to describe both snowflakes and snowdrops, in reality Dodoens dealt with two different genera: Leucoion bulbosum triphyllon (*Galanthus nivalis*), Leucoion bulbosum hexaphyllon (*Leucojum vernum*), and Leucoion bulbosum polyanthemon (*Leucojum aestivum*). Both genera are members of the amaryllis family, but they differ in that snowflakes have flowers with six equal segments, rather than the three large outer petals and three smaller inner petals of snowdrops. It

Like sunlight, the golden flowers of *Eranthis hiemalis* light up the author's garden in early spring.

This woodcut of *Leucojum vernum* first appeared in a book by Charles de l'Ecluse (Clusius), printed in 1583. (ILLUSTRATION FROM THE LIBRARY OF THE NEW YORK BOTANICAL GARDEN.)

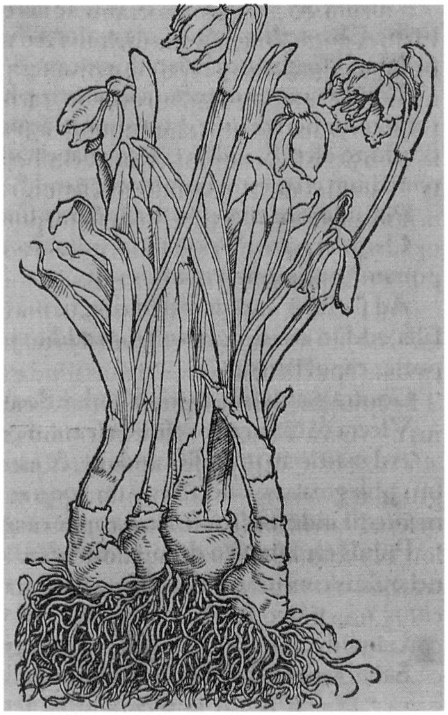

was Carolus Linnaeus, in *Systema Naturae* of 1735, who separated the two and created the new genus of *Galanthus* for snowdrops.

The spring snowflake, *Leucojum vernum,* flowers in my garden in February/March, at about the same time as the common snowdrop. The flowers are plump and bell-like, with a greenish dot on the tip of each petal. Whereas snowdrops have one flower to a stem, spring snowflakes can have two. Unlike the narrow, glaucous grayish leaves of snowdrops, the leaves of snowflakes are broad, a bright rich green, and grow from 6 to 8 inches tall, although larger specimens have been reported. Snowflakes favor more moisture than snowdrops and are native from western Russia to the Pyrenees and Belgium, growing in woods and meadows in damp places. It has been suggested that plants from the western part of this range have a green spot at the tip of each petal, while those from the eastern end are tipped with yellow. In my garden the yellow color seems more dependent on growing conditions than genetics, varying from season to season. A robust plant may have two flowers per stem, and these are sometimes given a varietal name, *L. vernum* var. *vagneri*. In my garden I combine this charming harbinger of spring with other early-flowering plants: the white flowers and deep green palmate leaves of the Christmas rose, *Helleborus niger;* along with winter aconite, *Eranthis hiemalis;* and Persian violet, *Cyclamen coum*. Another group is planted near a large oak, growing with Allegheny spurge, *Pachysandra procumbens,* our soft green, silver-spotted native counterpart of the glossy green Japanese import. Remember, both snowdrops and snowflakes go dormant by late May.

Winter Aconites

In the damp, chill days of first spring, when biting temperatures balance the lengthening daylight, our eyes seek out bright color as a compensation for the lingering last breath of winter. The fresh, pure white flowers of *Galanthus* spp. and *Leucojum vernum* are a welcome signal of the season's change, but both name and color remind us, too soon, that it is not yet spring. When the first of the winter aconites, *Eranthis hiemalis,* begin to show their bright yellow, buttercup-like flowers above a Toby-ruff, or frilled collar, of green leaves, then it seems as if the warming sunlight of true spring has come to touch the sodden brown remnants of last year's discarded leaves.

When purchased at the nursery, tubers of this plant look like the stick-like trash that is left after screening compost. I can't tell which side is up, and the shriveled warty lumps show none of the promise of a plump heavy daffodil or hyacinth bulb. All too often they have been dried beyond the point of resurrection. Purchase the tubers as soon as they are available in autumn, and plant equally promptly. But before planting, take the time to rehydrate the tubers by soaking them overnight in damp peat moss. If the peat moss is moistened with a dilute liquid fertilizer solution (one that is higher in phosphorus and potash than nitrogen, say 10-30-20 analysis), so much the better. Once rehydrated, the tubers look far more auspicious. They are also far more prone to fungal rot and should be planted within 24 hours of the soaking period. So purchase early, soak before planting, and do so in a timely fashion. While I cannot tell which way is up, the plant knows to send shoots up and roots down, even if the tuber is planted upside down. Purchase a minimum of 25 tubers, and be prepared for only a 20 percent success rate the following spring, for *Eranthis hiemalis,* even more than *Galanthus* spp., much prefer to be moved in the green than in the dry state.

Why fuss with a difficult plant? Because it isn't difficult, once you have it growing. In the spring tubers may be moved with ease, and the flowers on established tubers produce copious amounts of pale tan BB-shot-like seed that germinates freely in flower beds and mulched paths alike. This happens early in the spring (in late February in my garden). I've seen a neglected planting in Weston, Connecticut, with a scattered treasure trove of flowers, flung on the ground like golden coins, continuing their cycle of growth and rest with no attention whatsoever, not even the raking away of a heavy cover of oak leaves. In this setting the stems had etiolated in their search for light, well beyond the typical 2 to 3 inches. The winter aconite is frost-proof and cold hardy, blooming in February, a true clear yellow with no hint of a ruddy tone. Native of European woodlands in France, Italy, Yugoslavia, and Bulgaria, it has naturalized elsewhere on the Continent and in Britain.

It is wonderful in combination with snowdrops or the mauve flowers of *Crocus tomasinianus,* and lovely on its own. An outrageous, smashingly stylish pairing is the winter aconite with the elegant black, strap-like leaves of *Ophiopogon planiscapus* 'Ebony Knight'. The black mondo grass grows for me, but does not increase at any great rate. No matter, a small bijou planting was all that was necessary to create an acceptable display; in fact more might have been too much. Winter aconites are also exquisite scattered under the bare branches of early-flowering shrubs such as *Corylopsis spicata,* with its pale golden bells, or *Rhododendron mucronatum,* with lavender flowers. Since the tubers grow barely beneath the soil's surface, only an inch or two deep, it is important to site them where they will not be disturbed by cultivation during their dormant season. A mulch will also help prevent their being inadvertently disturbed.

There is a slightly taller, not quite so freely spreading species, *Eranthis cilicia,* that also has a fine bright yellow flower and more finely cut, bronze-tinted foliage. Similar in appearance but vegetatively more robust is a sterile hybrid between the two species, *Eranthis tubergeni* 'Guinea Gold', bred by the Dutch firm of C. G. van Tubergen.

Cyclamen

Unlike the majority of the early-flowering winter-hardy bulbs, *Cyclamen coum* has beautiful leaves that remain in good condition for eight months, right through the worst of winter. The Persian violet, native from Bulgaria through Turkey to the Caucasus and northern Iran (Persia of old), western Syria, and northern Lebanon, is a captivating flower, a sweetly fragrant hardy counterpart of the tender florist's cyclamen, *C. persicum,* which is grown as a potted plant for indoor use.

The leaves are roundish, somewhat leathery in texture, a dull somber green above, often with silver marbling or blotches, no two plants having identical markings. The reverse of the leaves is a deep purplish crimson. This is one geophyte well worth growing as a foliage plant. Belonging to the family *Primulaceae,* cyclamen have flowers similar to that of *Dodecatheon,* or shooting star, a related genus, looking somewhat like a badminton shuttlecock. Leaves appear in September to October, and the flower buds form in autumn, by November. Frost-proof, they stay through winter's coldest days to open into small, vivid, cerise-pink flowers in late February or early March. The tuber is rounded in outline, somewhat flattened above, with shoots emerging from the upper surface and roots from the bottom. While in England and Holland I have seen the tubers growing completely exposed, resting on the surface of the ground, in my garden I plant them about two inches deep in humus-rich woodland soil that is kept mulched with a layer of chopped oak leaves. It is important that the site have good drainage, as excessive moisture can lead to rotting of the tubers. This species is cold hardy and freely self-sowing. It is difficult to be sympathetic when someone complains about these as a "weed," as does my friend Nina Lambert in Ithaca, New York, who has the Persian violet seeding into her lawn. With reliable snow cover it should be hardy to $-10°$F or lower.

After pollination, the pedicel begins to coil, winding up like a watch spring. The seed takes several months to mature, ripening in late summer. Fresh seed, collected while still pale honey-colored before the capsule has opened and sown promptly indoors will germinate in a couple of weeks. There is an additional advantage to collecting the seed at this point: ants find the sticky coating on the seed attractive, and will carry it away. Soak the seed for a couple of hours in tepid water with a drop or two of dish detergent added. This will remove the sticky coating and

As if sprayed with silver paint while a maple leaf was held over them, the leaves of *Cyclamen coum* display their exquisite patterning.

The flowers of *Cyclamen coum* have an appeal far greater than their diminutive size.

any germination inhibitors it may contain. Old seed should be soaked in tepid water overnight or for 24 hours, but may still take months to germinate. Vigorous seedlings will often flower their second winter. Mice devour the first-year tubers (which look like little pink pearls) as some kind of toothsome caviar. It is best to grow the seedling plants in pots, or afford some type of protection such as planting in wire-mesh cages sunk in the ground until the second year, when the tubers begin to develop a corky covering. All cyclamen are under CITES Appendix II protection, and propagation from seed is the only method for production, as tubers of this genus do not make any offsets.

There are some selected forms available: 'Album' has white flowers with a magenta blotch at the opening and plain green leaves; 'Roseum' is similar to plants growing wild on the shores of the Black Sea in northern Turkey with rose-pink flowers that have a darker blotch and attractively silver-marbled leaves; 'Nyman's' has a broad silver band on the leaves with only the rim and central vein green.

I like this cyclamen with *Crocus tomasinianus,* especially the deeper-colored forms such as 'Barr's Violet', 'Ruby Giant', and 'Whitwell Purple' for a combination of mauve, lavender, and purple with the intense carmine-magenta of the cyclamen. Carla Teune, curator of the Leiden Botanic Garden in Holland, grows this cyclamen in difficult, dry conditions under an old beech tree, combined with the vivid electric-blue flowers of *Scilla sibirica,* another small bulb. This is possible because the fallen beech leaves are crisp and light, whereas those from Norway maples would choke and smother the tubers. Another favorite pairing in my garden associates the vivid fuchsia cyclamen with the 1-inch-long, perfectly formed bright yellow trumpets of *Narcissus asturiensis,* also in bloom in March.

Crocus

For the most part, crocus are plants that need an open sunny site and light, well-drained soil. However, *Crocus tomasinianus,* winner of a Wisley Award of Garden Merit as being worthy of inclusion in every garden, is quite content in woodland, multiplying freely by seed and offset, and adding its grace note of chalice-like, white-throated, soft mauve flowers to the spring garden. This charming crocus was named by Dean Herbert after his friend, the botanist Muzio de Tommasini (1794–1879) of Trieste, Italy, who was particularly interested in the flora of Dalmatia. (As an aside, Signor Tommasini always spelled his name with a double "m." The specific name of this crocus may be found with either one "m," as Herbert spelled it, or with two.) *Crocus tomasinianus,* native to the former Yugoslavia, east of the Adriatic, has a small corm with a finely reticulated tunic. When closed, in overcast, cloudy weather, the pale ashen-gray exterior of the petals, closely furled and pencil slim, are rather unimpressive. Then, as the skies clear the flowers open to reveal their clear, soft, washy, translucent lavender color. En masse, the display is very fine. There are some varieties and named forms with deeper, more saturated color: *pictus* has the outer petals tipped with purple; 'Barr's Purple' is pale without, rich purple-lilac inside; 'Taplow Ruby' is the deepest color form available, a dense rich reddish purple; 'Whitewell Purple' is a purplish mauve with bluish overtones; 'Ruby Giant' is a good deep purple color and is probably a hybrid with *Crocus vernus* (a closely related species from central Europe).

In my garden I have planted two named varieties of *Crocus tomasinianus* with *Scilla sibirica,* combined with the deep maroon flowers of *Helleborus atrorubens.* As this crocus is so early to bloom, in late February or early March, I use the paler type species in combination with plum-purple *Helleborus atrorubens* "of gardens" and the equally early acid-yellow flowers of *Adonis amurensis,* where a deeper hue would be too strong a contrast. I also use it underplanted in a broad sweep of woodland phlox, *Phlox stolonifera.* It seeds so freely (the rock garden at the Brooklyn Botanic Garden is crowded with it) that it is excellent for naturalizing. The leaves are quite narrow, with a central white stripe, and neatly die away in late spring.

Crocus begin the year, and as will be seen in a later chapter, they close it out. Only in summer are their chalice-like flowers in white, cream, yellows, blue, and violets to purple absent from the garden. They arise from a corm that is replaced each year, generally accompanied by offsets. Alas, crocus are a tasty tidbit for garden gastronomes, and mice, voles, and chipmunks eat their corms, while rabbits and deer dine on foliage and flowers. I try to console myself with the thought that the goats of Greece eat these flowers in their native haunts, but this is small consolation when I find new depredations each morning. Trying to find a sunny, well-drained location proof against these vandals is a logistical dilemma in my essentially shady garden. Grow crocus in a rock garden under a prickly mat of *Phlox subulata,* or where some other open site will permit the summer ripening their corms require. Remember their small stature, and avoid planting them where the flowers will be concealed by taller neighbors.

Usually the earliest to bloom in the new year for me is the celandine crocus, *Crocus korolkowii,* named for General Korolkov, who discovered it in 1882 in Turkestan. Native to Afghanistan and northern Pakistan, its flowers are a rich golden mustard yellow inside, feathered with purple-brown on the outside. On a cloudy February day when it is closed the appearance is quite inconspicuous, in contrast to its sunny display when open. In my garden these grow under some old field cedars, *Juniperus virginianus,* pruned high enough that the site is sunny, and quite dry in summer.

These flowers are closely followed by the Scotch crocus, *C. biflorus.* The tunic on this species is annulate (ringed): smooth, somewhat glossy, creamy beige in color, and split into a series of narrow rings on the lower third. If handled roughly the tunic will peel away, leaving the corm subject to bruising and desiccation. In the species the flowers are usually white, distinctly striped brown or purple on the outside. It is native to western Turkey, western Yugoslavia, northern Albania, and northeastern Italy, where it grows in open stony places and in scrubby brush. I planted it near a prostrate juniper and a low-growing cotoneaster. Over time, the shrubs have crept over the crocus, which early each spring push through to flower in late February or early March. There are a number of subspecies and cultivars. *C. biflorus* ssp. *adamii* is a strong purple-lilac inside, grayish-buff-feathered purple outside, while ssp. *alexandri* is white inside, heavily stained with violet outside. Lengthily named *C. biflorus* ssp. *weldenii* 'Fairy' has flowers that are white with a purple blotch inside, grayish, speckled with methyl-violet outside. All of these forms send up bunches of flowers, each corm begetting its own posy, crowding for space as they emerge in the spring. On mild sunny days the honey bees buzz about, eagerly gathering the first nectar of the season. These crocus are a charming addition to the herb garden, where they thrive in the sunny, well-drained site planted beneath a carpet of thyme.

Flowering as the snow melts in February is the snow crocus, *Crocus chrysanthus.* This native of Asia Minor, Turkey, and Greece was a particular favorite of the eminent English horticulturist E. A. Bowles. The snow crocus is quite variable, with a ground color of sulfur yellow, orange, white, or lilac, with the outside being speckled, feathered, or flushed with chocolate brown or bronze to purple. These markings can be anything from minimal to a heavy suffusion of color. The simplest way to distinguish this species from the Scotch crocus is that the former has a golden-yellow throat. Also, its flowers are more rounded. (I find that this is only helpful if I am comparing the two and see their flowers side by side.) The two species have been hybridized, an easy task since their natural range overlaps and they sometimes cross in the wild. Numerous cultivars are readily available: 'Blue Pearl' is a pale lobelia blue; 'Brassband' is a vivid Naples yellow with a bronze blotch veined with green; 'Cream Beauty' is Naples yellow; 'E. A. Bowles' is lemon yellow with the margins feathered in purple, and it is larger than 'E. P. Bowles', which is lemon yellow with a purple-brown blotch; 'Fuscotinctus' is Chinese yellow inside and lemon yellow outside, entirely striped and feathered in plum-purple; 'Gipsy Girl' is aureo-

The charming lavender flowers of *Crocus tomasinianus* combine well with the clear blue blossoms of *Scilla bifolia* in the author's garden.

Also in the author's garden, *Crocus tomasinianus* is paired with the bright yellow flowers of *Adonis amurensis*, resulting in a more vivid combination.

lin yellow strongly striped and feathered purplish brown; 'Ladykiller' is purple-violet with a white margin; 'Prinses Beatrix' is a clear lobelia blue with the characteristic golden-yellow base, and 'Snowbunting' has white flowers with gray feathering. These are the most frequently available, and comprise just over 10 percent of the registered cultivars. In Norwalk I had a small collection of these growing on the north side of the house. The site was open to the sky and very bright, with additional light reflected off the white house. The different snow crocus were grouped with a dwarf rhododendron 'Purple Gem', whose bronze-plum winter color provides an attractive background.

Another early species is *Crocus sieberi.* The corms are quickly distinguishable from the preceding two species as this one has a reticulate or netted brown tunic. The flowers are pale to deep lilac, with a yellow throat and a frilly, vivid orange-red stigma that protrudes from the unopened bud as if sticking out its tongue. Growing in the scrub and thin woods or mountain turf of the Balkans and Greece, this is adaptable to dry sites. The species itself is rarely grown; instead, several named forms with stronger markings are favored. 'Hubert Edelsten' has a yellow throat, soft lilac petals with the two colors separated by a white zone; 'Tricolor' is similar. 'Violet Queen' is amethyst-violet with a yellow throat and lacks the white chevron, as does 'Firefly', which is mineral violet. In his book *Crocus & Colchicum* Bowles wrote, "In 1923 I found two pure white youngsters among my seedlings, after thirty years of hopeful expectation. The better of these has increased freely and is the best white and orange spring Crocus I know. It is now known as 'Bowle's White'. . . ." This selection is a fine crocus, with a large globular pure white flower and an orange throat.

After these dainty flowers, the familiar "Dutch crocus" cultivars of *Crocus vernus* seem somewhat bloated, perhaps a little coarse. Even the corms, netted with brown hemp-like strands, are larger. They are charming in their own right; the important thing is to grow them separately from their smaller kin to avoid unkind comparisons. This is an easy enough matter since the Dutch crocus bloom later, flowering in March and April.

The true wild species, native from the Pyrenees to the Carpathian Mountains, sturdy enough to thrive in high alpine pastures at 7,500 feet, is difficult to obtain. Instead we are offered numerous cultivars: 'Jeanne d'Arc' is a large, pure white with a purple base; 'King of the Striped' is amethyst-violet with lighter stripes; 'Peter Pan' is ivory-white with short lilac stripes; 'Pickwick' is grayish white with mineral violet stripes; 'Purpureus Grandiflorus' is a uniform violet; 'Remembrance' is violet with a silvery sheen. Did you ever purchase a bag of mixed crocus, and the following spring discover the yellow-flowered ones in bloom two weeks or more before those with white, striped, or lavender flowers? Of garden origin, and properly named 'Golden Yellow', this is a cultivar of *Crocus flavus* cultivated since the seventeenth century. 'Mammoth Yellow' or 'Dutch Yellow' are invalid names by which it is often sold.

Dutch crocus, with their large flowers, are excellent in combination with shrubs. An attractive combination to try is that of the red twig dogwood, *Cornus stolonifera,* its polished red bark on young branches above a glowing pool of 'Golden Yellow', or very different with 'Jeanne d'Arc' emulating the snow so recently vanished. One of the delights of an early visit to Wave Hill was the contorted "Harry Lauder's walking stick" hazel, *Corylus avellana* 'Contorta' trailing pollen-dusted yellow catkins on its twisted bare branches over a pool of deep purple and lavender Dutch crocus. I have used 'Purpureus Grandiflorus' with *Yucca* 'Golden Sword', enjoying the purple flowers peeping through snow in contrast to the sculptural yucca foliage, with its soft buttery yellow markings.

Scilla

Among the small early bulbs are some with flowers of the same desirable electric blue as gentians, such as the charming Siberian squill, *Scilla sibirica.* Native from southern Russia, Crimea, and the Caucasus to Turkey and northern

Iran, with drooping, bell-like flowers of a brilliant Prussian blue, this bulb adds tremendous impact to the early garden. Growing only 6 to 8 inches tall, with three or four flowers to a stem, this is often offered as the cultivar 'Spring Beauty' or by its synonym, 'Atrocaerulea'. Plant the small bulbs with their papery, deep purplish-blue tunics in drifts and groups under shrubs where the following spring (in late March or early April) their flowers will pool beneath the radiant yellow bells of forsythia, softer yellow of *Cory-*

Together, *Crocus vernus* and the trailing tassels of contorted hazel create a charming combination.

lopsis spicata, drooping white racemes of *Pieris japonica* or *Leucothoe catesbei,* or the lavender blossoms of early azaleas. It is charming in combination with other bulbs such as early daffodils or the kaufmanniana or greigii hybrid tulips. This bulb multiplies freely, and in subsequent years the hair-fine, grass-like seedlings appear in profusion, ultimately to cast a blue haze that melts away at the end of spring. There is a white form, *Scilla sibirica alba,* which has a creamy-white tunic, is smaller in size, and is not so vigorous in growth.

A real favorite of mine is the 3- to 4-inch-tall, earlier-blooming *Scilla bifolia.* This has one-sided, reddish-stemmed racemes of small, upward-facing star-like flowers of a rich bright blue. It, too, multiplies very quickly from seed. This is enchanting with early hellebores, either green *Helleborus viride,* maroon *H. atrorubens* "of gardens," or the variable apple-green to white to pink flowers of *H.* x *orientalis.* There is a pink form, *Scilla bifolia rosea,* which I find to be a pretty enough pink in bud but a pale dirty off-white in flower. If I ever get around to it I plan to dig this

Annual Growth Cycle of *Crocus vernus*

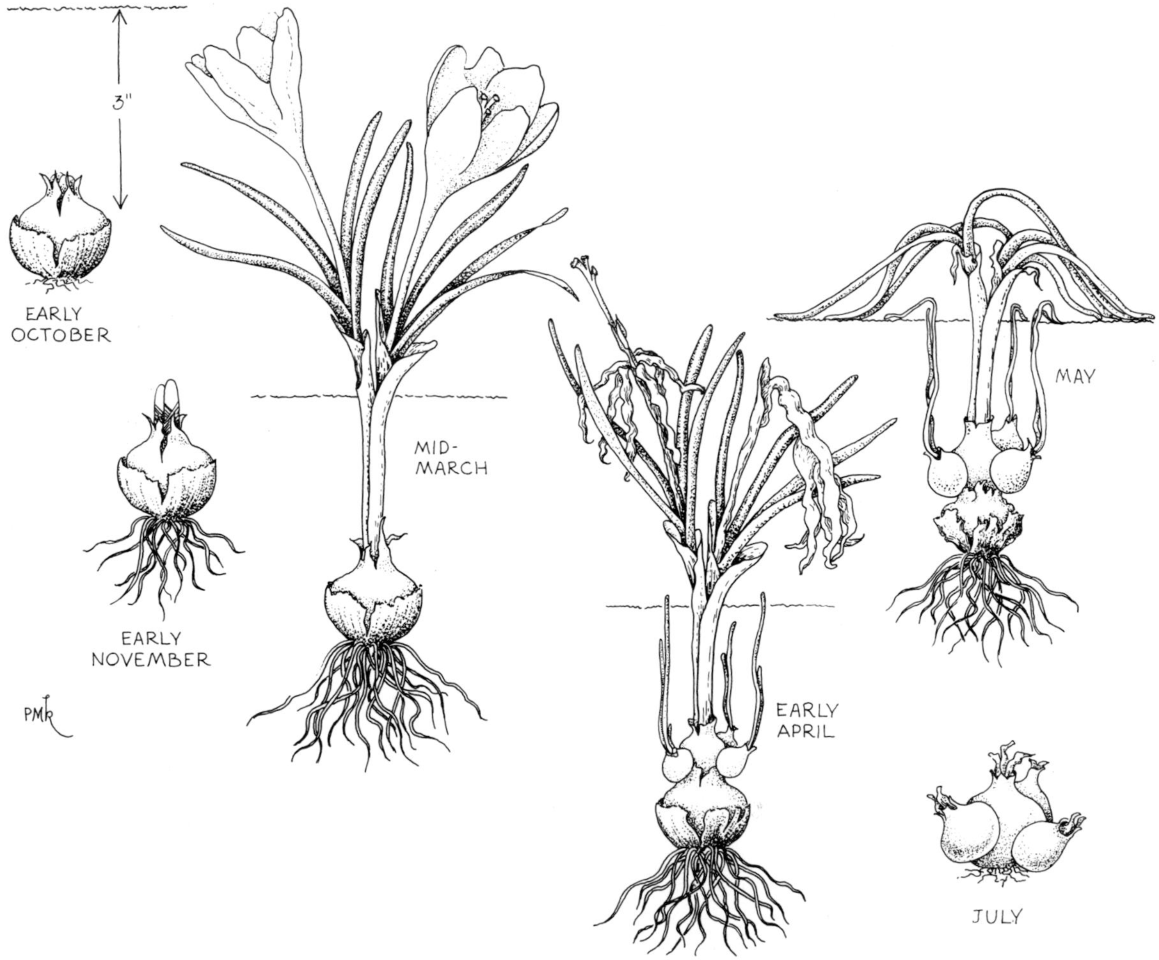

out, doing so while it is in bloom so I can distinguish it from the blue.

One bulb as eager for spring as am I, *Scilla tubergeniana,* was introduced by van Tubergen. Its buds are pushing up from between the glossy green leaves as soon as the shoots make an appearance in late March and open as they clear the ground. I prefer this older name to the tongue-twisting taxonomic revision of *S. mischtschenkoana.* Collected by Georg Egger, German consul in Tabriz, one of the towns of northwestern Persia, the first bulbs arrived in Holland mixed with *Puschkinia libanotica* (*P. scilloides*), which it rather resembles. Egger had offered to collect a very beautiful chionodoxa, but instead of going himself he sent a "trustworthy person" who mistook his directions, went to the wrong place, and collected the wrong bulbs, two years in a row! A small compensation was that each time, among the unwanted bulbs, five or six of an exceedingly early, free-flowering, unknown scilla were found. It must be appreciated that the two bulbs overlap in range in the Caucasus and northern Iran. Both have flowers of a pale transparent bluish white, like skim milk, with a line of turquoise penciled down the middle of each petal. While this may sound insignificant, I find that they provide a lovely effect if sited where early-spring sunshine can shine through and illuminate the flowers. The two can be readily distinguished upon close inspection, as in scilla the petals are separate and in puschkinia (named for Count Mussin-Pushkin, a Russian chemist, geologist, and plant collector) they are fused into a bell-like tube at the base.

Chionodoxa

Another related, also truly blue-flowered bulb, is glory-of-the-snow, *Chionodoxa.* The common name relates to its native habitat in the mountains of western Turkey and Crete, where it follows the retreating snow in bloom. In my garden it flowers in late March or early April. Like puschkinia, the base of the petals are fused, and the flowers face upward, which easily differentiates it from scilla. The most common variety is *C. luciliae* (*C. gigantea*), which should correctly have one or two soft lavender-blue flowers with a small white center. Confusingly, the plant generally offered under this name is instead *C. siehei,* which has up to 12 flowers in a one-side raceme of purplish-blue flowers with a large white eye. The confusion is decades old, as the original *C. luciliae* was introduced from western Turkey and described by Pierre Edmond Boissier, while the latter (sometimes referred to as '*C. luciliae* of gardens') was introduced by George Maw later in the nineteenth century. This sort of in-fighting is the taxonomist's delight and gardener's despair. In any case *C. siehei* is a vigorous plant, seeding freely. In Norwalk I once planted a mass of the typical blue form with a few water-lily tulips, *Tulipa kaufmanniana.* As the slightly taller creamy-yellow and rose-pink flowers of the tulip opened wide in spring sunshine above a pool of blue chionodoxa, the effect was exquisite. 'Naburn Blue' has a softer blue color, and 'Pink Giant' is taller, a fine pink with a white eye.

There is a naturally occurring hybrid between *Chionodoxa siehei* and *Scilla bifolia,* named x *Chionoscilla allenii* for James Allen of Shepton Mallet, who first noted their appearance in his garden in the late 1800s. It has upward of seven dark blue to violet-lilac flowers that appear in March on an 8-inch stem.

Chionodoxa sardensis has the most luxurious color of all, as it almost lacks the white eye, which has the effect of intensifying the clear rich blue willowware porcelain color of its flowers, four to twelve on an 8-inch stem. A delight at Wave Hill are masses of these flowering in a deep blue pool among the bare stems of viburnum, overhung by the shrub's international-rescue-orange berries. This species also increases freely, creating a vivid multitude in the early woodland garden.

The shift in the seasons is more noticeable now. The days are appreciably longer and sunlight warmer. Winter's silence is broken in the morning by the murmurous vocalizations of birds defining their territories and courting a

The electric-blue flowers of *Scilla sibirica* and a charming orange-flowered cultivar of *Tulipa kaufmanniana* combine attractively in front of a shrub border.

mate. And at dusk the shrill, insistent chorus of spring peepers begins, to be my lullaby at the onset of the second spring.

Plants in growth are no longer scattered, isolated events. Fibrous-rooted perennials such as spotted lungwort, *Pulmonaria saccharata;* many primroses, including *Primula abchasica, P. juliae, P. polyanthus, P. vulgaris,* and their cultivars; epimedium; and more are in flower. And another flush of geophytes add their blossoms to the woodland scene.

Crocus lend their spring flowers to a planting of heather in a rock garden setting. (ILLUSTRATION COURTESY OF THE NETHERLANDS FLOWER BULB INFORMATION CENTER)

At Wave Hill, in the Bronx, New York, *Chionodoxa sardensis* spills on the ground like blue pools beneath the early yellow flowers of *Jasminum nudiflorum*.

2

Second Spring

Anemone, Muscari, Brimeura amethystina, Pseudomuscari azureum, Hyacinthoides, Camassia, Leucojum aestivum, Fritillaria, Ornithogalum

THE FIRST passionate rush of spring is over. While nights are still chilly, the days have mellowed to shirtsleeve temperatures. The garden beckons. This is the time of year when I am lost to housebound tasks. Intending to wander through the garden "only for a moment" with my morning cup of tea, time slips away. Geophytes, with profound diversity, continue this second round of spring. There are more options for combinations as perennials, shrubs, and small trees begin their growth. Dates are vague, as so much depends on the conditions of the winter preceding: bitter temperatures and snow cover will delay events, but the sequence will be the same. Entries from my garden notebook reveal the flowering of snowdrops, snowflakes, and winter aconite commencing with a month's variation in different years. In 1990 they were in full flower by February 17; after the snowy winter of 1986 they did not bloom until March 20, even later in 1993. The geophytes of first spring flower with a trickle, tantalizing us with their early development. By second spring the weather is more benevolent, and across the country flowers come to the garden in a flood.

Anemone

Very different in shape from the other spring geophytes are those of the windflowers, *Anemone* spp., which resemble little daisies. Wood anemone, *Anemone nemorosa,* is found in various forms over all of Europe, northern and western Asia, in woods and wet meadows. The slender, creeping, forking rootstock is a glossy chestnut brown. The flowers, one or very occasionally two on a 3- to 10-inch stalk, may be white, rose, lavender, or blue, as much as 1½ inches in diameter. As expected, so wide-ranging a plant has a number of selected forms. These cultivars include: *alba*

At Wave Hill two sturdy plants growing in happy combination: the dusky blue flowers of *Muscari armeniacum* and green *Helleborus foetidus.*

A wet meadow in Washington State is covered with a haze of *Camassia* in bloom. (C. COLSTON BURRELL)

plena, which has double white flowers; *bracteata,* with a Toby-ruff of green bracts beneath white flowers; *flore-pleno,* which is double flowered; *rosea,* with pink flowers; 'Allenii', with especially fine, deep-colored blue flowers; and 'Robinsonii', with blue flowers flushed rosy mauve on the underside. Given the woodland conditions to its liking this little windflower will run about, coming through a loose ground cover of myrtle, *Vinca minor,* or other such, or in pleasant association with shrubs. I especially like the blue forms in combination with the silvery-gray fronds of Japanese painted fern, *Athyrium goeringianum* 'Pictum'. This type of pairing is desirable, as the windflower is a spring ephemeral and vanishes in late spring. If a planting is to be increased by division, do so as the leaves are beginning to yellow, as this responds poorly if moved while in full growth.

There is a pleasant little pale yellow-flowered hybrid between *A. nemorosa* and *A. ranunculoides* named *A. intermedia,* naturally occurring in Silesia, where the two species share the territory. *A. ranunculoides* is itself a charming yellow-flowered anemone found in damp woods and meadows over almost all of Europe and western Asia. It has been in cultivation in England long enough to have naturalized in several parts of the country. From the creeping horizontal rootstock arises a slender stem 3 to 10 inches tall with one or sometimes two or three yellow blossoms measuring about an inch across. It is appealing in combination with the pale yellow *Primula vulgaris* of English hedgerows and small, dark-leaved, purple-flowered *Viola labradorica.* It is interesting that windflowers have, among the different species, flowers in all three primary colors of yellow, blue, and red.

In nearby Connecticut woodlands I find the little *Anemone quinquefolia* growing wild. The small white flowers are dainty, one or occasionally two arising from the creeping, white, stick-like rootstock. This does not respond well to drying out, and the briefer the time it is out of the ground the better. A dainty, shy little thing, most often it is cultivated in native plant gardens.

The commonly available anemone in most garden centers and catalogs is the Grecian windflower, *A. blanda.* It has a natural range from Greece through Asia Minor to the Caucasus and Kurdistan, where it brightens the landscape in February and March. The buttercup-like foliage is pretty, but it is the 2-inch-diameter daisy-like flowers, with 9 to 14 narrow petals in shades of blue, lavender, pink, or white, that give the plant its attraction. The deepest blue form is the cultivar 'Atrocaerulea'. When this is offered it is usually as relatively small, roundish tubers. Other forms include: 'Scythinica', which has petals that are white on their upper surface, blue underneath; var. *alba* is, of course, white flowered, as are 'Bridesmaid' and 'White Splendour'. 'Pink Star' has soft creamy-yellow-centered pink flowers, 'Charmer' has deep pink flowers, and 'Radar' is an intense cerise-pink-flowered form. The white forms apparently make large tubers, as they are offered as cut-up portions; the pink and lavender forms are sold as irregular but intact tubers.

All of these arrive at the nurseries in a desiccated, shriveled state. It will aid in their growth that vital first season if the tubers are soaked in damp peat moss overnight before planting. If I am really in a rush, I soak them in tepid water for an hour or so to rehydrate them more quickly, but I feel that the gentler overnight method is better for the tubers. Once soaked they should be planted promptly; left for several days at this point the tubers can begin to mold and rot. Even after they are soaked it is difficult to ascertain which way is up. If in doubt, plant sideways, as the plant will send the shoots up, its roots down, and, over time, the tuber correctly orients itself.

The Grecian windflower is superb in many situations. The daisy-like flowers look delightful with primroses, especially polyanthus and juliae species and cultivars, as long as some attention is paid to particular shades, as red-flowered primroses will appear exceedingly harsh and unpleasant with pink and lavender windflowers. Lavender and blue shades look especially good combined with a ground cover of myrtle, *Vinca minor,* or in association with yellow daffodils, or the soft lavender of *Crocus tomasinianus.* Either of the white cultivars looks beautiful as a companion for the deep maroon-flowered *Trillium cuneatum.* The combination of azaleas and windflowers is a pleasing one, especially with other small bulbs such as *Scilla sibirica,* with its small blue bells, and early herbaceous perennials such as epimedium, whose foliage will provide interest after the bulbs are dormant. This type of simple plant community provides a more interesting display than the stereotypical "foundation planting" of azaleas alone, tightly wedged up against a house and lacking any other companion plants.

A. apennina, from southern Europe, is the counterpart to the Grecian windflower. This charming little tuber with soft sky blue flowers, about 2 inches in diameter, composed of 10 to 15 petals, is found in deciduous woodlands and rocky sites in the higher mountains. Use it as you would the blue forms of *Anemone blanda.* It also has some color forms: in var. *alba* the flowers are white inside, pale blue outside; 'Petrovac', from Yugoslavia, is a multi-petaled deep blue; 'Plena' is double flowered; and 'Purpurea' has violet flowers.

Muscari

Grape hyacinth, *Muscari armeniacum,* is one of the easiest bulbs to grow. It is perhaps *too* easy, as its proclivities toward intemperate increase can overrun the space allotted to it. The round, fleshy bulbs produce numerous offsets and the resulting bulblets thrive. Growth is vigorous in a wide variety of sites, despite its habit of sending foliage up in the fall. The grassy leaves can become quite tattered over the winter, but this does not inhibit flowering. The tight spikes of lavender-blue flowers, rimmed with white and constricted at the mouth, appear in April to early May in my garden. In its native habitat on the north side of the Mediterranean — Greece and Yugoslavia, east through Turkey to the Caucasus — it is found in woodland and meadows. In gardens it is equally adaptable to sunny or lightly shaded sites. At Keukenhof, the 70-acre, 6-million-bulb display garden of the Dutch bulb growers in Holland, grape hyacinths are used in brightly hued combination, a river of smoky blue flowing between red and yellow double tulips. My friend Sydney Eddison of Newtown, Connecticut, uses grape hyacinths at the front of her perennial border, in bright contrast to the foamy yellow blooms of *Draba sibirica.* Basket-of-gold, *Aurinia (Alyssum) saxatilis,* would provide a similar effect. An attractive small grouping in Stan and Helen Barnes's Connecticut garden had grape hyacinth with the soft blue flowers of forget-me-nots, *Myosotis sylvestris,* and the rosy-red blossoms of wild columbine, *Aquilegia canadensis.* Vigorous enough for waste places and roadside banks, it is handsome with the chartreuse bracts of cypress spurge, *Euphorbia cyparissias.* Do not, repeat *do not,* move this rampageous spurge into your garden no matter how attractive you find the combination. Upgrade to a more refined species, perhaps *E. myrsinites.* In which case a better behaved grape hyacinth would probably also be a good idea. I like to use this bulb underplanted beneath myrtle, *Vinca minor,* as the ground cover's similarly colored flowers appear at the same time. A paler blue form, 'Cantab', is very handsome with daffodils, less harsh in appearance than the typical color. This species is the one you are most likely to find at garden centers and nurseries when bulbs arrive in the fall. There is a white form, *Muscari armeniacum* 'Album', which is less vigorous, and also less invasive. There are several others worth seeking out. *Muscari botryoides* is similar, with sky blue flowers rimmed with white. It also has the common name of grape hyacinth; the edges of its leaves roll inward, helping to distinguish it from *M. armeniacum.* Introduced to Europe in 1576, it has a pleasing fruity fragrance when you kneel to the flowers. Often this species has two flower spikes per bulb.

Muscari latifolium is readily distinguished from the common grape hyacinth, as it has only one, or rarely two, broad leaves rather than the four to eight narrow leaves of the latter. Its flower spike is impressive, reaching nearly 12 inches tall, with somber, blackish-violet fertile flowers on the lower part of the spike, and blue sterile flowers toward the tip, resulting in a conspicuous two-tone effect. It is striking in combination with white-flowered *Arabis procurrens* or *Aubretia deltoides,* and I grow it with magenta-red *Primula polyanthus* and maroon *Trillium cuneatum.*

The tassel hyacinth or feather hyacinth, *Muscari comosum,* has been bounced by the taxonomists into *Leopoldia comosa.* Introduced nearly 400 years ago, in 1596, the species is rarely grown in favor of a sterile cultivated form called 'Monstrosum' or 'Plumosum'. The flowers are transformed into a mass of branching, thread-like petals, forming a feathery purple mass. It is attractive, and combines handsomely with the vivid fuchsia flowers of the hardy *Geranium sanguineum* 'Max Frei'.

I am waiting, as I write this, to see the flowers of *Muscari ambrosiacum,* which I brought back from Holland in September 1992. However, to be accurate I should now call it *Muscari muscarimi,* the latest name change returning it to that genus from its sojourn in *Muscarimia.* Taxonomic correctness is important, but as a gardener I want to know where to find it in a catalog! The lilac flowers are said to fade to creamy white ("rather dingy" is how Mevrouw van der Zalm described it) and more sweetly scented than the poet's narcissus. All too often we neglect fragrance in our pursuit of showy flowers, yet smell is the most evocative of our senses.

Brimeura amethystina

On the basis of their constricted flowers as contrasted with the open bells of hyacinth, grape hyacinth were split off into their own genus. Also detached from hyacinth is *Brimeura amethystina,* which looks rather like a miniature bluebell. This may still be found in catalogs under its older name of *Hyacinthus amethystinus.* Whatever you call it, this is a dainty bulb, growing about 6 inches tall and flowering in May with a loose one-sided raceme of a dozen or more bell-like flowers that can vary from pale china blue to deeper blue. Its native haunts in the high mountain meadows of the Pyrenees supplied the common name of alpine hyacinth, which suggests its usefulness in the rock garden, perhaps planted under a ground cover of thyme. This small bulb does not appreciate a hot summer baking, and will do well in light shade.

Pseudomuscari azureum

Compared to the alpine hyacinth, *Hyacinthella azurea* is an orphan child, moved from one genus to another. Originally *Hyacinthus,* then *Muscari,* even *Hyacinthella,* it has been deemed invalid and is now designated *Pseudomuscari azureum.* It does look very much like a grape hyacinth, but with flowers more bell-like and open at the mouth. It is easily grown in the rock garden, and I like to group a handful of the bulbs between tussocks of blue sheep's fescue grass, *Festuca ovina glauca.* The bright sky blue flowers, neatly penciled with a darker stripe on each petal and tightly packed on an erect 4-inch spike, appear in late March. It needs a sunny site with well-drained soil.

Hyacinthoides

Similarly at the mercy of the taxonomists are the English and Spanish bluebells. Originally classified as *Scilla,* then moved to *Endymion,* they are now classified as *Hyacinthoides,* where one might hope they will be permitted to remain. I remember with delight a bluebell woods I saw in Holland one May many years ago. Under the bare branches of massive beech trees the woodland was awash with their blue flowers. This would have been *Hyacinthoides non-scriptus,* the sweetly scented English bluebell. Growing 15 to 18 inches tall, the tip of the flower stalk nods gracefully. It increases freely by means of both seed and offsets, and as the bulbs pull themselves deeply into the soil it can be difficult to dislodge from an unwanted position. I usually patrol my woods after the blooming season, snapping off spent flower stalks to inhibit its spread. With its proclivity for expanding far and wide, it is best used in an informal, naturalistic setting such as a woodland garden or with shrubs. I like to grow it interplanted with glaucous blue-leaved hosta such as 'Halcyon' or 'Blue Cadet', even with the larger *H. sieboldiana*. The bulbs' flowers are handsome with the newly arisen hosta foliage, which matures and conceals the yellowing bulb foliage. With the addition of a fern such as the fine-textured lady fern, *Athyrium felix-femina,* the garden looks attractive for an extended period.

The Spanish bluebell, *Hyacinthoides hispanicus,* is somewhat smaller, about 12 inches high with an upright flower stalk, and is not fragrant. Also useful for semi-wild, informal garden use, it typically has blue flowers. There are selected forms such as 'Blue Giant', 'Blue Queen', 'Danube', 'King of the Blues', 'Myosotis,' and 'Sky Blue'. Pink and white forms are available with descriptive names such as 'Queen of the Pinks', 'Rosabella', 'Peach Blossom', 'Alba', 'Mount Everest', and 'White City'. Spanish bluebells are lovely with azaleas and rhododendrons (but be careful in matching pinks), pieris, and other shade-tolerant, spring-flowering evergreen shrubs.

Camassia

Similar in appearance to a larger, looser wood hyacinth is a purely North American genus, camassia, or quamash, or, occasionally, wild hyacinth. While frequently offered in catalogs and nurseries, this bulb is not common in gardens. Since it is a reliable, attractive addition to the late-spring garden, this is difficult to explain. There are several species native to the Pacific Northwest. *Camassia quamash* (*C. esculenta*) is found from British Columbia southward down the coast to California, and inland to Montana and Utah. American Indians of the region ate the onion-like bulbs boiled or roasted, and it was served to Meriwether Lewis and William Clark when they reached the Oregon Territory on their westward journey of exploration from St. Louis in 1804. It is quite variable, ranging from 8 to 24 inches tall, with star-like pale to deep violet-blue, or white flowers in April or May. In the wild it is found in wet meadows or along streams in open, lightly shaded woodlands but grows well with average moisture in cultivation. There is one cultivar, 'Orion', with clear violet flowers. I like it in a mixed border, combined in groups of six or more bulbs with perennials and shrubs — perhaps yellow ranunculus or trollius, bronze tulips, coppery *Iris fulva,* yellow *Iris pseudacorus,* purple-leaved *Berberis thunbergii atropurpurea,* or deciduous azaleas. Camassia are also good as cut flowers.

Other species are sometimes available. *Camassia leichtlinii* is taller, reaching 3 to 4 feet high, with deep violet-blue to white flowers. As chance would have it, the white-flowered form was discovered first. Thus it, rather than the more common blue, is regarded as the type. Some of the cultivars — 'Blauwe Donau' ('Blue Danube'), with lavender-violet flowers; 'Alba', with snow-white flowers; 'Semiplena', with creamy-white, semi-double flowers — are periodically available. *Camassia cusickii,* from northeastern Oregon, has rather large bulbs, with sizable specimens weighing as much as a half-pound. It grows about 2½ feet tall and has pale gray-blue flowers. 'Zwanenburg', introduced by van Tubergen at the turn of the century, has wisteria blue flowers.

Leucojum aestivum

The summer snowflake, *Leucojum aestivum,* is a charming addition to the open woodland or lightly shaded border. Naturalized in England, native to western, central, and southern Europe, and eastward to Turkey and the Caucasus, this attractive geophyte was introduced into cultivation in 1594. It is larger and more floriferous than the spring snowflake, with strap-like leaves similar to a daffodil, growing 18 inches tall with three to five plump, green-tipped, bell-like white flowers dangling from the arching stem in May. The bulbs look very much like those of narcissus, and should be planted early in autumn. They require a moist site with midday shade and grow well near a pond or in a wet meadow. There is one cultivar, 'Gravetye Giant', introduced by William Robinson and named for Gravetye Manor, his garden in Sussex. It is even larger, up to two feet tall, with seven good-sized flowers.

Fritillaria

Quite different from the delicate star-like flowers of camassia or the daisies of anemone are the sturdy, square-shouldered bells of *Fritillaria.* This genus was named by Matthias de L'Obel, or Lobel, coming from the Latin *fritillus,* a dice box, in reference to both the boxy shape and checkered patterning of the flower. The Spanish Netherlands in the sixteenth century were unsettled and chaotic, yet this was the time and place where three men founded a botany based on personal observation and investigation of their local flora rather than the ancient authority of Pliny and Dioscorides. Lobel investigated the plants of southern France, especially about Narbonne, Charles de l'Ecluse, or Carolus Clusius, studied those of Austria-Hungary; and Rembert Dodoens examined those of the Netherlands. Though published in separate volumes under their individual names, their botanical writings are so interrelated that it is difficult to know what to attribute to whom. They corresponded regularly, and shared their information, their publisher, and even the illustrations to their books. Their work formed the basis for the later system of Linnaeus, which culminated in the formation of modern botanical taxonomy. Lobel's arrangement, based on differences in leaf structure, was an attempt to create a system of classification "according to their kind, and their mutual relationship."

Thoroughly distributed across the northern hemisphere, different species of *Fritillaria* are found in Europe, Japan, China, and the western coast of North America. Within the genus are some easily grown reliable performers, and others that frustrate the most skilled grower. Many are inhabitants of woodland, and prefer a cool, lightly shaded situation. They prefer adequate, if not abundant, moisture while in active growth. In general, these are the easier species to cultivate. There is no tunic, and the scales are loosely attached. Thus the bulb is somewhat fragile, and prone to desiccation, especially in the dwarfer species. Accordingly, plan to purchase and plant promptly, as soon as the bulbs are available in the autumn.

Widely available, *Fritillaria meleagris* has many common names: guinea hen flower, snake's head fritillary, checkered lily, and leopard's lily. The last is possibly a corruption of "leper's lily," referring to the small bells that lepers were required to wear to give warning of their approach. The species name, *meleagris,* is derived from the Greek word for guinea hen. The small whitish bulb, generally with some hairy roots left from the previous season's growth, is poisonous, as are those of many other species. Indigenous in much of Europe, it needs conditions that approximate those of its native haunts in wet meadows and open woodland. It grows well in shady gardens where the checkered purple flowers associate well with hellebores, especially the long-lasting pink, plum, and greenish-white flowers of *Helleborus* x *orientalis.* Since it grows only 12 to 15 inches tall, with inconspicuous thin, grayish leaves on the stem, plan to use it toward the front of an area in minimum groupings of ten or more. If planted in grass the site should stay damp: in England *F. meleagris* has naturalized in wet meadows, especially at Christ Church and at Oxford. There is wide natural variation in the depth of the purple-pink flower color, which has resulted in the selection of particular forms. Classically named varieties include 'Adonis', with creamy-white flowers, checkered in pale purple; 'Aphrodite' has pure white flowers without any markings; 'Artemis' has flowers with a very pronounced checkering of purple with green; 'Charon' is quite dark, mallow-purple checkered black; and 'Saturnus' has rather large, red-violet flowers. Unfortunately, named forms must be purchased from English sources, as they are not generally available in the United States. What is offered here are *F. meleagris alba,* with white flowers having pale green tessellation, and "Mixed Varieties" with "many interesting color variations," suggested by another vendor as "a good

A feather from a guinea hen displays the neat, tidy markings of this barnyard fowl.

The tessellated markings of guinea hen flower, *Fritillaria meleagris,* leave little doubt as to how it got that common name.

way to explore the species." These mixes will include forms that vary from deep purple-black with very faint markings to strongly tessellated flowers to white with green checkering. I always mean to separate the different forms, but tend to think of it after the flowers have faded.

Very different is the crown imperial, *Fritillaria imperialis.* Growing a stately 3 feet tall, just three bulbs will create an imposing display. It was introduced to Europe in 1554 by Ogier Ghiselin de Busbecq, who is also credited with introducing the tulip. This is one of the flowers often included in the Dutch and Flemish flower paintings of the seventeenth and eighteenth century. A client of mine once brought one from the garden into her studio to paint. By the following morning the pungent scent had permeated the entire room. All parts of the plant — bulb, leaf, flower — have a strong, musky, skunk-like odor.

The large smelly bulbs are usually individually wrapped in tissue, and root growth often begins while the bulbs are still in boxes at the nursery. Prompt planting is a must. Carla Teune, curator of the Leiden Botanic Garden, says that if you can grow potatoes, you can grow crown imperials. They need a rich, well-drained soil in a sunny site. Since they root vigorously in autumn, feed them at that time with a fertilizer high in phosphorus and potash. Alternatively, feed in spring with a complete fertilizer including a moderate level of nitrogen. One common recommendation is to plant them sideways so water will not collect between the scales. This is pointless, as over time the bulb will right itself. Instead, be sure the site is not waterlogged. Deep planting with 6 inches of soil over the bulb, and spacing 8 inches apart, is necessary for these massive bulbs. In spring a stout bronze bud emerges from the soil and develops quickly. The glossy green leaves ascend the stem, which is topped with four to six or more pendant flowers, crowned with a pineapple-like tuft of leaves. Another, less familiar common name is 'Tears of Mary.' Legend has it that the flowers were originally erect, and white in color. But the plant refused to mourn when Christ passed it on the way to Calvary. Ever since, it blushes (the flowers are typically a rich orange), nods its head in shame, and the large white nectaries, each with a clear drop of nectar, are its unshed tears. Cultivars include 'Aurora' and 'Orange Brilliant', with orange-red flowers, and 'Rubra Maxima', with very large, angular, flame-orange flowers with faint purple veining, shaded carmine-purple on the reverse of the petals, and introduced in 1665. Likewise, 'Flava' and 'Lutea' also date from the mid-seventeenth century. Both have yellow flowers, the latter with faint purple veining. Unlike most fritillaria, which are fertilized by bumblebees, crown imperial can be pollinated by a small bird. Bluetits, *Parus caeruleus,* were observed pollinating crown imperials at Cambridge University in 1986, 1987, and 1988.

Arriving in Europe by way of Constantinople (now Istanbul) in the sixteenth century was another stately species, *Fritillaria persica.* This bulb has a more Victorian appearance, for rather than the fresh, bright green of the crown imperial, its numerous leaves are a soft gray-green, often with a lengthwise curl. They are scattered up a 3-foot-high stem, which is completed by a long spike of 7 to 20 or more small, somber, dark plum-colored, bell-like flowers, rather than a leafy tuft. The form offered by nurseries is an exceptionally fine deep-colored one named 'Adiyaman' after a town in southern Turkey. A group of three or more makes an elegant addition to the garden. Again, plant early to protect from desiccation. Native to southern Iran and Turkey, Israel, and Jordan, this species will tolerate hotter summers. However, the flowers will last better in a lightly shaded site.

One I am very fond of is *Fritillaria pallidiflora.* This is rare in cultivation, although it can be increased by seed, which is produced quite freely. The squarish, bell-like flowers are quite large in proportion to the 15-inch height. One to four to a stem, they are a pale greenish yellow or straw yellow, just barely tessellated with reddish brown outside, and freckled with the same color inside. Native to the Tien Shan and Ala Tau Mountains of central Asia, it is found at almost 12,000 feet. Obviously it is winter hardy and has an aversion to hot summers, growing best in cool, moist, but well-drained conditions in a soil with ample compost. I grow it in light shade with a permanent mulch of oak leaves and small twigs. Yellow hose-in-hose primroses add to the spring display. To provide interest after the bulb is dormant, large, hairy-leaved *Heuchera villosa* and ferns share the same space.

A relatively recent re-introduction, and in apparently good supply, is *F. michailovskyi.* Discovered in northeastern Turkey in 1905, it was brought into cultivation with the 1965 Turkish expedition of Brian Mathew, John and Helen

Tomlinson, and Margaret Briggs. This dainty bulb grows 4 to 8 inches tall, with one to four flowers in May/June. They are a glossy yellow inside, and a rich purplish brown outside, edged in bright yellow. One charming combination at the New York Botanical Garden's Thomas Everett Memorial Rock Garden pairs this with ferny-leaved, soft yellow-flowered *Corydalis cheilanthifolia*.

Other species of fritillaria are offered on an irregular basis. One handsome, temperamental small charmer is the black sarana, *Fritillaria camschatcensis*. This is the only species that occurs on both the Asian and North American continents, and is native to Japan, where it grows at low elevations in moist meadows with sedges and grasses as well as in the mountains in central and northern Honshu and Hokkaido, being especially common around Sapporo. I saw a wonderful display of it at the Rokku Mountain Alpine Botanic Garden outside Kobe, Japan, but suspect it was cultivated. It is also found in eastern Siberia, Kamchatka through the Kuril Islands to Alaska, into Washington and Oregon. In very cold climates it will be summer blooming and thrive in full sun, but more typically it appears in early to mid-spring and grows best in a cool, leafy soil in partial shade. The flowers, one to three or more on a 6-inch-tall stem, are the deepest color of any in this genus, a deep maroon-purple, almost black. It resents transplanting and quite often will not flower the first couple of years after being moved. While the bulbs are poisonous, they are made harmless by cooking. Roasted, it was such a staple food of the northern regions that early European explorers gave it the name of Eskimo potato.

Fritillaria thunbergii is widely cultivated in Japan and China, and has become naturalized in suitable locations. It has two to six white flowers faintly tessellated or veined with pale purple, on stems 1 to 2 feet tall. Deeper planting, with about 6 inches of soil over the bulb, seems to improve flowering. It has in the past been called *F. verticillata* var. *thunbergii*, as the two species are so similar. I grow *F. verticillata* under Allegheny spurge, *Pachysandra procumbens*. As it grows 15 inches tall, the flower stalk easily reaches above the ground cover. I find the greenish-white, faintly checkered flowers rather modest, but enjoy the attractive curl to the tips of the slender gray leaves, reminiscent of graceful flourishes on an illuminated manuscript. Another species native to Japan is *F. japonica*, with one or two bell-shaped, drooping white flowers lightly tessellated with brown and purple. Found in lightly shaded thickets and open woodlands, it is scarce in cultivation.

A North American species, checker-lily *Fritillaria affinis*, also known as *F. lanceolata*, is native from British Columbia south to California. It is extremely variable, with dwarf forms from exposed grasslands to giant forms generally found in woodlands, ranging in height from 6 inches to over 3 feet tall. Color can be anything from yellow-green or green to deep purple, with, or possibly without, tessellation. Wayne Roderick, who has studied the California native flora since boyhood, finds it easy to grow in the University of California Botanic Garden, and even considers this an aggressive species. It thrives in their basic mix of one part good garden soil, one part coarse sand, and one part humus. Remember though, this species is found in the San Francisco area, so he is growing a locally native plant. *F. affinis* 'Wayne Roderick' is a sterile triploid form found in Marin County, with flowers gray-purple on the outside, blotched with green at the base, and unevenly checkered on the upper half. It produces numerous "rice grain" offsets as its means of propagation.

Roderick finds most of the species of *Fritillaria* native to the Pacific coast difficult if not impossible to grow in gardens. Part of the difficulty is that bulbs offered for sale are commonly desiccated beyond viability. Even if healthy bulbs can be obtained, none are as easy in cultivation as *F. meleagris*. In addition to *F. affinis*, he finds *F. purdyi* more adaptable in gardens, perhaps because it is found in a wide range of habitats. It grows from a 1,000-foot elevation in Lake County to over 7,000 feet in Mendocino County, with the bulbs wedged between rocks with 3 to 4 inches of scree on top of the rocks. He grows it in equal parts of their basic mix and crushed road rock. These two native species,

The sturdy, cool yellow bells of *Fritillaria pallidiflora* add a charming touch to the author's woodland garden.

The fresh white flowers of *Ornithogalum umbellatum* are a charming addition to hosta and ferns in the Connecticut garden of Pierre and Susan Bennerup.

with modifications for southern California or the northwest, could be grown and enjoyed by people who are instead cultivating more familiar bulbs such as daffodils and tulips.

Two I would like to try are *F. pyrenaica* and *F. pontica*. *F. pyrenaica* is native to south-central France and northwestern Spain. The solitary flowers are heavily tesselated dark purple to brown outside, citron-green inside. The plant grows 6 to 12 inches tall. There is one rather rare, highly desirable form with pale yellow flowers, the cultivar 'Old Gold'. *F. pontica*, from southern Albania, southern Yugoslavia, northern Greece, and northwestern Turkey, grows wild in damp scrub or woodland but not in dry shade. It is reputedly easy to grow if given light shade. It flowers in April/May, with one to three apple-green flowers, citron-green inside. Its characteristic feature is that the beautifully shaped pale green bells are overtopped by a whorl of three gray-green leaves while the rest of them are scattered up the 12- to 18-inch stem.

Ornithogalum

Star of Bethlehem is a name applied to several different white-flowered *Ornithogalum*. There are about 150 species native to Europe, Africa, and Asia, many of them quite hardy. Native to southern Europe but naturalized in many areas, silver bells, *Ornithogalum nutans,* grows 12 to 18 inches tall with 3 to 12 white flowers in April/May, each with a broad green midrib on the reverse of the petals and held close to the stem on short pedicels. The leaves die away quickly, often about the time the bulb flowers. It grows best in shade and will naturalize in woodland, where it combines attractively with hosta and other coarse-leaved plants such as Siberian bugloss, *Brunnera macrophylla,* with its blue flowers resembling forget-me-nots. More widespread, native to most of Europe, North Africa, and portions of the Middle East, including Turkey, Syria, Lebanon, and Israel, *Ornithogalum umbellatum* is very similar in appearance and time of bloom. It grows 6 to 10 inches tall, with numerous 1-inch-wide flowers on each stem. Each flower is on a pedicel held well out from the stem, pure white inside, with a green stripe down the center of the petals on the outside. They provide a glistening display while open and then fold into a disappearing act, opening at midday or early in the afternoon and closing at dusk. This species can be very invasive through self-sowing, and is best used in a wild garden or beneath shrubs where such increase is not a problem. It also grows well in grass, and can become a nuisance in the lawn. The leaves of both these species have a silver-white line on the upper surface, similar to crocus.

Several tender species are grown for the florist trade, widely used as cut flowers since they last for several weeks. They are excellent in mild winter areas of the South, and in California. *Ornithogalum arabicum* is a Mediterranean species, pleasingly fragrant with pure white petals and a striking glossy black ovary clearly visible in the center. Each individual flower is about 2 inches wide, with the spike 20 to 30 inches tall. The lower flowers have a longer pedicel, producing a somewhat flattish appearance. It needs a warm, sunny site with a good summer baking. Otherwise in subsequent years it may grow well but flower poorly. Chincherinchee, *O. thyrsoides,* has large white or creamy-white flowers, each about 1 inch wide on stalks 2 feet high. This is a tender bulb, and needs a sheltered, well-mulched position in marginal areas. It can be treated like gladiolus, with the bulbs dug in early autumn and stored in a frost-free location for the winter. The large bulbs can be planted in a sunny site in spring, with ample moisture in summer while the leaves are growing, but avoid a soggy site. It will then flower in late summer. A native of the southwest Cape of South Africa, it can only be left in the ground in regions with mild winter. Under such conditions it will increase quickly.

This is a hectic time of year. The garden requires, nay, demands, attention — admiration of emerging growth and fresh flowers, nurturing seedlings, cosseting tender plants not sturdy enough for the outside world, commencement of weeding, mulching, fertilizing. It is important to tend established garden comrades. If old clumps of bulbs are overcrowded, the period after they bloom and before they go dormant is the most suitable time to separate them. Now is the time to mark and move the white forms of guinea hen flower. Fertilizers are best assimilated and utilized while the geophytes have leaves in active growth. Look around the garden and observe where plantings seem in need of improvement — more snowdrops clustered around the oak tree, purple and lavender crocus to be planted under the yellow *Corylopsis spicata*. Then page ahead in your calendar to August/September and make a note of what to do. We need to constantly look ahead from the "now" in the ongoing dance of the seasons.

3

Daffodils, Hyacinths, and Tulips

THE BIG THREE OF SPRING

DAFFODILS, hyacinths, and tulips are familiar to gardener and nongardener alike. Apartment dwellers purchase them coaxed into early bloom in pots, and as cut flowers to adorn a room. These are the bulbs commonly used for formal bedding out in elaborate patterns of color in public parks and gardens. The classic example is Keukenhof at Lisse, in Holland. It is open for only a few months in the spring when the millions of bulbs that were planted the previous autumn blossom in a tapestry of color. This extraordinary display is guaranteed since all the bulbs are planted fresh each year. For the home gardener this is neither practical nor desirable. We inhabit our gardens year-round, so our goal is a garden that pleases us in all seasons. With a massive display of bulbs needing fresh plantings each autumn, the only possibility for summer interest would be an equally tremendous planting of annuals. For most gardeners the combination of these bulbs with annuals will be on a smaller scale, and their association with other perennials, shrubs, and a scattering of annuals will provide the most satisfactory long-term results.

Daffodils

Perhaps the most common and widely recognized bulb of all is the daffodil. It is among the first flowers we learn to name as children. In autumn its big brown onion-like bulbs provide a promise of the seasonal journey, flowers to follow winter's end. When I see bunches of golden daffodils and branches of pussy willows for sale in shops I know that spring is here. Readily obtainable, simple to plant, reliable in flower. What more could be asked? Only some thought on how to make effective use of their bright spring display, and conceal the disreputable yellowing foliage as it ages.

"Daffodil" and "narcissus" are both used as common names. When italicized, *Narcissus* is the botanical Latin name of the genus. This confusion is sometimes compounded by another everyday name, "jonquil," often used in the South to refer to yellow-flowered narcissus. There is one classification of species narcissus called *N. jonquilla*, with several sweetly scented deep golden-yellow flowers on a tall stem.

Daffodils grow well in sun or deciduous woodland shade. When planted in a woodland daffodils have a tendency to face sunward while in bloom. While in growth they will tolerate surprising amounts of water. Mike Salmon of Monocot Nursery in England told me of finding wild daffodil species blooming completely underwater on the Iberian Peninsula. The critical point is that these same bulbs were dry while dormant in summer. While daffodils can tolerate very moist soils when in growth, winter wet can lead to bulb rot. Avoid planting in heavy wet soils; either plant in a different location or make a raised bed so as to improve drainage. The majority of daffodils are cold hardy. More, they demand a period of cold if they are to flower. In mild winter areas such as southern California, the bulbs are sold "precooled," given a necessary chilling by the wholesaler before they are sold. Along with other bulbs in the Amaryllis family, such as *Galanthus,* snowdrops, daffodils are not eaten by chipmunks, voles, squirrels, rabbits, or deer and are thus an excellent choice for areas where these animals are a problem.

In a formal planting use daffodils in groups of a minimum of ten or more of a kind, with the bulbs placed close together, only inches apart. In groupings with naturalistic design plant in drifts, like schooling fish, with a few gathered in smaller clumps hinting at natural increase. Plant three times as deep as the bulb is high, perhaps a little deeper in light sandy soil, more shallowly in a heavy clay. Rather than use the so-called naturalizing mixtures, which flower in random display, I prefer to buy separate varieties and plant them in distinct groups. This allows me to create an effective display rather than an erratic one. Be discrimi-

Noted author and gardener Sydney Eddison effectively combines tulips and daffodils with peonies, daylilies, and other perennials in her Newtown, Connecticut, flower border.

One sure way to shorten the life of your daffodils is to "tidy up" the foliage.

A traditional way of planting daffodils is in an infrequently mown field or orchard, as here in New Canaan, Connecticut. Caution: Do not use the hay for animal feed if daffodil leaves are mixed with the grass.

In New Canaan, Connecticut, the author used daffodils at the edge of a client's pond, where the combination of sunny flowers and spring-green grass and willow foliage would create an effective display.

nating about color and time of bloom: I can never forget the jarring riot of color I saw one spring where an orange and yellow large-cup daffodil had been combined with purple rhododendrons in front of a red brick building.

Daffodils can be used in many different ways. They are elegant in a formal border, interplanted with peonies and daylilies to disguise the aging bulb foliage. It is poor technique to fold, braid, or tie up bulb foliage, as it reduces the ability of the leaves to send food down to the bulb for next year's bloom. As has been mentioned, daffodils are very suitable in woodland plantings, used with hosta, astilbe, or ferns as companion plants to hide their old yellowing leaves. For example a group of daffodils might be centered in a clump of three astilbe. Then as the bulbs' flowers fade the emerging leaves and later flowers on the herbaceous perennial take their space and add interest to the shady garden. Daffodils can be planted in turf, but then the grass should not be mown until the bulb foliage has ripened. A location with rough, coarse grass, such as an orchard or a meadow, is more suitable than a lawn right next to the house, where the unkempt grass would be quite obvious.

The eleven-division classification of daffodils is based on the form of the flower: relative length of trumpet or corona to the perianth (petals), shape of the flower, number of flowers to a stem, and parentage from wild species. Thus the first three divisions are based on the length of the corona, the fourth contains double daffodils, the next five categorize hybrids showing the characteristics of particular species, the tenth contains species daffodils as they are found in the wild, and the last division is a resting place for daffodils that do not fit in the other categories.

The trumpet daffodil of Division I, with one flower per stem and corona equal to or longer than the perianth segments, is most familiar and a reliable stalwart in cultivation. Early blooming, not fragrant, this is the "host of golden daffodils" of Wordsworth, the daffodils spilling down the grassy knoll at the Brooklyn Botanic Garden, the cut flower of the florist. They are useful in the perennial border, in large-scale informal designs, and in combination with shrubs and trees.

Many cultivars exist, in variation on the theme of yellow, white, and bicolor, growing from 12 to 18 inches tall, depending on the variety. When we imagine a daffodil, it is a golden-yellow trumpet daffodil that comes to mind. This "standard" is personified by 'King Alfred', which was introduced in 1899, but today there are only a handful of the authentic cultivar being grown. What is offered should more properly be referred to as the "King Alfred type." 'Dutch Master' and 'Unsurpassable' are sunshine yellow, 'Arctic Gold' is goldenrod yellow, while 'Bestseller' is a softer, primrose yellow. 'Beersheba' and 'Mt. Hood' are classic whites (the latter will open ivory-cream and then fade to white), and there are bicolors such as 'Spellbinder', with white trumpet and lemon-yellow petals, and 'Foresight', with white petals and a yellow trumpet. Pink daffodils, trumpets such as 'Mrs. R.O. Backhouse' and large cups such as 'Louise de Coligny', 'Salome', 'Pink Charm', and 'Roseworthy' have the finest color when the flower first opens, and under cool conditions, so they are best used in a shaded situation.

Large-cup, Division II, daffodils also have one flower per stem, but length of the corona is more than one-third but less than equal to the perianth segments. Similar in height to the trumpet daffodils, the flowers appear later in the daffodil season and can be yellow, as in 'Carlton'; white, as in 'Ice Follies'; or bicolor, as in 'Ambergate', 'Carbineer', and 'Delibes', with an orange cup and yellow petals, 'Royal Orange', with orange cup and white petals, or 'Spring Queen', with pale lemon-yellow cup and white petals.

There are fewer cultivars offered of short-cup, Division III, daffodils than of Division I and II. They are late blooming and have one flower per stem, with a cup a third or less than the length of the petals. 'Barrett Browning' has a red-orange cup and yellow petals, and 'Audubon' has a pale yellow cup edged with orange-red and white petals.

Next come the double daffodils. Regardless of the proportion of corona to perianth segments, number of flowers to a stem, or parentage, all are grouped in Division IV. One of the earliest double cultivars, which has been given specific ranking, is *N. eystettenis,* or 'Queen Anne's Double Daffodil'. Mentioned by Lobel in 1581, it is named for Basil Bessler's herbal, the *Hortus Eystettenis* of 1618, in which it was first depicted. Growing about 7 inches tall, the cup has been replaced by six gradually diminishing soft yellow layers, creating a six-pointed star. This is named for Queen Anne of Austria, and confusion can readily arise since there is Queen Anne's (of England) Double Jonquil, which is a late-flowering, fully double, rounded little flower on 6- to 8-inch-high stems. Possibly identical is 'Pencrebar', reintroduced by Alec Gray in 1929 after it was found growing in a Cornish garden of the same name. Another early double is 'Van Sion', highly valued when it was introduced in the 1500s and still available today. It was registered as *N. telamonius plenus,* but to gardeners and bulb producers alike it remains 'Van Sion', after Vincent van Sion, the Fleming who lived in London and grew the first bulbs of this cultivar in England in 1620. Each spring I see a sturdy clump with many raggedly double yellow flowers cheerfully blossoming next to a stone wall here in Wilton, Connecticut. Some other readily available varieties include: 'Earlicheer', which is ivory-white with some lemon-yellow petals mixed in; 'White Lion', which is waxy-white with some pale yellow petals in the center; 'Golden Ducat', which is a sport of 'King Alfred' and just as golden yellow; 'Cheerfulness', which has fragrant white and light yellow flowers; and 'Yellow Cheerfulness', which is yellow. To my eye, double flowers have an air of cultivation about them, so as to appear better suited to more formal sites.

Triandrus hybrids, Division V daffodils, have *N. triandrus* as a parent, and like the species have one to several small, nodding, fragrant, fuchsia-like white to pale yellow flowers late in the season, on stems 10 to 14 inches high. 'Angel's Tears' is a cultivar name inappropriately given to the species *N. triandrus albus.* Supposedly this took place when a Spanish boy, Angel Gancedo, burst into tears from fatigue and temper after a difficult climb to collect the bulbs for Peter Barr in 1887. Newer forms include milky-white 'Petral', ivory-white 'Ice Wings', and yellow-flowered 'Liberty Bells'. I have not found these easy to keep, and it is possible that they need sharper drainage than I have been providing. James S. Wells, in his book *Modern Miniature Daffodils,* suggests that the bulbs are relatively short-lived, and Michael Jefferson-Brown, in his *Narcissus,* writes that some, such as white-flowered 'Thalia', a familiar cultivar from early this century, are vulnerable to a debilitating virus that has infected commercial stock.

Among my favorites for informal naturalistic use are those in Division VI, bred from *N. cyclamineus,* which have petals that reflex back "like a mule about to kick," according to one old book. They have one or two flowers on stems 7 to 10 inches tall and are among the first to bloom. All of them have character and personality, bulbs that multiply well, and flowers that last for a long time. I find them superb in the woodland garden, where I grow them in combination with later-appearing, taller-growing native perennials such as *Caulophyllum thalictroides,* blue cohosh, whose emerging shoots, neat foliage, and attractive blue fruits in autumn fill the space once occupied by the now-dormant daffodils. They are excellent in combination with shrubs, and can extend the rather narrow interest of a typical foundation planting of azaleas, rhododendrons, pieris, and mountain laurel. Many of these are lower-growing cultivars, often a foot or less in height. These hybrids prefer partial shade and a soil that does not dry out in summer. They are suitable for use in small spaces as well as for mass plantings. The species itself is among the first to bloom. One long-lasting yellow-flowered cultivar with only slightly reflexed petals, 'February Gold', blooms in late March or early April in my Connecticut garden. 'Peeping Tom' is also yellow, with an extra-long trumpet; 'Charity May' is a uniform soft buttercup yellow; 'Jenny' has white petals and a creamy-white trumpet; 'Jack Snipe' has a yellow trumpet and white, typically reflexed petals. One choice cultivar is 'Tete-a-Tete', which is excellent not only for garden use

In the author's garden a spritely combination pairs *Narcissus* 'Jumblie' with the blue daisy-like flowers of *Anemone apennina*.

At Wave Hill, in the Bronx, New York, an old, still-popular cultivar of narcissus, 'Actaea', blossoms with the faded rose-colored sepals of *Helleborus niger*, a pairing as appropriate today as it would have been centuries ago.

but also in containers for early bloom. The flowers, on 6- to 8-inch stems, frequently appear in pairs, although sometimes singles or triplets appear. Another aptly named cultivar is 'Jumblie', with pairs of flowers tangled together on 5- to 7-inch stems. I have grown this interplanted in a jack-in-the-box manner with *Anemone apennina* and achieved attractive results. This was easily accomplished. At planting time I dug the hole and planted the daffodil bulbs. After filling the hole halfway, I set the anemone tubers in place and finished filling the hole. The jumbled golden flowers of 'Jumblie' and the blue daisy-like flowers of the windflower appear together. 'Dove Wings' has creamy-yellow petals that fade to white, and a white trumpet. I use it with the green-flowered *Helleborus foetidus,* bear's foot hellebore, to create a cool and elegant effect.

Jonquils, *N. jonquilla* hybrids, are placed in Division VII. They flower later in the season than trumpet, long-cup, or cyclamineus daffodils, and have two to six strongly scented, sweetly fragrant flowers to each 8- to 18-inch stem. The perianth is flat, rather than reflexed like triandrus hybrids, and their rush-like leaves are dark green. They can be grown, even naturalized, almost anywhere in the South, where not all daffodils are easy to cultivate. A light airy mulch of pine straw to keep the soil cooler in hot summers is helpful. 'Trevithian' is the standard, an older cultivar with sweetly scented lemon-yellow flowers, usually in pairs on an 18-inch stem. 'Baby Moon' has small, deliciously scented buttercup yellow flowers on 5- to 6-inch stems in late April and is charming in the rock garden; 'Lintie' has an orange-yellow cup and yellow petals; 'Pipit' opens a soft lemon-yellow with the cup fading to white; and 'Quail' is soft golden yellow and will waft the most delicious, tantalizing fragrance across the garden on each passing breeze.

Paperwhites are tazetta daffodils, grouped in Division VIII. These are bunch-flowering hybrids of *N. tazetta,* with four to eight or more very fragrant flowers to a stem, and often two or three 14- to 18-inch stems to a bulb. The cup is quite shallow and the perianth segments are often crinkled. As they are less cold hardy than the other groups, these are best used for indoor bloom in cold winter regions, outdoors only in the South or similar mild winter areas. Basically, they are Mediterranean in origin: native in locales such as Iran, Kashmir, and Lebanon, and the French and Italian Riviera, and grow best under mild, sunny conditions. The species, *N. tazetta,* is naturalized in China and Japan, having been introduced in the thirteenth century, possibly even earlier. Flowering time is quite variable, from December through April.

This is a popular division, familiar when coaxed into bloom indoors in a bowl of pebbles to help fidgety gardeners survive cold winters. 'Cragford' has a small, flattened orange cup and creamy-white petals; 'Geranium' has sweetly scented flowers with a geranium red cup and white petals; 'Scarlet Gem' has primrose-yellow flowers and a flattened cup of tangerine red-gold; and 'Grand Soleil d'Or' (often offered simply as 'Soleil d'Or'), sometimes called Chinese sacred lily, is a glowing golden yellow with an orange cup, deliciously scented. 'Bridal Crown' is a double white. The familiar "Paperwhite" (a generic name) may be one of several cultivars. Relatively recent introductions from Israel are 'Galilee' and 'Ziva', with white flowers and cups; 'Omri' and 'Nony' (which have floppy foliage, as does 'Galilee') have a creamy-yellow cup. Tazettas will generally flower in four to six weeks after potting up. If grown indoors in pebbles and water, discard the bulbs after flowering, for they will have exhausted their food reserves and will be too weakened to salvage for another season. All will grow outdoors in the milder parts of the South, the Gulf states, and those portions of Washington, Oregon, and California that border the Pacific Ocean. Around Los Angeles an early form of *N. tazetta,* 'Soleil d'Or', or 'Autumn Sol', also called the Chinese sacred lily, with white petals and mandarin-orange cup can be in bloom by Thanksgiving, even earlier in Santa Barbara.

Pheasant's eye daffodil, *N. poeticus recurvus,* is the last to bloom, flowering in late May or early June. The flowers, one per 16- to 18-inch-high stem, have a glistening, crystalline white perianth and a small ruffle of a cup, greenish yellow edged with red. It is native to Europe, from central and southern France and northern Spain through the Alps down to southern Italy, through the Balkans, and into Greece. The bulbs resent digging, and are best when deeply planted in a site that never dries out and then left undisturbed. Limited in number of cultivars, Division IX contains 'Actaea', which was introduced in 1927. This old, strongly fragrant variety is one that I have found surviving and flowering in long-abandoned gardens under brambles. The cup is yellow, and rimmed in crimson red. 'Cantabile' has a green cup that fades to yellow in sunny sites, thinly edged in deep red.

The split corona, or butterfly, daffodils are in Division XI. They have a divided corona, torn into segments for at least one-third of its length, laid flat against the perianth, giving the appearance of a daisy. 'Cassata' has a white cup tipped with pale yellow and white petals; 'Pico Bello' has a white cup with central orange band and white petals; 'Valdrome' has a deeper yellow cup and soft yellow petals. The daffodils in this classification seem less persistent in the gar-

Annual Growth Cycle of Narcissus

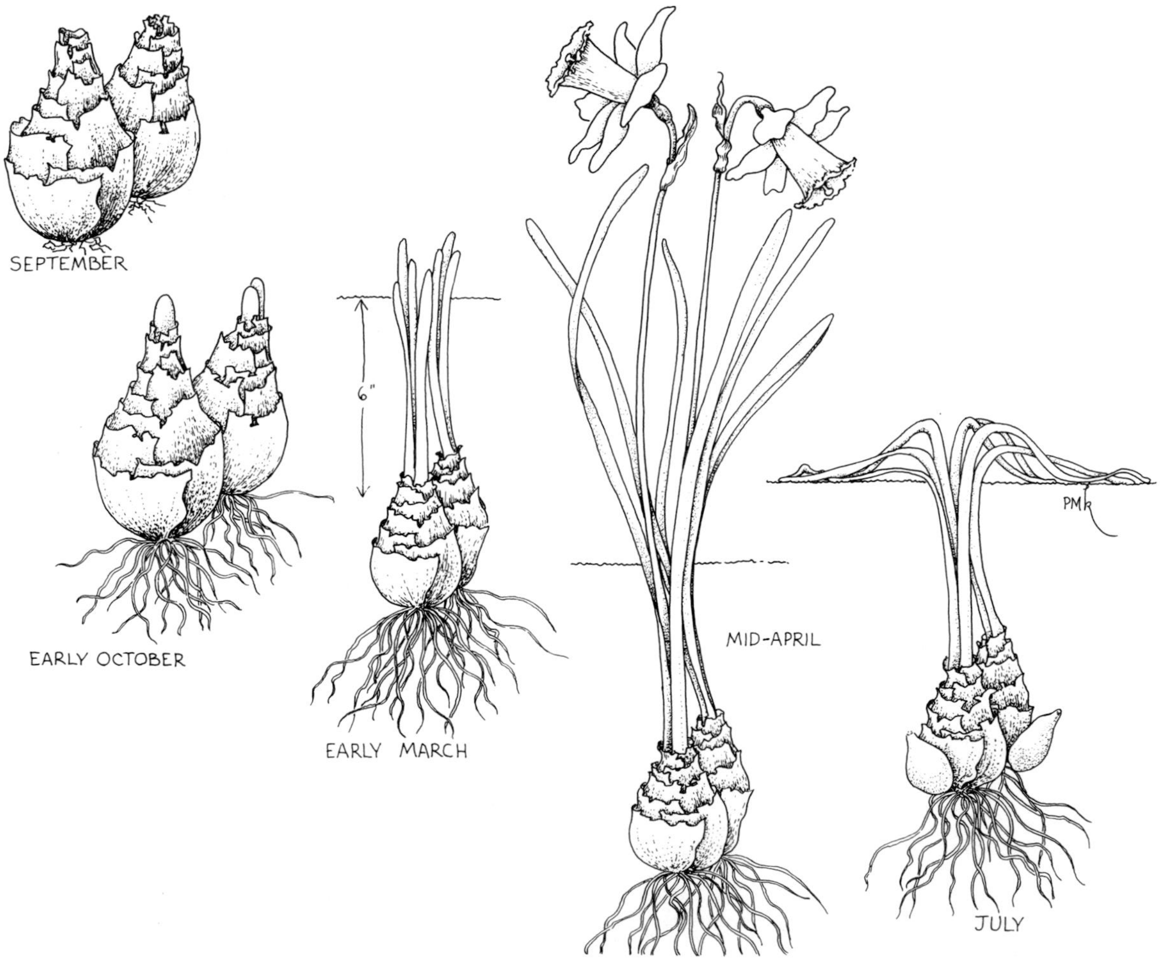

den than, say, trumpet or poeticus cultivars. They weaken, cease flowering, and vanish after several years. I use them in more formal settings, rather than woodland or naturalized groupings.

Species daffodils Division X, are any that occur in the wild. Here are grouped *NN. cyclamineus, jonquilla, tazetta,* and others, some of which are parents of the hybrids. There is, as might be expected, a good deal of diversity. The hoop petticoat daffodil, *N. bulbocodium,* grows 8 inches tall with a funnel-shaped cup and petals reduced to narrow spikes. As it prefers full sun and a sandy, gritty soil, this would be a good choice for the rock garden. *N. asturiensis* (*N. minimus*) is an exemplary miniature of the trumpet daffodils, growing only 3 to 4 inches tall with a perfect little yellow trumpet. Absolutely hardy, I have had this flower outdoors in late February or early March. The dainty size suggests its use in pots, flowering year after year under alpine house or cold frame conditions. *N. pseudo-narcissus* is the Lent lily, found wild in English woodlands in March. About 12 inches tall, the trumpet-like flowers have a lemon yellow cup and sulphur yellow petals.

Daffodils have much to recommend them. They are reliable in bloom, with many of the cultivars and species often making offsets and increasing in number from year to year. They can be grown in sunny situations, provided the soil does not bake dry in summer, and are even more at home in deciduous woodlands. Most are hardy in cold winter areas, and there are varieties that tolerate mild winters. The flowers are excellent for cutting; bulbs can be coaxed into early bloom indoors. Better yet, daffodils are pest-free, untouched by voles, chipmunks, mice, rabbits, or deer. So excellent a plant should find its place in any garden, to brighten the spring scene year after year.

Tulips

Tulips, along with dahlias and German or bearded iris, appear in a rainbow of colors. It is small wonder that tulips are as popular as they are. With strong-stemmed, cup-like flowers in white, ivory, cream, yellow, orange, red, pink, lavender, and purple, they have tremendous appeal in the spring garden and as a cut flower. Alas, the modern hybrids are not as persistent a flowering plant as could be wished, and their flowers are a dietary delight for deer and rabbits above ground while below ground voles and chipmunks dine on the bulbs. These are edible, and anecdotes from the seventeenth century exist, possibly apocryphal, one about an Antwerp merchant who, mistaking for onions some tulip bulbs sent from Constantinople with a consignment of cloth, roasted and ate a number of them to great financial loss. The Dutch were obliged to eat tulip bulbs during the German occupation of Holland in 1944 and 1945 at the height of the winter of starvation, the *hongerwinter.* A pamphlet published January 23, 1945, concerning food supply during the war was written by the Rubber Society at Delft, which was trying to supply staff members with extra food supplies "in the form of Tulipbulbs, food that — if well prepared — is eaten nowadays in great quantities in the big cities." Noting that the nutritional value of the tulip is 'almost 1.8 times that of potatoes," the pamphlet goes on to suggest methods of preparation. The thin brown tunic was removed and the bulbs sliced in half to permit removal of the inedible immature yellow shoot in the center. Eaten raw the bulbs are hard to digest, and recipes suggest boiling and mashing, separating the scales and roasting into tulip chips, or grinding and drying into a coarse flour to be used for making bread and pancakes. Eight bulbs at one meal was considered a rather good portion. Gladiolus were also eaten, but never narcissus, which are poisonous.

Tulips made their entry into the gardens of western Europe about 400 years ago. While Turkish historians mention the flower as early as the middle of the fifteenth century, this is the period when the conquest of the Crimea led to the introduction into European Turkey of tulip species from the Black Sea area and beyond. Muhammed II, conqueror of Constantinople, was a keen gardener with a special interest in tulips. Their journey to western Europe began when Ogier Ghiselin de Busbecq, ambassador from the Emperor Ferdinand I to the court of Suleiman the Magnificent, brought seeds and probably also bulbs back to Vienna in the mid-sixteenth century. Only five years later, in the garden of Councillor Hewart, Konrad Gesner saw a tulip with a single large reddish flower. His illustration, the earliest known of a tulip in western Europe, appeared in his book, *De Hortis Germaniae Liber* of 1561. By this time a prominent German family of merchants and bankers, the Fuggers, were growing tulips in Augsburg, and the following year an Antwerp merchant received a cargo of bulbs from Constantinople.

In 1573, one of Europe's premier botanists, Carolus Clusius, founded a *Hortus medicus,* or physic garden, in Vienna. A professor of botany with a very special liking for geophytes, he received a large quantity of tulip seed from de Busbecq, who was due to leave for France the next year. The tulip seed was somewhat shriveled, and as he was dubious as to its viability, Clusius didn't get around to sowing it until 1575. Germination was excellent, and beginning in 1580, the tulips began flowering with yellow, red, white, and purple flowers, and even some with mixed colors. This is the first mention of the "breaking" of tulips, a virus-induced color patterning, which resulted in the tulipomania of the 1630s. Only cultivated tulips are known to be susceptible to the virus disease resulting in variegated flowers.

In the autumn of 1593, at the age of sixty-six and crippled from a fall, Clusius became a professor of botany at the University in Leyden. He requested that the Curatores of the University grant him the use of a garden temporarily being used as a Hortus medicus. He wanted this space to cultivate his bulbs, for which plants he had a great fondness. A re-creation of this small fenced garden can be found today in the Clusius garden, across a small canal behind the botanic garden. In its day the fence could not protect his choicest bulbs, many of which were stolen by thieves who climbed into the garden by night. By 1603 the inventory mentions 600 tulips, early and late, rare and common varieties. Thus from Flanders was the tulip introduced into its spiritual home, Holland, with which it has been associated ever since.

Cultivated tulips were brought to Russia from western Europe by Dutch merchants in the sixteenth and early seventeenth century. An official reference to cultivated tulips in Russia dates back to the 1701 inventory of Nizhni Park, located in the St. Petersburg suburb of Petrodvorets. They reached England at about the same time, roughly 1578, from Vienna. The first record of a tulip bulb flowering in France dates from 1608. Within a few years, the French were exchanging tulip bulbs for fantastic sums. There were instances of single bulbs being traded for a mill, a brewery, and used as a dowry. The craze spread northward through Flanders to Holland, where the drama was played out — the *Tulpenwindhandel,* or Tulipomania. It was at its height for only three years, between 1634 and 1637, but prices for rare bulbs had begun to climb to absurd heights even earlier through the enthusiasm of Dutch amateurs. Johann Beckman, in his *History of Inventions and Discoveries,* published in London in 1846, wrote that the speculation "was followed not only by mercantile people, but also by the first noblemen, citizens of every description, mechanics, farmers, turf-diggers, chimney-sweeps, footmen, maid-servants, old clothes-women, etc. At first everyone won and no one lost." Tulips were the "junk bonds" of the seventeenth-century horticultural world!

The most popular, called at the time "florists' tulips," were divided into three classes: roses, bybloemens, and bizarres. Roses had a white background color, which was marked with some shade of rose, scarlet, crimson, or red. Bybloemens also had a white ground, but the marking color was some shade of purple or black. The nearer the rose class approached scarlet, and bybloemen deep purple or black, the better. Bizarres had a yellow ground marked with shades of orange, scarlet, brown, and black. A feathered flower had the markings confined to the edges of the petals only, while a flamed flower had in addition a central pillar or beam of color in each petal. The classes also in-

In Holland, beheading tulips is a springtime chore in the bulb fields. The result is more robust bulbs to send to market. (ILLUSTRATION COURTESY OF THE NETHERLANDS FLOWER BULB INFORMATION CENTER)

Still unmistakable today, this woodcut of *Tulipa praecox alba* first appeared in print in 1583, in a book by Charles de l'Ecluse (Clusius). (ILLUSTRATION FROM THE LIBRARY OF THE NEW YORK BOTANICAL GARDEN)

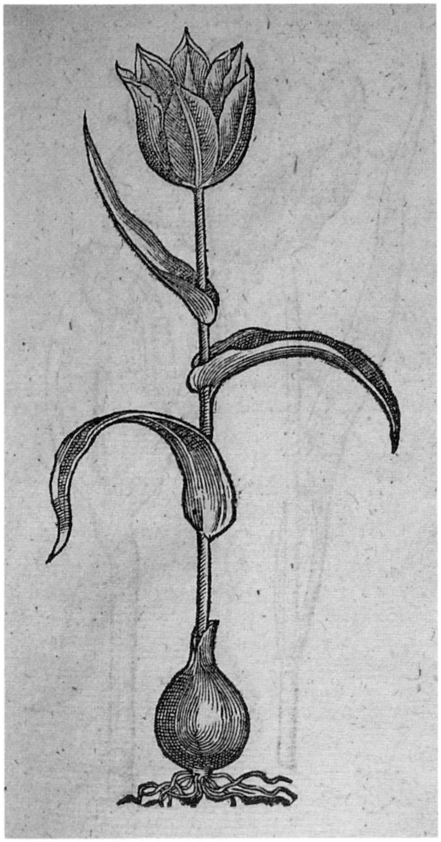

cluded breeders, or mother-tulips. The breeder was the seedling form of the flower, of one uniform color, and had no stripes or markings. The foliage was a solid shade of green. We know now that the markings are virus induced, and seedlings are free of the disease. When a flower broke, or *rectified,* as enthusiasts described it, it had a variegated flower and mottled foliage. Thus the speculation, with enormous sums exchanged even for a breeder, in the hopes that it would rectify into some elegant new variety.

In the early days of the mania sales took place between the end of June, when the bulbs were taken out of the ground, and September, the month for replanting them. Subsequently the pace became even more frenetic: deals were made year-round, with delivery promised for the summer. Farmers lacking ready cash bartered livestock and household goods in anticipation of huge profits. Beckman gives the price for one bulb of 'Viceroy' at: 2 loads of wheat, 4 loads of rye, 4 fat oxen, 8 fat pigs, 12 fat sheep, 2 hogsheads of wine, 4 barrels of 8-florin beer, 2 barrels of butter, 1,000 pounds of cheese, a complete bed, a suit of clothes, and a silver beaker — the whole valued at 2,500 florins. One bulb of 'Semper Augustus' fetched nearly twice that amount, together with a fine new carriage and pair. Such trades underscore the frenzy and widespread participation, as lack of money did not hinder speculation. Neither cultivar is grown on a commercial scale today, but only by amateurs for exhibition purposes, or in the Hortus Bulborum of historical cultivars at Limmen.

Suddenly, early in 1637, the crash came. The market was flooded as everyone wanted to sell and no one wanted to buy. On February 24, delegates from the principal towns of Holland met in Amsterdam to decide what was to be done. They agreed that all sales of tulips made before the end of the previous November should be binding. Transactions after that date could be canceled by the buyer if that notice was given before March. In April the Court of Holland declared that vendors who could not make their purchasers pay up could dispose of their bulbs as best they could and claim the difference. But often transactions had been for bulbs the seller did not actually possess, and the purchaser never intended to receive. It was all trading on futures, and the bubble had burst.

It is not surprising to learn that tulipomania left in its wake a small but violent band of tulip-phobes. Chief among them was Evrard Forstius, like Clusius also a professor of botany in Leyden, who reportedly could not see a tulip without attacking it furiously with his stick.

Today tulips have a more modest value, securely founded on their beauty in the garden. Modern development seeks to produce sturdy flowers with good color on strong stems, accomplishing these results through selective breeding rather than disease. About 1885 the famous firm of E. H. Krelage acquired from an amateur tulip grower, Monsieur Lenglart of Lille, a marvelous collection of healthy, vigorous tulips then known as "Flemish Tulips." Krelage renamed these, with the permission of Charles Darwin's son, "Darwin Tulips." They were an instant success and, as "Single Late Tulips," remain popular today. The crossing of 'Duc van Tol' cultivars with "Darwin" in the late 1920s resulted in "Mendel Tulips," which today are placed in "Single Early" for the earlier-blooming cultivars, while later-flowering ones, chiefly the result of hybridization between single early and late-flowering tulips, are placed in "Triumph Tulips."

Like narcissus, tulips have a registry of their own, lengthy lists of correctly named cultivars and species. Both genera contain a diversity of species, and there are seemingly endless possibilities for hybridization and selection. Although this does seem rather complicated, basically, there are fifteen categories of tulips. Single Early bloom in April, and this is a venerable category, with 'Yellow Prince', a synonym of 'Gele Prins', dating from 1785, still available today. Double Early tulips, short-stemmed, also bloom in April. 'Murillo', with white flowers flushed with pink, is a very famous Double Early developed in 1850. Its "sports," or variations, number in the dozens and include yellow and orange 'Marechal Niel', blood red 'Oranje Nassau', and deep rose 'Peach Blossom'. Tulips in Single Early and

Double Early categories are a good choice for coaxing into early bloom indoors.

Following these into bloom are the Triumph and Darwin hybrids. 'Kees Nelis', blood red edged orange-yellow and introduced in 1951, is the first Triumph hybrid. It is so famous that the house in Hillegom, Holland, where its hybridizer, an individual named 't Mannetje lived, has this tulip embossed on the wall above its front door. Late-flowering tulips bloom in May and include Single Late tulips with oval-shaped blossoms quite different from Darwins, and Peony Flowered, or Double Late tulips. Lily Flowered tulips, with pointed, reflexed petals, were originally called *retroflexa,* and date back to the nineteenth century. Fringed tulips have crystal-like fringes on the edges of their petals; Viridiflora tulips have green markings on the petals. Parrot tulips with extravagantly fringed petals date back to at least the late seventeenth century. Each Parrot variety is a sport from Single Early, Triumph, and Darwin tulips.

The term "Rembrandt tulips," if strictly applied, should be employed only for Darwins that have broken as a result of viruses. As this lily mottle virus seriously affects lilies, never grow Rembrandt tulips near lilies in case the virus should be transferred. These broken tulips with flowers striped or marked brown, bronze, black, red, pink, or purple on red, white, or yellow ground are no longer grown for commercial purposes, and will possibly be dropped from the next edition of the Classified List.

Planted at the New York Botanical Garden each year, tulips create a Persian carpet of color employing the same technique utilized at Keukenhof. And this is the best method, used in smaller numbers, to produce a stunning display in the home garden. Treat tulips as annuals: plant them in the fall, enjoy the display in the spring, and then discard them. While someone is always ready to tell me of a friend whose tulips flower reliably year after year, experience in my own garden and that of clients is otherwise. The first year after planting the display is excellent. Every bulb flowers, height and color is uniform within each variety, and the results are well worth it. The next year perhaps 60 percent of the bulbs flower. Some flowers are small, and the nonflowering bulbs send up only a single large leaf. By the third year perhaps about 30 percent are flowering. I have tried fertilizing more heavily, planting more deeply than usual, and so forth, and it just is not worth it. So I regard these bright flowers of the May garden as transients, temporary residents in the garden who cheer me with their flowers, to be replaced with new bulbs in the fall. Most of my geophyte budget goes for permanent denizens of the garden, but I always include a portion for tulips, unequalled for their colorful spring display.

This practical method allows utilization of that same space for annuals in the summer. It is a simple matter to plant marigolds or zinnias, and easy to pull the annuals for new bulbs in the fall. If perennials had been overplanted instead, new bulb placement would be awkward if not impossible. However, like any other bulb, tulips look better in combination than in isolation. Traditionally, they are combined with early, half-hardy annuals. Certainly wallflowers, *Cheirianthus,* in warm yellows and orange are splendid with tulips of a deeper orange or red hue. Forget-me-nots, sky blue, look charming with white, pink, or lavender tulips. Other good companion plants include arabis, candytuft, English daisy, pansies and violas, and primroses. Virginia bluebells, *Mertensia virginica,* is a shade-tolerant, ephemeral native geophyte often combined with May-flowering tulips. The golden daisy-like flowers of leopard's bane, *Doronicum caucasicum,* are charming with the early, dwarfer hybrids such as the orange and purple 'Princess Irene'. Azaleas create a fine background, but care is necessary in choosing tulip varieties, as some of the pink azaleas have a harsh bluish tint difficult to match. Soft pale pinks with white tulips create a delicate effect, while very different results are achieved from deep purple tulips, which also look striking with the fine lace-like foliage of a burgundy cut-leaf Japanese maple.

There are some tulips that I do find to be a more permanent addition to the garden: kaufmanniana, fosteriana,

and greigii hybrids and their original species. These dwarf early-flowering varieties are a charming addition to the rock garden or in the front of the border, and they are also useful for forcing. The key is good drainage and a sunny site where they can receive a good ripening in summer.

Kaufmanniana hybrids are very early (blooming in late March or early April), very dwarf hybrids of *Tulipa kaufmanniana,* native of the western Tien Shan Mountains of central Asia. Called the water-lily tulip, the species has a carmine rose exterior, creamy white with a deep golden-yellow base inside the flowers, which open wide in sun-

In spring the tulip walk at the New York Botanical Garden is a Persian carpet of color.

In the soft light of an overcast spring day, tulips, violas, and flowering cherries create a welcoming entrance display at the New York Botanical Garden. The tulips are a mixture of 'Shirley', a Single Late that starts pale yellow and fades to white with a flamed purple edge, and a deep maroon late-blooming Triumph cultivar, 'Negrita'.

light. There are naturally occurring varieties that are a rich buttercup yellow suffused with cherry. I once planted a dozen of these with about 50 bulbs of *Chionodoxa lucillae* and very much enjoyed the water-lily tulips flat open above the blue glory-of-the-snow. Cultivars are usually soft rosy pink or red outside, golden, cream, or white inside, like 'Ancilla', 'Brilliant', 'Cherry Orchard', 'Heart's Delight', and others. While the leaves on *T. kaufmanniana* are plain green, the varieties and hybrids will sometimes have mottled foliage.

Fosteriana are large-flowered varieties and hybrids, blooming in early April, with arguably its best-known cultivar 'Madame Lefeber', often incorrectly called 'Red Emperor'. The brilliant red flower with a yellow-bordered black blotch at the base is familiar, and a vivid partner to yellow trumpet daffodils, as their flowering periods overlap. Other varieties include the self-explanatory 'Golden Eagle', 'Golden Emperor', 'Purissima' = 'White Emperor', and more. *T. fosteriana* is native to central Asia.

Greigii tulips and their cultivars always have an attractive chocolate-brown mottling or striping to their leaves, and flower in April, later than kaufmanniana. 'Carioca' has flowers with a porcelain-rose exterior, edged with buttercup yellow, and buttercup yellow inside. Many cultivars in this class have an edging of a contrasting color to the petals, while others are a single color, for example 'Oratorio', with a rose exterior and apricot-rose interior. *T. greigii* itself has a deep fiery vermilion red color inside and out, marked at the base with a black blotch. It is also found in central Asia.

A major player in the European introduction of these species was the firm of C. G. van Tubergen, who in the period 1897 to 1914 brought into general cultivation a considerable number of previously unknown geophytes from central and western Asia. Taking Tashkent as a starting point, and collecting in Turkestan and Bokhara during the spring months of those years, P. L. Graeber gathered, among others, several varieties of *Tulipa kaufmanniana* and *T. greigii, T. korolkowii, T. hoogiana, T. tubergeniana,* other tulips, *Colchicum luteum,* and iris. A. Kronenburg,

an Austrian by birth who lived in Beirut, Syria, was commissioned in 1898 to collect in Syria and Palestine. In the autumn of 1901 he went to the Caucasus and collected quantities of *Tulipa eichlei,* staying in a hotel run by Joseph Haberhauer in Samarkand-Bokhara. In the summer of 1904 Haberhauer wrote to van Tubergen, saying that in the souk each spring, the peasants sold as cut flowers tulips that were larger and more brilliantly colored than any he had seen in gardens. The dry bulbs he sent that autumn proved to be the species we now know as *Tulipa fosteriana*. These were not instances of a few bulbs collected for study.

At home in the short turf of a buffalo grass lawn in Colorado, *Tulipa humilis* is multiplying both by seed and offsets. (SANDY SNYDER)

A warm combination of 'Orange Elite' tulips (a greigii cultivar), and the yellow daisies of *Doronicum caucasicum* brighten a spring garden in Westport, Connecticut.

Huge quantities were dug for export and resale. It is just this sort of massive collection from the wild that has endangered native populations, taking them to the brink of extinction.

Gardeners should concern themselves with this and purchase species bulbs labeled "of propagated origin." A letter from Mike Read of the British Flora and Fauna Preservation Society in early 1991 indicated that funding had been secured for at least the first year's work of an "Indigenous Propagation Project." This would have profound benefits, not only for the plants but, significantly, for the local people in Turkey who depend on sales of the bulbs for an important portion of their income. However, with the unsettled conditions in the region, most especially the Gulf War and its aftermath, horticultural endeavors such as this become minor issues.

I believe that much of the difficulty in growing tulips as perennials is the result of where we grow them. How do conditions differ in our gardens from those where tulips developed in the wild? Research conducted by Z. P. Botschantzeva, in Tashkent, central Asia, provided some interesting information. June through September, there is no summer precipitation in Tashkent. With *Tulipa kaufmanniana*, root formation within the bulb started in the fourth week of June, developing very slowly. In October, with autumn's lower temperatures and increased soil humidity, they grew more quickly and began to function immediately to carry water and nutrients from the soil to the bulb. Inception of flower buds occurs after leaf initiation, around mid-August, and is completed by the beginning of September. Flowers appeared aboveground in mid-March and wilted by the first of April. By early May the upper third of the leaves had turned yellow and dry, and by early June all aboveground organs had dried off but the seeds were still damp. *Tulipa fosteriana* followed the same cycle, on a slightly later schedule: root formation initiated in the first days of July, completed in October. Flower differentiation started in early June, with winter dormancy from November till early January, and flowering early in April.

Simply because the bulbs are out of sight does not mean events are not occurring. If the "dormant" bulbs in the ground are overwatered, it can skew their growth. In gardens, if the weather should prove dry, natural rainfall will be supplemented by irrigation. Conversely, if held for sale at too high a temperature the embryo flowerbud can blast and wither, and the bulb will produce only leaves the following spring. By nature tulips are ephemerous, typical of perennial plants that grow under the severe climatic conditions of central Asia with a pronounced summer dormant period. A large part of the region — Turkmenistan, Tajikistan, Uzbekistan, and southern Kazakhstan — is a vast desert with enormous mountain ranges in the east and south. It is only with falling temperatures and the first rains of autumn that the bulbs have functional roots. Many of these central Asian species occur on stony mountain slopes.

Not unexpectedly, it is in rock garden settings where these species tulips have full sun and sharp drainage that they perform as the perennials they indeed are. For my friend Sandy Snyder in Littleton, Colorado, where the climate is similar to that of central Asia, planting 2,500 tulips, crocus, and bulbous iris in her buffalo-grass lawn created an alpine meadow effect. She used *Tulipa tarda, T. humilis,* and *T. linifolia*. Over the years the bulbs have increased well, twenty- to thirtyfold in the first five years, to fortyfold since her original planting in the autumn of 1984. The grass is not cut until the bulb foliage is completely withered. I had good results with *T. aucheriana* on a west-facing, very sandy slope. The original three bulbs not only bloomed year after year but produced daughter bulbs that quickly reached flowering size. Two produced four flowers apiece, and one had five flowers. Then the deer came.

Hyacinths

The more than 200 hyacinth cultivars incorporated in the 1991 "International Checklist for Hyacinths and Miscellaneous Bulbs" of the Royal General Bulbgrowers' Association are selections of a single species, *Hyacinthus orientalis.* It is difficult to imagine the fat, overstuffed flower spikes of hyacinth as we see it today as a slim and graceful wildling with a lax raceme of two to 15 flowers. Since only *Hyacinthus orientalis* is involved, the development of modern cultivars ranging from white and yellow, pale pink to red, pale to deep blue and purple, has been accomplished solely by selection. A true bulb, the papery tunic is red-violet in forms with red and blue flowers, white where the flowers are yellow or white. Originally found in central and southern Turkey, northwestern Syria, and Lebanon, it has become naturalized in parts of southern Europe. Happily, the strong sweet fragrance of the wild type is retained in its modern descendants.

This is one bulb that lends itself to formal bedding, and at Keukenhof hyacinths are used in precise designs, easily producing colorful patterns in the May garden. The challenge is to do otherwise and devise an informal configuration. Whether formal or informal, do not buy the top-size bulbs. These will be 19 cm and over in diameter, and the resulting congested flower stalks are gross and require staking. I find them much more attractive in subsequent years when they have dwindled and assumed a more graceful appearance. First size, 18/19 cm, and second size, 17/18 cm, produce quite satisfactory displays. Even inexpensive third size, or bedding hyacinths, 16/17 cm and 15/16 cm, will produce fine spikes and create a good show when planted in beds and borders.

A catalog of hyacinths printed in Holland in 1808 lists numerous varieties, many of which are no longer available. As recently as 1973 a major Dutch bulb firm was offering four different dark blues, six light and medium blues, four whites, three yellow and salmon, four dark red and crimson, four deep pink, three pale pink, and two purple and violet cultivars. These thirty different cultivars represented only van Tubergen's wholesale offering of single-flowered hyacinths; they listed another half-dozen with double flowers. A current American retail catalog offers only six single-flowered cultivars: white 'Carnegie', primrose-yellow 'City of Haarlem', soft lilac-blue 'Delft Blue',

In precise, soldierly array, hyacinths at Keukenhof, in Holland, parade along a path.

A casual mixture of hyacinths in shades of blue, lavender, pink, and rose create a softly harmonious display in this New Canaan, Connecticut, garden.

At Stonecrop, the superb garden of Frank Cabot in Cold Spring, New York, the elegant reflexed petals of 'White Triumphator' tulips establish a cool display with *Dicentra spectabilis alba*.

Also in the Cabot garden, *Tulipa* 'Red Shine' provides a fiery, luminous display in front of *Berberis* 'Crimson Pygmy'.

dark salmon-apricot 'Gypsy Queen', deep rose-pink 'Pink Pearl', and mallow-purple 'Violet Pearl'. This is a very meager representation of the 203 cultivars listed in the 1991 "International Checklist" and includes no doubles. The only double I have seen was 'Hollyhock', looking most attractive coaxed into early bloom at Rob Proctor's house in Denver one snowy March. He had obtained the bulbs from the Daffodil Mart. Regardless of whether the bulbs come from a neighborhood garden center, by mail order from another state, or across national borders, what is important is what we do with what we have available.

One serene planting in a client's garden used groups of white hyacinths in a ground cover of myrtle, *Vinca minor,* with groups of white *Narcissus* 'Mt. Hood'. They were followed in summer with *Caladium* 'Candidum', which has a white leaf. Edged with myrtle, a circular bed set in a brick terrace had a planting of mixed medium and light blue, rose-pink, and soft violet hyacinths, followed by white-flowered impatiens. In my woodland garden I have used 'Violet Pearl', finding the hyacinth flowers a fascinating contrast to the wine-red new shoots of a species peony, *Paeonia obovata alba.* Another charming combination paired soft lilac-blue 'Delft Blue' and 'Blue Magic', a deep violet-blue hyacinth, with grape hyacinths. Hardy annuals such as pansies are attractive with hyacinths while both are in bloom, but will do little later on to conceal their aging foliage.

These are major bulbs, like big-league players come up to bat when spring is in full swing. Daffodils with the golden hue of yolks from the fresh-laid eggs of free-range hens, growing in a grove of white-trunked birches, summon spring. Tulips with colors from a pirate's treasure chest — gold, ruby-red, tourmaline-pink, amethyst-purple, ivory-white — ornament gardens. Hyacinths as ramrod straight as soldiers on parade scent the gently warming days. The woodcuts in old herbals depict some of the geophytes we grow today. These establish a connection with those who have gone before us. A couple of links in the chain is the diplomat enamored with a new bulb, who shares seed with an aging professor. Both men are equally absorbed by the beauty of the tulip's flowers, and unaware, innocent, of events that wait down the halls of time: the lunacy of the tulipomania, and the infinitely more stable commercial trade of modern times. These bulbs are not dusty relics to be kept as curiosities but splendid additions to landscapes large and small, more beautiful in combination than in isolation. The locket-like white flowers of *Dicentra spectabilis* 'Pantaloons' are more beautiful in combination with lily-flowered 'White Triumphator' tulips than by themselselves. Display the vivid flowers of Tulip 'Red Shine' against the coppery bronze foliage of *Berberis thunbergii* 'Crimson Pygmy' and see how they glow. Think in terms of color and combination, for these are bulbs to use in the perennial border. Their flowers add interest when other, fibrous-rooted perennials are just beginning their growth. Remember to look beyond the moment, and consider what will follow afterward, when the bulbs are dormant. Create a sequence so that foliage and flowers of summer-flowering geophytes, perennials, annuals, and shrubs can fill in the bare spaces, and relinquish it again when spring comes around once more.

4

Offbeat Bulbs

THE NEGLECTED NATIVES

Dicentra, Erythronium, Claytonia, Arisaema, Sanguinaria, Trillium, Polygonatum, Smilacina, Uvularia, Apios, Helianthus

WE TEND to compartmentalize plants, fitting them into segregated categories that serve to define them in our minds. Thus *Arisaema triphyllum,* jack-in-the-pulpit, and *Sanguinaria canadensis,* bloodroot, are perceived as "wildflowers." They also fit the category "geophyte," as they have an underground corm or tuberous roots for food storage. These and other geophytes are excellent additions to the gardener's repertoire of plants for the woodland garden.

A deciduous woodland is made up of several plant groups: canopy trees that shade all the plants beneath; understory trees, which grow in the shade of the forest canopy; and shrubs, which provide the lowest woody layer. Beneath these three groups of woody plants are the herbaceous plants. These sometimes fleeting, usually spring-blooming forbs (herbs other than grasses) are the ones most closely connected with the concept of "native wildflowers." Such familiar and popular plants as *Sanguinaria canadensis,* bloodroot; *Trillium* species; *Arisaema triphyllum,* jack-in-the-pulpit; *Erythronium americanum,* dogtooth violet; and *Dicentra cucullaria,* Dutchman's breeches, are the ones that come immediately to mind.

In a forest, flowering is concentrated in spring when the greatest amount of sunlight is available to the lowest layer of plants. Even though the days are shorter than in summer, even though the sunlight is weaker, filtered as it slants through more of the atmosphere, this period of time before the tree and shrub layers leaf out is when energy is most available. The sequence of awakening growth in spring climbs upward from the ground, first the herbaceous plants, then shrubs, next understory trees, and last the canopy. Some herbaceous plants, spring ephemerals such as *Erythronium americanum,* dogtooth violet, and *Dicentra cucullaria,* Dutchman's breeches, follow the familiar pattern of other spring-flowering bulbs such as *Galanthus nivalis,* snowdrops, and *Narcissus* spp., daffodils, in that they emerge early in the year, flower, set seed, and go dormant by early summer, hidden underground until the wheel of the seasons turns again. So immediately we have two categories of woodland herbaceous plants: those that go dormant in late spring/early summer and those that go dormant later, in autumn. In winnowing through the plants it becomes possible to select for more than flowers, choosing those with attractive summer foliage such as *Sanguinaria canadensis,* bloodroot, or the sealing-wax-red fall berries of *Arisaema triphyllum,* jack-in-the-pulpit.

We overlook what is under our feet. Certainly as far as the nursery industry is concerned, interest centers on those predominately spring-flowering geophytes imported from Holland. In our need to categorize, wildflowers originating in North America are classified first and foremost as *native,* and their development as bulbs, corms, tubers, or rhizomes is disregarded. Yet these plants of forest and grassland may well become the next great source of garden introductions. Many fine native plants are overlooked, excluded from their gardens by individuals who feel they are not interested in wildflowers or assume that something foreign and exotic must have more cachet, more appeal than a plant that grows locally in field or forest. Perhaps we should remember that the English, long regarded as inspired gardeners and designers, have a very limited native flora, which is one of the main reasons they were such avid collectors of plants from Asia, Europe, and North America. A more valid reason not to purchase wildflowers is based on ethics, for these plants — *Trillium* spp.; *Sanguinaria canadensis,* bloodroot; *Arisaema triphyllum,* jack-in-the-pulpit; *Fritillaria* spp.; *Erythronium* spp., dogtooth violets; *Dicentra cucullaria,* Dutchman's breeches; and more — are commonly offered for sale as wild collected material.

During the time of spring when our native woodland plants begin their growth, the trees are still innocent of leaves, but on the forest floor the first green shoots testify to the awakening of certain North American bulbs.

Dicentra

Commonly called Dutchman's breeches for the fanciful resemblance of its flowers to pantaloons hung on a laundry line, *Dicentra cucullaria* is a true bulb. It occurs in great colonies, often on stony slopes with relatively shallow soil layers. Since the surrounding soil is so thin, and there is no tunic on the bulb, the scales may be exposed to sunlight. In such cases they will "sunburn" and turn red. Duchman's breeches is one of the first plants to appear in the spring, when from a loose cluster of scales looking like grains of rice arise ferny leaves and a loose raceme of two-horned white flowers, indeed resembling pantaloons hung on the wash-line to dry. The dainty white flowers and fern-like, gray-green foliage are quietly attractive. Early into growth, this bulb is also early into dormancy. The leaves will yellow and dry in May. For this reason it is wise to combine a group of this bulb with some other plants that will be in growth later in the season. This not only serves to prevent inadvertent disturbance of the site later in the year, but will also provide interest in the garden past the first flush of bloom. I plant this in combination with primroses, violets, and early trillium species such as *Trillium cuneatum.* If it is grown on its own, locate it near a stump, fallen log, or stone that can serve as a useful marker when the plants are dormant. I sent some of these to my friend Carla Teune, curator of the Leiden Botanic Garden. We both found it amusing that I sent Dutchman's breeches to Holland. But they vanished from a case of finger blight — someone found them attractive and dug them up.

A close relative is squirrel corn, *D. canadensis.* The flowers are similar, as is the foliage. Underground, the bulb looks like a loose collection of yellow corn kernels. Both of these species are readily cultivated in regions of the country where the summers are not unduly hot.

Erythronium

I have occasionally found Dutchman's breeches growing and flowering together with dogtooth violets, *Erythro-*

nium americanum, but the latter more commonly grows in moist wooded areas with deeper soil. This species is found in eastern North America, from Nova Scotia to Minnesota, Florida to Alabama. Appearing after crocus are in bloom in our gardens, these wildlings look like miniature yellow lilies, often with a brownish stain or flush on the outside of the petals. They are also ephemeral and go dormant in late spring. Its underground structure, a corm, does indeed bear some resemblance to a dog's canine tooth, while other common names, such as trout lily, adder's tongue, and lamb's tongue, refer to the green and brown mottled leaves. *Erythronium americanum* can be disappointing since it is a shy blooming corm, which forms extensive colonies of foliage, many plants sending up a single leaf, and sparse in flower. Unlike other species of erythronium where offsets are sessile, clinging to the parent and producing a tight cluster of new plants, this species produces long slender offshoots, or runners, which produce new corms at some distance from the original. These will often bury themselves fairly deeply before storing sufficient energy to send up a pair of leaves and a single flower. The corm can be as much as 12 to 15 inches below the soil's surface, and the stem leading up is about the diameter of a strand of spaghetti. It is necessary to be quite careful when moving these. When the plant is strong enough to send up a pair of leaves, it will also flower before going dormant. I was fascinated by a rock outcrop near the Merritt Parkway in Greenwich, Connecticut, which had a patch in heavy bloom each spring. Upon investigation I discovered that the corms had somehow become established in a soil-filled crevice, and their being confined in this manner was apparently what made the difference. In the garden I planted some with a piece of flat slate at the bottom of the hole (tipped at an angle so water would run off) and the next year these also began to flower more freely. This genus is one that resents disturbance, and will flower better the second and subsequent years following planting. Should you want to raise erythronium from seed, sow the seed when ripe. Germination will occur the following spring. A few of the largest bulbs will flower the third year, but in general it will take four years for seed-raised bulbs to reach blooming size. There is a very similar, more freely flowering species, *E. umbilicatum,* native from Virginia to Florida.

The first year after planting flowering will be sparse, and even within the garden, digging and separation of an established clump generally results in a less floriferous performance the following spring. It is prudent, therefore, to decide where the corms are to be planted at the outset and leave them alone thereafter. There is no protective tunic, and dormant corms from vendors are easily bruised, and subsequently subject to mold and fungal rot. Additionally, if not displayed loosely packed in wood shavings they can quickly begin to shrivel. Because of these difficulties it is best to acquire and plant erythronium as early in the autumn season as possible.

There are several other native species. Common to central and eastern North American woodlands (Ontario and western New York to Kentucky, Arkansas, and Texas) is *E. albidum,* with attractive white flowers having a hint of transparency to their petals. This is not as free-flowering in cultivation as other, more desirable western American species such as *E. revolutum,* native from California northward to Vancouver Island. This is an attractive, easily grown species with beautifully mottled leaves and from one to three deep rose-pink flowers. Some selections have been made, and are available as 'Pink Beauty' and 'Rose Beauty'. There is a white cultivar, 'White Beauty', but it is not widely offered. Another deservedly popular, readily cultivated species from the west is *E. tuolumnense,* from Tuolumne County, California, which has one to four golden-yellow flowers and plain green leaves. 'Pagoda' is a hybrid of this species and *E. revolutum* 'White Beauty', with yellow flowers and mottled leaves.

There are two western species very difficult to accommodate in cultivation. *E. grandiflorum* is native to the Cascade Range of northwestern California and Oregon north into Washington, where it is found in the Olympic Mountains. It has glossy green leaves with no mottling, and from

One of the earliest of our native bulbs to bloom, Dutchman's breeches, *Dicentra cucullaria,* dangles its flower laundry in the spring breezes.

Attractive in combination with soft lavender *Jeffersonia dubia,* the yellow lily-like flowers of *Erythronium umbilicatum* provide a seasonal display in the author's garden.

As red and glossy as sealing wax, the fruits of *Arisaema triphyllum* glisten in the early-autumn sun.

Filling the meadow, the white flowers of *Erythronium montanum* truly look like an avalanche spilling off the Cascade Mountains behind them. (SUE OLSEN)

one to five yellow flowers on stems that may reach 12 inches tall. In the wild it is found at altitudes up to 9,000 feet. Another species from the same mountain ranges, profuse on Mt. Rainier and Mt. Hood, *E. montanum* is called avalanche lily. The white flowers, one to five on a 12-inch stem above unmottled green leaves, emerge as the snows retreat, literally budding and blossoming in the icy meltwater running down the slopes. As might be expected from such high mountain plants, they are difficult to cultivate at lower elevations and do not grow well in gardens.

There are as well several European and Asiatic species. Long popular in European gardens is their native, *E. dens-canis,* introduced to gardens as early as 1596. It has rosy-mauve, lilac, or carmine flowers and mottled foliage. In common with the other species, it does not like being moved. As might be expected from so long a period of cultivation there are several named forms, not generally available. 'Frans Hals' and 'Lilac Wonder' are described as imperial purple, 'Pink Perfection' is an early-flowering clear pink cultivar, 'Purple King' is cyclamen-purple, 'Snowflake' is pure white, and 'White Splendour' has a dark brownish-red basal spot. The one I have seen offered, though rarely, is the pink 'Rose Queen'. Provide them with a partly shaded location that will not parch, even when the bulbs are dormant in summer. They combine nicely with various of the woodland shrubs such as azaleas and hydrangeas, and I like to use ferns to fill the space when the erythronium are dormant. Deer eat these more expensive hybrids and imported species, although they do not appear to trouble the locally native one.

Erythronium dens-canis var. *japonicum* is native to Japan and Korea, and has violet-purple flowers with a dark marking inside at the base of the flower, and strongly mottled leaves. It has been reliable for me, making large clumps after several years. Of course, when I lifted and split them (to have some new plantings elsewhere in the garden) the following year's display was a stingy ghost of the attractive, established original planting.

Claytonia

When I supply myself the treat of an expedition to the woods in early spring, accompanied with a sense of gleeful delight, it is not childish "playing hooky" but serious "research." A look at wild plants emerging from their winter sleep, perhaps nestled amid the roots of a large beech or the deep humus collected in a tumble of rocks, their association with uncoiling fern fronds, all suggest their proper placement in my garden. Sometimes their release from competition in the wild to luxurious accommodations in cultivation results in a population explosion. This may, or may not, be a problem.

Spring beauty, *Claytonia virginica,* sends up a dainty little stem, 4 to 6 inches tall, with a pair of narrow glaucous leaves. A raceme of delicate five-petaled flowers, translucent whitish pink, crowns the stem. And underground is a small tuber that can out-propagate crabgrass and chickweed. In lightly shaded woodlands, open grassy thickets, semi-shaded rough areas at the edge of a meadow, this charming little plant will fill in as a ground cover, carpeting the space with its exquisite little flowers, which then disappear back underground to wait for the following spring. It multiplies at an astonishing pace, but is not a problem as plants with more extensive roots might be. The spring beauty appears, flowers, and like a well-mannered guest disappears in a timely fashion, allowing ferns and other herbaceous plants their time in the shade.

Arisaema

I exchange plants with friends in Holland, England, and Japan. My husband claims that I am sending them plants I trip over on the way to the mailbox, and there is some truth in what he says. Our native *Arisaema triphyllum,* the familiar jack-in-the-pulpit, is rare and exotic to them, an easily cultivated tuber with a bizarre flower. It has a three-part leaf, only one in the case of immature and male plants, two when the flattish tuber has reached sufficient size/mass to become female. The leaflets are arranged in a T, which distinguishes it from trillium, whose leaflets are spaced equidistant from one another. The leaf is a good contrast to the lacy texture of ferns or astilbe. This species grows 1 to 3 feet tall. The flowers, which appear in May, have a spathe, which may be either pale green or a rich chocolate brown, striped in white. Female plants have large dense heads of bright red berries in the autumn. I have found jack-in-the-pulpit to be a very obliging plant. It can be dug in full bloom, put in a pot for entry in a show, brought home and replanted, and never wilts, flags, or shows any sign of stress. If plants are obtained locally as container-grown specimens, there should be no problem planting them even while in full growth. Dormant tubers can be planted in spring or fall. Rooting occurs from the upper surface, so soil amendment should be in the few inches above rather than beneath the tuber.

Arisaema dracontium, the green dragon, is our other native species. It has a plain green leaf-like spathe tightly rolled around the spadix, which extends beyond this wrapper like a small child sticking out its tongue. Both species prefer dappled woodland shade, and soil high in organic matter, which does not dry out. They are easily raised from seed: in the autumn clean the pulp from around the ripe seed, soak it in tepid water, and rub away any remaining pulp with a paper towel. Be careful to wash your hands after handling the pulp. Crystals of oxalic acid, which are present in all parts of the plant, can cause an unpleasant prickling, itching sensation in your mouth, tongue, and lips, much the same as the effect of eating chili peppers. Euell Gibbons, in one of his books on wild-gathered food, says that the tuber is edible if boiled in three changes of water to remove the crystals. That may be, but I would imagine after such treatment it would have the same gourmet appeal as library paste. The crystals (also present in *Diffenbachia,* accounting for its common name of "dumb cane") explain why deer, rabbits, voles, and chipmunks leave arisaema strictly alone.

Sow the seed in a light, gritty mix. Germination will occur within a few weeks if the mixture is kept indoors under grow lights, the following spring if placed outdoors in a cold frame. Seedlings have a single leaf and form a small tuber the first season. Young plants are neuter. In a couple of years, when the tubers first flower, the spadix will have only male flowers. As the tuber gains size and stores more food, the same plant will flower as a female and bear the cob of bright red berries in autumn.

Sanguinaria

Bloodroot, *Sanguinaria canadensis,* is named for the orange-red sap that oozes forth when the plant is damaged or the tuber is cut or bruised. I find the most vigorous wild colonies near a woodland glade or by the side of a road, where openings in the canopy allow additional light to reach the forest floor. From the growing point a pinky-orange bud quickly pierces the soil in early April, with the single leaf protectively furled like a cloak around the fragile flower bud. Rapidly it unrolls, releasing the flower stalk to expose the chaste white, eight-petaled daisy-like flower with a central boss of golden stamens. You must look quickly, as the petals soon drop and flowers last only four or five days. Fortunately the foliage, gray-green leaves as much as a foot across, remain through the summer, and their bold form offers good contrast to ferns, especially the silver fronds of *Athyrium goeringianum* 'Pictum', Japanese painted fern, or the glossy dark green of Christmas fern, *Polystichum achrostichoides.* They are also elegant emerging from a polished green carpet of myrtle, *Vinca minor.*

The single-flowered plants are fertile and reproduce by seed. Fresh seed germinates easily, and self-sown seedlings can often be somewhat weedy. The seed has a fleshy little appendage called an elaiosome. This is attractive to ants, which gather the seed, a process of seed dispersal called myrmecochory. Germination is more difficult if the elaiosome dries out, so seed must be gathered and sown promptly. In my area germination in the wild occurs in March of the following year. Division of the tubers is

Annual Growth Cycle of *Arisaema triphyllum*

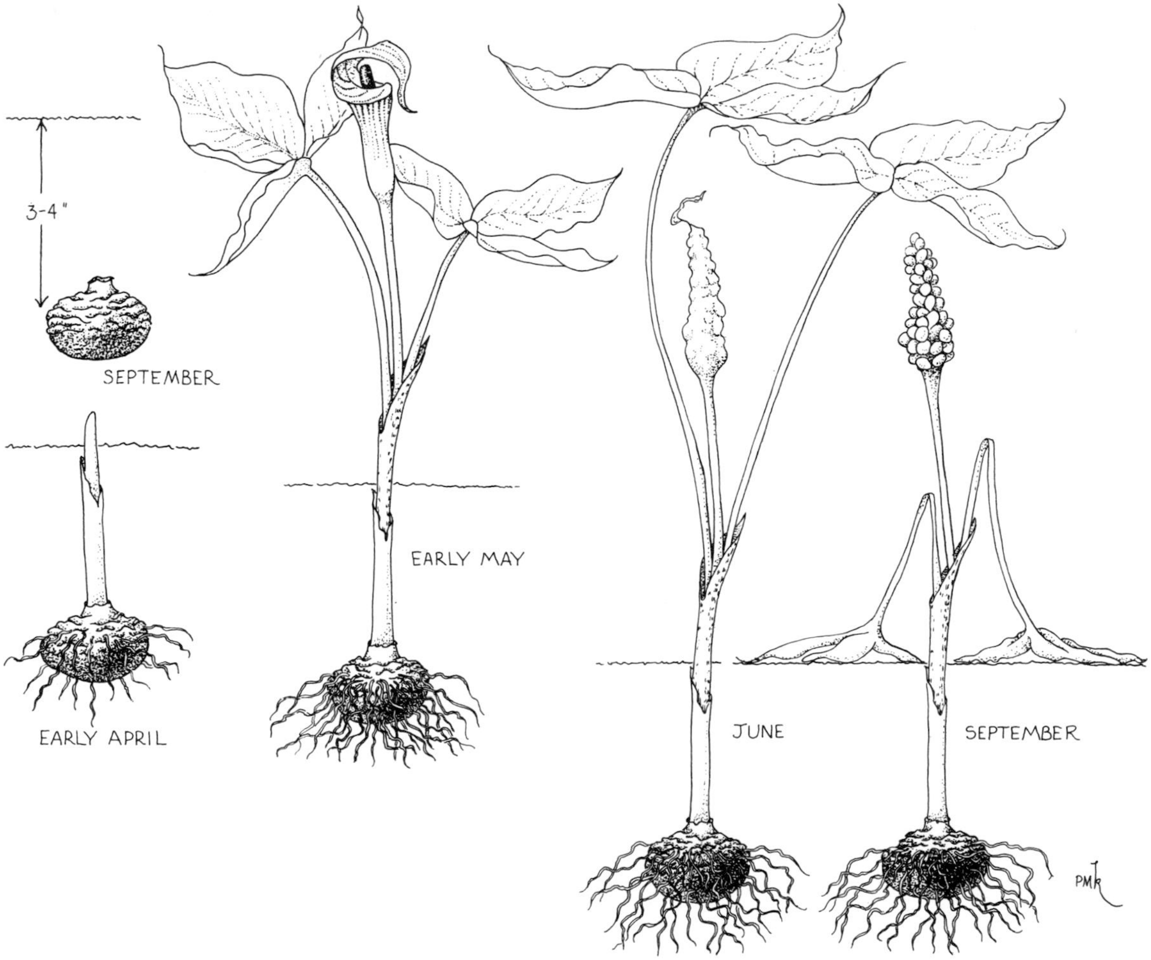

another means of increase. There frequently appears a semi-double form with from 14 to 16 petals, named *Sanguinaria major flore pleno* in 1732 by the German botanist Johann Jakob Dillenius. A fully double form exists, with 48 to 60 petals, where even the stamens have been changed to a petaloid form. *S. canadensis multiplex* (regularly misnamed *flore-pleno*) has peony-like flowers that last for about a week; it is sterile and can only be propagated by division. It would have difficulty surviving in the wild, and it is the admiration of gardeners that has increased its population. It was first brought into cultivation by Guido von Webern, who discovered a colony growing on property he purchased in Dayton, Ohio, in 1916. He sent a specimen to the Arnold Arboretum, in Boston, where it was officially described by E. H. Wilson in the 1923 issue of *Gardener's Chronicle*. Occasionally I hear of a new clone being discov-

As full and plump as can be, the flowers of *Sanguinaria canadensis multiplex* are delightful in the author's shady spring garden.

Not worms, the small white structures on this *Sanguinaria canadensis* seed are the fleshy arils that attract the ants who disperse the seed.

Unfortunately lasting for only a brief period, the daisy-like white flowers of *Sanguinaria canadensis* create a crisp display with electric-blue *Scilla sibirica* in this New Canaan, Connecticut, garden.

ered in the wild, so it is something that occurs on a regular basis. The large, heavily veined, grayish umbrella-like leaves are a handsome addition to the summer garden, unless the weather is hot and dry for an extended period and the plants go dormant early. I like to combine their foliage with just about any fern, epimediums, or astilbes. There is considerable variation, in that some clones have deeply cut, almost finger-like lobes, while others are almost orbicular. The branching tuber is oriented horizontally just below the surface of the soil and should be planted quite shallow. The sterile double form is vegetatively quite vigorous and branches even more than does the single. Often rot can set in where tubers overlay one another, and large pithy desiccated patches develop at the back end of the tubers. Von Webern's colony died around 1966 after he had died and the tubers were no longer separated. They should be lifted, separated, and promptly replanted every four years or so, in late summer or early autumn when the foliage begins to yellow. Generally this poppy relative is otherwise free of problems, although one year almost all of my double form just died out for no reason I could determine. At the same time this happened in the garden of Richard Redfield, a highly accomplished gardener in Scotland, Connecticut. So perhaps it was like the flowering of bamboo, one of those infrequent occurrences that serve to keep gardeners from becoming too complacent.

Trillium

Perhaps the most adored of our spring wildflowers is trillium, an elegant, readily recognized member of the lily family. Many species are easily cultivated and make a handsome addition to the shady garden. Unfortunately, of the plants offered for sale it is certain that the majority are collected from the wild. Production from seed is slow, offsets are not formed with anything approaching the rapidity of *Sanguinaria,* and micropropagation is, at present, ineffective because of a benign fungus usually present in the plants' tissues. It is feasible from seedlings, which are free of the fungus, but this does not allow for selection of superior-flowering forms. Collection of stock plants from threatened habitats provides material for research into methods of ethically satisfying the demand for these desirable shade garden plants.

The genus *Trillium* occurs in temperate forests in the northern hemisphere. About 40 species are distributed disjunctively between Asia (the Himalayas and East Asia) and North America, with the majority of its approximately 30 species being found in the latter region. From a short, roundish, often knobby rootstock one or a few shoots develop per year. The simple erect stem of trillium arises from the apex of a short, stout rhizome, usually just one per year, sometimes two, rarely several. Each shoot ends in three leaves, equidistant from one another in a whorl. A single, terminal, trimerous flower — three sepals, three petals — is at the top of the stem. Flower color varies from white to rose pink, green to chartreuse to yellow to maroon. There are two types: pedunculate or sessile. In pedunculate varieties, such as *T. erectum* and *T. grandiflorum,* there is a short stem or peduncle between the flower and the foliage. Generally these have unmottled foliage and the flowers open wider. In sessile species, such as *T. luteum* and *T. cuneatum,* the flower is directly above the leaves, held more erect, rarely opening wide, and usually these species have foliage that is mottled light and dark. Sessile-flowered trillium are found only in North America, pedunculate species are found in both North America and Asia.

In its early stages of growth a trillium tuber will stand erect, with roots emerging equally from all sides. From two to five roots are produced each season, according to the size and vigor of the plant, and live from two to ten years. Individually, roots grow about 4 inches in the first year, and increase their length still more and send out some branches; they apparently live three or four years or even longer. When the roots have attained a considerable length they begin to contract. This contraction draws the tuber down into the ground. Since only the young roots contract the pull is exerted only at the growing end. Roots grow from the crown end on the lower side of a horizontal tuber. In *T. sessile* the tuber is either erect or horizontal. The annual growth of the tuber is slow, probably less than an inch since, in general, it grows only enough to make room on its surface for the bases of bud sheaths.

The storage structure in trillium consists of a stout subterranean stem provided with a relatively large terminal bud or crown, and perennial roots. Carl Purdy, the well-known horticultural authority on California *Liliaceae,* felt that in his experience trillium rootstocks seldom persist entire for more than 15 years even in well-drained, gravelly soil, and in ordinary garden soil probably five years or less. As growth goes on at the crown end the base rots away, generally leaving a smooth scar. In the autumn the underground terminal bud contains not only the young stem-buds for the next growing season but also two or more young stem buds for the second season in advance.

There are two types of fruit — non-pulpy fruits are green, turning yellow or white at maturity, and their shape varies from globose to ovate. There is no mechanism for dehiscence, and the fruit opens through pressure of the enlarging seeds and degeneration of the wall tissue. Usually the seeds are dropped simultaneously as a large, somewhat viscous conglomeration, although sometimes they fall in smaller portions, each of which usually corresponds to the seed mass of a single placenta. Partly, at least, the attraction for ants is chemical, caused by the fatty oils in the appendage, which must be considered as a true elaiosome. Because of the elaiosome the seeds are picked up from the ground and carried away. It is important for gardeners to collect ripe seed as it matures within the capsule, before opening, if they are successfully to collect ripe seed before the ants.

In June 1934 the U.S. Department of Agriculture published a pamphlet, *Bulbs from Seed,* written by David Griffiths, advocating seed propagation for trillium and other geophytes. His research was done with *Trillium sessile californicum* and *T. grandiflorum.* From an individual wild-collected tuber he produced four blooming stems in six years. He found that reproduction from seed required six years to bring to blooming (that is, salable) size. Fresh seed was sown in drills about six per inch in rows 6 inches apart in a 3-foot-wide bed. Then they were left for four years without disturbance. At that time they were lifted and re-set one inch apart in rows spaced 6 inches.

Obviously, growing trillium from seed is not an undertaking for the impatient gardener. When possible, sow the seed as soon as it is ripe in August, as it requires one or even two periods of cold before it will germinate. Dry seed loses viability rapidly — delays of six years in its germination have been recorded. If seed must be stored, then it is best to package the whole berry with peat moss and refrigerate. Sow widely spaced, at least ½ inch apart, since seedlings will remain in the pot for a couple of years. Sink the pots in a cold frame and try to ignore it. Trillium seed exhibits complete double dormancy. It needs a cold period followed by a warm period to allow the roots to begin growth, then another cold period and a second warm period before seed leaves appear. Thus the first leaves will not appear until a period of almost 18 months after sowing. A further period of three to six years will then be needed to flower them. You can speed things up by placing the fresh seed in a small plastic bag of barely damp peat moss and chilling it for six to eight weeks in the refrigerator. Next keep the bag and its contents at room temperature for six to eight weeks, and then sow, but be careful as roots may be present. Put the seed pot in a cold frame for the remainder of the winter for the second temperature cycle. Germination should then occur the spring following sowing. Seedling plants remain in a pot or nursery row for at least two years, until the tubers have formed sufficient storage mass to compete in the rough-and-tumble of the garden.

Perhaps you feel that this is too long to wait. All I can say is that if you make a start and sow seed each year, in six years and thereafter you will have trillium flowering from seed. This might be hastened somewhat with a program of light, regular fertilization. The one caveat is that the trillium seed germinates best if it is fresh. Then the first year it will send down a radicle, and the second year will produce

In the author's garden, the backlit flowers of *Trillium cuneatum* resemble a candle's flame.

Existing now only in memory and pictures such as this, *Trillium grandiflorum* as it flowered along Route 480 in northeastern Ohio before the site became a housing development.

the first, single leaf. Old seed can take two or more years to break dormancy. In the wild it takes from eight to ten years for a plant to reach reproductive maturity, that is, flowering, from seed. Plants can be budded from the rhizome, but this produces only one or two buds per year for each rhizome. It is a generous friend indeed who offers you a trillium.

One piece of lore associated with trillium is that you should never, ever pick the flower, as this will kill the plant. Deer, who never seem concerned with this sort of information, occasionally dine on trillium in my garden. Naturally, they prefer the fully double *Trillium grandiflorum* 'Flore Pleno'. Perhaps the extra petals provide additional flavor. Happily enough, and in contradiction to the folklore, the following spring the tubers produced leaves but no flowers. Beginning in 1972 a study was conducted in Ohio with *T. grandiflorum* as the study species. The different treatments consisted of: no picking, picking flower only, flower and one leaf, flower and two leaves, flower and all three leaves, repeated picking over several years. As might be expected, picking flowers only had little effect on flowering in subsequent seasons. When both flower and all leaves were gathered one year the results were a very significant reduction in the rate of flowering one year after treatment. Where complete picking was done two years in a row the percentage of blooming plants dropped sharply. When culling was done three years in a row flowering not only subsided but recovery was slower. Complete picking for two years produced a drastic reduction in the rate of flowering, but the plots recovered to the normal flowering rate in four years. Complete picking for three consecutive years produced a significant reduction in the number of plants, from 195 in 1972 to 119 in 1975, but amazingly, one plant still flowered even after this severe treatment. Although the percentage of flowering returned to normal in six years, when the project was terminated in 1981, nine years after the start of the project, the total number of plants had not recovered significantly.

Trillium cuneatum flowers mid-March to late April, on stems 15 inches tall. The flowers are sometimes fragrant, sometimes have a fetid odor, and their color is very variable but always contains purple pigments, commonly greenish brown to brownish purple. It has short, stout rhizomes. Found in rich deciduous forests in the Southeast — North Carolina, South Carolina, Kentucky, Tennessee, Alabama, Georgia, Mississippi — this has been a reliable performer in my garden, flowering in combination with *Anemone blanda* 'White Splendour', primroses, and broad beech ferns.

Trillium erectum flowers early April to early June, with wide morphological variation of sepals, petals, and petal color, as well as leaf variation. Color of petals may be reddish purple or dark purple, pink, cream, or white, narrow or broad. Usually this species is found on mountain slopes in deciduous, mixed, and coniferous forest from the East Coast to the Midwest. Wild sweet William, *Phlox divaricata,* with its soft blue flowers, forms a pleasant association. I like the typical deep rich oxblood-maroon form in combination with the clear pink flowers of *Pulmonaria rubra,* and the white or cream-colored forms with the blue forget-me-not-like flowers of *Brunnera macrophylla.* And, as with all trillium, ferns add attractive foliage for a pleasing summer combination.

Wake-robin, great trillium, snow trillium, call it what you will, *Trillium grandiflorum* is magnificent. The showy, white to pink flowers, often later aging to rose-purple, blooms in early April to early June, depending on the locale. In the wild this is found in sites with rich, moist soil in deciduous woodlands. When our son attended Case Western Reserve University in Cleveland, Ohio, we would drive back and forth every May and August. And on May 10, off Route 480 in northeastern Ohio I saw literally acres of *T. grandiflorum* in bloom, white flowers as far back into the woods as I could see. (The next spring the woods were gone, and small tract houses had been built, within sight and sound of the tractor trailers on the highway.) Their native distribution is similar to that of *T. erectum.* In cultivation I think my favorite combination is with the soft blue flowers of *Phlox divaricata*. The western *T. ovatum* is quite similar, but with smaller flowers, which spread wide from the base, whereas wake-robin is erect at the base. There is a stunning, fully double form, *T. grandiflorum flore-pleno*, with rows of petals decreasing in size to give a star-like appearance. This is vegetatively fairly vigorous and produces more offsets than the type, probably because it is sterile and produces no seed.

Trillium luteum is a sessile-flowered trillium growing 15 inches tall that flowers in mid-April to early May, with petals bright lemon yellow or greenish yellow. It has a strong citrus, lemony fragrance. Found in deciduous southern forests — North Carolina, Kentucky, Tennessee, Georgia — usually rocky and moist, on calcareous or granitic substrata, this is easily accommodated in my more eastern garden. I grow it in combination with blue-flowered *Phlox stolonifera;* or with hosta that have small to mid-sized yellow leaves, such as 'Kabitan' or 'Wogan Gold'; dark green *Liriope muscari;* and the evergreen Christmas fern, *Polystichum achrostichoides.*

Trillium sessile, often confused with *T. cuneatum,* flowers on foot-high stems in late March to mid-May, with purple to greenish-yellow (forma *viridiflorum*) petals, and has a spicy, slightly pungent odor. Naturally occurring in low, rich, moist woods in valleys or on hillsides, in rocky or calcareous and rich alluvial soil, it is clearly adaptable to a variety of sites. The distribution is from New York and Pennsylvania south and westward to Maryland, West Virginia, Virginia, North Carolina, Michigan, Illinois, Indiana, Ohio, Kentucky, Tennessee, Alabama, Missouri, Arkansas, Kansas, Oklahoma.

Not all trillium are easy to cultivate. *Trillium undulatum,* the painted trillium, is a plant of cold pond banks, often found in the wild growing under hemlock trees near acid bogs. The wavy-margined white petals, stenciled with a crimson V, are attractive. But attempts to establish this species usually result in its languishing decline and disappearance.

Of the few Asiatic species, not all are worth cultivating. The accurately named *Trillium smallii* and *T. apetalon* either have reduced petals or lack them entirely. Most attractive is *T. kamtschaticum,* with good-sized white flowers.

Polygonatum, Smilacena, Uvularia

Simple, not extravagantly showy, Solomon's seal, false Solomon's seal, and merrybells are easy to establish and demand little care. They are welcome in my garden for their neat, attractive appearance, which is sustained over an extended period. They make a good foil for other showier plants whose interest quickly wanes, and are especially useful in disguising the summer bare spots left by spring ephemerals such as snowdrops or Dutchman's breeches. I plant them in combination with ferns, trilliums, bloodroot, astilbe — in fact, with just about any shade-tolerant perennial.

If they are available as container-grown plants, all three genera can be planted while in growth. Otherwise I prefer fall planting, as the foliage is changing from green to golden yellow. But should the need arise, they can be moved from a site about to be "developed" if they are carefully dug and attention is paid to watering while they become re-established in their new site. The typical prescription for other forest dwellers — dappled shade, soil high in organic matter, moist but well drained — suits these also.

Both Solomon's seal, *Polygonatum* spp., and false Solomon's seal, *Smilacina* spp., are named for a fancied resemblance of the warty leaf-stem scars on their ivory-white, knotty rhizome to King Solomon's ring. Both of these members of the lily family have extended interest, adding subdued flowers in spring, assuming a quiet, stately form in the summer, and providing attractive fruits for the autumn garden. *Polygonatum biflorum* grows 1 to 2 feet tall, with many ovate-oblong leaves alternating up the arching stems. Small greenish-white bells, paired or solitary, dangle inconspicuously from each leaf axil in May or June, to be followed by blue-black berries. This spreads fairly quickly

Unquestionably a favorite with all who see it, double-flowered *Trillium grandiflorum flore-pleno* needs the protection of gardens for its increase.

Trillium luteum has pale lemon-yellow flowers, most appropriate with its delicate, citrus-like scent.

Vigorous, coarse, weedy — all are appropriate epithets for *Helianthus tuberosa*. In the right place, however, its cheery yellow daisies are welcome, and a token of summer's end, flowering when the cicadas sing.

to make an excellent woodland ground cover, and also reproduces well from seed. Much more stately is great Solomon's seal, *P. canaliculatum.* The strong stems, growing as much as four feet tall in rich sites, have two, three, or four green-tipped white flowers to chime fairy music as they dangle from the leaf axils, to be followed by blue-black berries. The leaves turn a wonderful old-gold color in autumn. This can be propagated by division in spring, or from seed. I like this arching above clumps of hosta, in combination with ferns, or on its own at the base of some rough-barked oak. The stem arches backward with the tip toward the back of the rhizome, which grows horizontally, close to the soil surface. It is important to remember when planting so that in subsequent years it grows in the chosen direction.

False Solomon's seal, or false spikenard, *Smilacina racemosa,* makes large colonies in rich woodland. The tiny white flowers are in a terminal panicle, much like astilbe, at the tip of a 2- to 3-foot-tall stem, to be followed in autumn by speckled beige berries that turn red in autumn. The ovate leaves alternate up the stem. False Solomon's seal, *S. stellata,* is much smaller, only 12 to 15 inches tall. The flowers are larger but less numerous, and are followed by green berries with dark brown stripes. The white flowers, appearing in May/June, are welcome, as not many other plants flower in shade at this time.

Closely related are the happily named bellworts, *Uvularia* spp. The family resemblance is obvious from the running rootstocks to the arching stems clad with alternating oval/ovate leaves. Great merrybells, *U. grandiflora,* has lemon-yellow flowers in April/May, hanging from the tips of thin branches at the top of the 18-inch-high stalk. The leaves are perfoliate, as with bellwort or merrybells, *U. perfoliata.* This flowers later, in May or early June, and is smaller throughout, with flowers of a paler yellow. Palest of all is wild oats, *U. sessilifolia,* which carries one or two straw-colored flowers in April/May on slender drooping stalks about 12 inches tall. All of these make attractive colonies in combination with other woodland natives such as trillium, arisaema, sanguinaria, and with exotics such as hellebores, hosta, epimedium. They can be propagated by division in spring or fall, or by prompt sowing of the few seeds that are produced in a fleshy, winged capsule in autumn.

Apios

One late-flowering geophyte for thickety places is the groundnut, or Indian potato, *Apios americana.* You should consider carefully, though, if you indeed want to invite this attractive vining plant into the garden. Sometimes, especially where it has hitched a ride as an unsuspected passenger lurking in the soil around the roots of a shrub, it has been most unwelcome. Underground are a series of edible potato-like tubers. They transplant with ease, and are difficult to discourage thereafter. This is a scandent plant, which means it depends on adjacent woody plants for support, prefering to grow with its roots well shaded, but the leaves and flowers up in the sun. I have it at the head of my driveway, clambering through a juniper. The stems are about 6 to 8 feet long, with pinnately compound leaves. In summer, short, dense racemes of fragrant, pinkish-brown pea-like flowers appear in the leaf axils. The evergreen juniper provides the interest when the geophyte is dormant in winter, a time when northeastern gardeners expect the least display from their plants.

Helianthus

In August and September the roadsides in New England produce a wonderful gardenesque display as asters and goldenrods provide a wealth of bloom. Another member of the daisy family that also flowers at this time is the Jerusalem artichoke, *Helianthus tuberosa.* The common name is supposedly a corruption of the Italian *girasole articiocco,* the vegetable that turns to the sun. An alternative legend has the common name derived from "the artichoke-apples of Ter-Neusen." About 1620, tubers were distributed under this name from the garden of Petrus Hondius, in Ter

Neusen, Holland. Rather than the flower, which is the edible portion of real artichoke, it is the smooth skinned tuberous roots of Jerusalem artichoke that are eaten. Like dahlia tubers, those of Jerusalem artichoke are high in inulin, a polysaccharide that undergoes hydrolysis to a dextrorotatory form of fructose. Jerusalem artichoke tubers are particularly recommended for diabetics, and, extracted as alant starch, the inulin is used as an ingredient in baking diabetic bread.

The original European reference to it appears in the writings of Samuel de Champlain, who in 1605 mentions that roots tasting like artichokes were cultivated by the native Americans. His observations were made at what is now Nausett Harbor, Massachusetts. Interestingly enough, speculations on the origins of agriculture theorize that it arose from two directions, one from seed propagation and the other by root culture. The simple act of digging for roots would be a primitive form of cultivation. The soil is loosened, competing vegetation removed, and small tubers left behind have a better opportunity to grow. Jerusalem artichoke was more quickly accepted as a food plant than the potato, finding ready approval in France, England, and Sweden within 40 years. Today the situation is reversed.

This species of sunflower is a polyploid, with 102 chromosomes acquired as a result of hybridization. In his book *The Sunflower,* Charles B. Heiser, Jr., theorizes that the two species involved were *H. hirsutus,* a perennial species with 68 chromosomes, and either our familiar common sunflower, *H. annuus,* or a diploid perennial species such as *H. giganteus* or *H. grosserratus,* all of which have 34 chromosomes. If the annual species, then it was brought east by trade from its native range, and the Jerusalem artichoke is a species that has existed for only a few thousand years.

This is a robust perennial, growing 6 to 10 feet tall, and generally considered too invasive for garden situations. The sturdy stems are topped with clusters of 3-inch-wide yellow daisies. It occurs along roadsides, at the edge of woodlands, in open fields. It can be useful in naturalistic plantings, or for use in rugged places along a roadside or driveway. I once saw a wild population most attractively mingled with the tall wand-like stems and beaded seed heads of bugbane, *Cimicifuga racemosa.* Since it multiplies so freely by increase of the tubers, most often it is seen as large stately colonies. Given the rich soil of a garden, it will cheerfully propagate all the more vigorously. You can try to control it by dining on the tubers: they can be eaten raw in salads, boiled and mashed, and even make a fine pickle. They do not store well for extended periods, so it is preferable to dig small quantities as autumn progresses and consume the tubers reasonably promptly. I once grew this on an extremely spartan diet, actually the outside curve of a gravel driveway. It only reached about 4 feet tall and did not outgrow its alloted triangle of space.

As has been mentioned, in a woodland it is important to keep in mind the sequence some geophytes follow of early growth and flowering, followed by summer dormancy. Other plants are necessary to conceal bare ground after the ephemerals have made their more fleeting appearance. Familiar perennials such as ferns, hosta, astilbe, aruncus, and epimedium, and native geophytes such as bloodroot, have attractive foliage that conceals the absence of summer-dormant geophytes. Honesty, also called money plant, *Lunaria annua,* is a biennial that grows quite well in moderate shade and even establishes as a self-sowing colony. It provides double value with spikes of lavender or white flowers in spring followed by attractive, glowing silver seed pods in autumn.

We often overlook the geographic origins of exotic geophytes we purchase, and ignore the indigenous varieties. Over the millenia these have adapted to local growing conditions, and many of them are highly suitable for gardens. Do not be turned off by the term "native plant," as any species of geophyte is native somewhere! Instead, explore our local flora and discover North American geophytes for your gardens. (Others, such as *Lilium* and *Crinum*, are to be found in different chapters.)

Native Geophytes for Seasonal Interest in Woodland Gardens

SPRING BLOOM, EPHEMERAL

Dicentra canadensis — squirrel corn
Dicentra cucullaria — Dutchman's breeches
Erythronium americanum — dogtooth violet

SPRING BLOOM, GOOD SUMMER FOLIAGE

Arisaema triphyllum — jack-in-the-pulpit
Polygonatum biflorum, P. canaliculatum — Solomon's seal
Sanguinaria canadensis — bloodroot
Smilacina racemosa — false Solomon's seal
Trillium species (especially those with mottled foliage such as *T. cuneatum, T. luteum)* — trillium, birthroot, wake-robin
Uvularia grandiflora — great merrybells

FRUITING EFFECT

Arisaema triphyllum — jack-in-the-pulpit
Polygonatum biflorum, P. canaliculatum — Solomon's seal
Smilacina racemosa — false Solomon's seal

5

Hardy Summer Bulbs

Allium, Nectaroscordum, Lilium

ONE BULB we are all familiar with is the lowly onion. Along with leeks and shallots, garlic and chives, these are the kitchen bulbs that play a major role in cuisines around the world. Their ornamental cousins can similarly enhance the garden. Luckily, they do not have the strongly odiferous properties we associate with onions, for in most instances it is only if the foliage is crushed that it smells. Rather, their interesting flowers supply a pleasing addition to the late-spring and summer garden.

The ornamental onions are true bulbs, and like the majority of other hardy bulbs they are planted while dormant in the fall. Sometimes they are also available, still dormant, in early spring. They range in size from an individual plump white handful down to a silver-skinned pea, indicative of the variation in size and stature of the flowering plants. Individually, each flower looks like a star or a little bell. They are gathered in an umbel — all the flowers arise at the top of the stem from a single growing point. This may be few flowered, as in *Allium moly,* or form a crowded sphere of flowers resembling a dandelion gone to seed, as in *A. giganteum.* A client who told me she had a short attention span and was "into" instant gratification asked that I include "high tech" plants in the design for her garden. After pondering this unique request I was positive that ornamental onions exactly fit the bill, as their spherical flower heads balanced on a slender stalk certainly have a somewhat abstract, geometrical appearance. The most common colors are lavender, lilac, mauve, or purple, but there are species with true blue, pink, white, or yellow flowers. Some are excellent as a cut flower, either fresh or dried.

Only a relative handful of the more than 500 species are in cultivation. But what options these provide: there are tall ones, short ones, and some in between. Smaller species are appropriate in the rock garden, while larger ones are suitable for the perennial border. The majority are plants of sunny, well-drained places, and especially those from central Asia and the Mediterranean region need a dry period in summer while they are dormant. Species from other parts of Europe and eastern Asia accept summer moisture, but none grow in damp shade. A few are invasive: chives, *A. schoenoprasum,* is a notoriously free-seeding species, while rocambole, *A. scorodoprasum,* proliferates by forming bulbils (small aerial bulbs) rather than flowers in an umbel.

Their major drawback as an ornamental is that the foliage of many of the taller species withers early, turning yellow and vanishing as the bulb is in bloom. In a herbaceous border this can be disguised by planting together with a perennial that has ample foliage for both. One combination I enjoy is *Allium christophii* planted jack-in-the-box fashion with sage, *Salvia officinalis.* Usually the allium has lost its leaves by the time its flowers appear in May, so the low, gray foliage of the herb conceals the bulb's bare ankles. Another possibility would accent the silver foliage of *Artemisia* 'Valerie Finis' with the allium's starry purple flowers. I use this allium and other large varieties in groups of five to ten. Smaller species provide a better display in the border when they are planted in groups of ten or more. In the rock garden, however, modest numbers are often satisfactory.

Suitable for the rock garden, *Allium acuminatum* is widespread in the Pacific Northwest. Only 3 to 6 inches tall, it has an umbel of deep pink flowers 2 inches in diameter in the spring. This small charmer is delightful with early dwarf dianthus in complementary shades of pink. *Allium cernuum* is another native from North America, flowering in July with nearly 30 to 40 white to deep pink flowers nodding at the top of a 12- to 18-inch-high stem. This species is useful for naturalizing as well as in the rock garden or in front of the herbaceous border with low-growing perennials.

Flowering in late summer, *Allium beesianum,* from western China, has bright blue flowers on stems 6 to 10 inches tall. Deep cobalt-blue-flowered *Allium cyaneum* is smaller, only 4 to 6 inches high, and is attractive with creeping thyme, *Thymus serpyllum.* Delightful in the rock garden, these are rarely offered except by specialty nurseries or at rock garden society plant sales.

While there are yellow-flowered allium, the color is not common, and not all are good plants for the garden. Probably the best is *Allium moly.* The loose cluster of bright yellow flowers is carried on a 6- to 8-inch stem in summer. Native to southwestern France and eastern Spain in light open woodland, this is useful in semi-shade beneath deciduous shrubs. I grow the more vigorous cultivar 'Jeannine', introduced by Michael Hoog in 1978, with *Corylopsis spicata,* 'Variegated Wahoo', a soft yellow variegated hosta, and the yellow-flowered *Corydalis lutea.*

Variable from pale to deep yellow, *Allium flavum* flowers in July. The tall form stretches 15 to 20 inches high and is excellent in the perennial border, which is where Fred and Maryann McGourty use it to good effect. I combine it with the yellow-variegated foliage of *Canna* 'Nirvana' and the glaucous blue leaves of rue. Lower-growing selections such as 'Minor', 'Minus', 'Nanum', or 'Pumilum' may be only 2 to 8 inches high, clearly preferable in the rock garden. Plant where re-seeding is acceptable.

Allium karataviense is one of my favorites. Unusual for an allium, it has very ornamental foliage. Nearly 8 inches long and 5 inches wide, the two or three broad blue-gray leaves flushed with purple almost rest on the ground, still looking good when the bulb is in bloom. The star-like flowers are rosy white to pink, in umbels 4 inches across on stems 8 inches high in late spring. They are useful for dried arrangements. This species is particularly suitable for containers. I grow it with *Artemisia* 'Valerie Finis' and *Geranium* 'Johnson's Blue'. The old-fashioned house plant Moses-in-the-cradle, *Setcreasea pallida* 'Purple Heart', is an attractive companion, spreading to fill bare space after the allium is dormant. Native to central Asia, this species needs a site that is dry in summer if it is to repeat its display in subsequent years.

Also native to central Asia and northwestern Iran, star of Persia, *Allium christophii,* needs similar growing conditions. Commonly offered as *A. albopilosum,* it has stems 2 feet high with a fat umbel of purple star-like flowers 10 inches across in May. It is an excellent cut flower fresh or dry. I do not deadhead since the seed heads are so attractive. In a friend's garden I saw it gone to seed in front of a red cut-leaf Japanese maple and the effect was stunning. In my garden I combined this with red-bronze *Berberis thunbergii atropurpurea* 'Crimson Pygmy', low-growing *Iris sibirica* 'Little White', and green-flowered *Nicotiana* 'Lime Sherbet'. With *A. macleanii,* this is one of the parents of *Allium* 'Globemaster', an expensive onion costing more than ten times as much per bulb as its star of Persia parent. The huge umbels are aster-violet, and because it is sterile the flowers last for an extended period.

A dramatic species, *Allium giganteum* is the one featured in all those come-on advertisements with "flowers as large as a child's head" and an illustration of a somewhat intimidated-looking three-year-old clutching the stem of an onion towering over him. This species has dense spherical umbels of purple-violet flowers 4 to 6 inches across on a flowering stalk that can be 4 feet high. (In fact, *A. christophii* has larger flowers, but on a shorter stem.) This was stunning in Kurt and Hannah Bluemel's Maryland garden in June, flowering with purple Japanese iris and deep yellow *Achillea* 'Coronation Gold'. At Wave Hill in the Bronx an attractive, more subtle association uses this allium with rich purple Siberian iris and a tall glaucous blue juniper. Deep reddish foliage creates a good background: consider using *A. giganteum* with the purple-leaved smokebush, *Cotinus coggygria* 'Royal Purple'; *Berberis thunbergii atropurpurea;* or bronze fennel, *Foeniculum vulgare* 'Bronze'.

Allium aflatunense should be similar, flowering in May with lilac-purple flowers in a dense umbel on stems 2½ feet tall. In fact, what is offered under this name is sometimes an imposter with *AA. rosenbachianum, macleanii,* and others masquerading as the real thing. To the alliophile this is no doubt a disgrace, but it is of less import to the pragmatic gardener. 'Mother of Pearl' and 'Purple Sensation', selections made by Jan Bijl (who also produced 'Globemaster'), both have violet-purple flowers. It has also been used in breeding. 'Gladiator', with rose-purple flowers, and 'Lucy Ball' with dark lilac-purple flowers, are hybrids with *A. macleanii.* 'Rien Poortvliet' is a sport of 'Gladiator' with amethyst-violet flowers. These all grow 2½ to 3 feet tall.

I have not seen *Allium macleanii* myself. It sounds attractive, having a dense spherical umbel of mineral-violet flowers with a deeper violet line down the center of each segment, growing about 2½ feet tall.

Allium rosenbachianum has a large, loose umbel of dark violet flowers with darker midveins, on 2- to 2½-foot stems. There is a white form, *A. rosenbachianum* 'Album', with whitish flowers with darker midveins. I intend to try this with *Artemisia* 'Powis Castle', since this sort of double-decker planting is a good way to compensate for the allium's scanty foliage. I also want to see if the silvery foliage of the artemisia and the white allium flowers will look as good as I imagine, or if amethyst-violet *A. christophii* still is best. Flowers appear in late spring, and the dried flower heads remain attractive until brought down by winter snow.

Allium schubertii reminds me of fireworks. This is a funny allium, with very attractive dried flower heads. Up to 10 inches in diameter, the enormous umbels look quite loose and open, since individual flowers are on pedicels of unequal length, anywhere from 1½ to nearly 8 inches long. Coming from the Mediterranean region, Syria, and Israel at low elevation, it is not reliably hardy in regions with cold winters and wet summers.

Called the drumstick allium, no doubt because of its tapering umbel of deep purple flowers, *Allium sphaerocephalon* blooms in late June or early July. The dense clusters of flowers are 2 inches across on stems 2 feet tall, sometimes more. This is useful in a naturalized or meadow setting as I saw it at the Berry Botanic Garden in Portland, Oregon, in combination with grasses, California poppy,

The airy yellow bells of *Allium flavum* are attractive in the author's garden, combined with *Canna* 'Nirvana' and the glaucous foliage of rue.

In spring the soft mauve flowers of *Allium karataviense*, bright purple flowers of *Geranium* 'Johnson Blue', and silvery leaves of *Artemisia* 'Powis Castle' coalesce in a very satisfactory manner in the author's garden.

Rather a thug, *Allium schoenoprasum* is aggressive enough to partner with *Artemisia ludoviciana* 'Silver Queen', assertive in its own right. (PHOTOSYNTHESIS)

Elegantly displayed like substantial purple soap bubbles, *Allium giganteum* float above the rich yellow flowers of *Achillea* 'Coronation Gold' in Kurt and Hannah Bluemel's Baldwin, Maryland, garden.

Even in this skeletal stage the seedhead of *Allium christophii* is attractive.

larkspur, and butterfly weed. Growing at the Denver Botanic Garden, in Colorado; Holden Arboretum, in Mentor, Ohio; and wild along the Colonial Highway near Gloucester, Virginia, this is obviously an adaptable plant, and one that multiplies. It is good as a cut flower, fresh or dried.

Ramps, *Allium tricoccum,* is the focus of a spring festival in the Appalachian mountains. Eating the odiferous bulbs is believed to protect the diner from colds, perhaps because no one will get within sneezing distance! Native to eastern North America, this species sends up a pair of broad green leaves in spring, making large colonies on the woodland floor that quickly wither. Then in midsummer an umbel of white flowers cluster atop a 12-inch stem, pale and pretty in the heavy shade. This redolent resident of nearby woodlands multiplies quickly. I restrict its spread in my garden by enacting a modest festival and dining on the slender bulbs.

Nectaroscordum

Originally ranked with allium, now placed in a separate genus, is *Nectaroscordum siculum.* This is the sort of discussion I am happy to leave to taxonomists and botanists, as long as I can be sure of getting the plant I have in mind for my garden. The umbel has pendulous flowers, dangling on long slender stems from the top of the stalk. The individual flowers remind me of little bells, greenish, strongly flushed with purple, and edged in white. It grows about 3 feet tall and flowers in late May or early June. I grow this tightly wedged between a small shrub with red-purple leaves, *Berberis thunbergii atropurpurea nana,* and blue Lyme grass, *Elymus arenarius,* with glaucous blue-gray foliage. The colors harmonize very nicely, and the planting still looks attractive when the bulbs have gone dormant. This is, no doubt, the subspecies *bulgaricum,* from the Crimea, northwestern Turkey, and southeastern Europe. The other subspecies, *N. siculum* ssp. *siculum,* is native to the Mediterranean area and has green-tinged cream or whitish flowers, often pale pink outside.

Lilium

Widespread in North America, Asia, and Europe, with showy, sometimes fragrant flowers, it is little wonder that lilies are so popular a garden flower. If allium have plebeian connotations, "below the salt," so to speak, then lilies must be considered elegant royalty. Numerous hybrids have been developed, as might be expected from so diverse a genus. Many of these are easily cultivated, useful in the herbaceous border, cottage gardens, naturalistic plantings, even as container plants, and raised for the cut flower trade. These selections are more readily available than the wild species.

Lilies are true bulbs. Their fleshy scales overlap one another but each only partially encircles the bulb, and they lack a tunic. While they like a moist soil, the site must be well drained. Wet bulbs rot. Old directions often suggest digging out beneath the planting depth and filling the space with coarse gravel or small stones. This only creates a sump, or reservoir, where water can collect, and reduces the rooting area immediately adjacent to the bulb. A better idea is to improve drainage for the site, perhaps by creating a raised bed or improving the tilth of the soil with compost or other organic matter. Alternatively, choose another location, for good drainage is critical. Some lilies root only from the basal plate, while others additionally root along the underground portion of the stem. Assuredly, the latter should be planted more deeply to allow these roots to form and function in fattening the bulb for next year's growth. In general, plant a flowering-size bulb two to three times deeper than the height of the bulb. A 2-inch-tall bulb would have 5 inches of soil above it. Fertilize at planting time as described in Appendix 1: "Planting, Cultivation, and Propagation Techniques."

Formerly, lilies were available only in autumn. As they go dormant rather late, often the ground would be frozen by the time bulbs arrived. With improved cold-storage techniques the bulbs can be safely stored over winter and sold at garden centers before growth begins in spring.

has fragrant drooping trumpet flowers of a dull purplish pink. Olympic Hybrids is a grex of vigorous lilies with fragrant, trumpet-shaped flowers in shades of white, cream, yellow, and greenish to pink, suffused with yellow in the throat, with a pink or purplish suffusion outside.

If consistency is important to you, then select named clones, distinguishable in print from a grex or strain by the presence of single quote marks around the name. 'Black Dragon' has intensely fragrant flowers with a powerfully sweet perfume materializing at dusk and dawn. The flowers, 12 or more on a 5- to 6-foot-tall stem, are white inside and purple-brown outside. 'Black Magic' is similar. 'Limelight' has slightly drooping, fragrant, trumpet-shaped flowers, yellow flushed with a hint of green; 'Green Dragon' has fragrant, wide trumpet-shaped flowers that are white inside and chartreuse-green outside, while 'Honeydew' has narrow trumpet-shaped flowers of a soft greenish yellow with a green stripe down the back of each petal.

I find these tall lilies excellent back-of-the-border plants, perhaps faced down with phlox to conceal their sparse foliage. The range of phlox cultivars from white, pale through deep pinks, to magenta provides potential combinations with any of these trumpet lilies. *Phlox* 'Bright Eyes' has medium pink flowers with a darker eye, an elegant combination for 'Black Dragon', while 'Green Dragon' would look particularly cool with white 'Mt. Fuji'. Copper King Strain grows and flowers well in light shade, where it would combine handsomely with the tall white wands of bugbane, *Cimicifuga racemosa,* and the tall, raggedy yellow daisies of *Inula magnifica.*

Oriental hybrids, Division VII, are mid- to late-summer-flowering hybrids of *L. auratum, L. japonicum, L. speciosum,* and *L. rubellum,* including those with *L. henryi.* They are valuable additions to the late-summer garden. Most of these have outward-facing flat or bowl-shaped flowers such as the well-known 'Empress of India', with deep rich red bowl-shaped flowers edged in white, with wart-like papillae at the base of the petals. Eight to 10 flowers, 10 inches across, are displayed on 4- to 5-foot-tall stems. 'Black Beauty' is an easily grown cultivar, blooming in midsummer with green-centered, very dark red flowers edged in white. One of the most popular, both in the garden and in the florist trade, is 'Casa Blanca', with sweetly scented pure white flowers with white papillae at the base and recurved tips to the petals. Three feet tall, it blooms midsummer to autumn. Everest Strain has green-centered fragrant white flowers spotted with maroon. Each petal has a rather crinkled texture. The 5- to 6-foot-high stems bear as many as 14 flowers in August/September. Imperial Crimson is a grex of flat-faced flowers, deep crimson with a white margin to the petals. Imperial Gold has white flowers with a central golden band to each petal, maroon spots, and recurved tips. Imperial Silver has white flowers with dark red freckles. The three grex, with large (8- to 12-inch diameter) fragrant flowers that appear in late summer, are derived from *L. auratum* and *L. speciosum.* The same cross produced the late-summer-blooming Jamboree Strain, with 14 or more fragrant crimson flowers with darker warts and narrow white margins to the recurved petals. Excellent for container use are the low-growing Little Rascal series. Only 18 to 24 inches tall, 'Red Rascal' and 'White Rascal' have up to a dozen 5- to 6-inch-diameter flowers in early August. 'Star Gazer' and 'Journey's End' are often sold under one another's name. No matter which you grow, they are both fine plants, excellent for forcing and for container use. Both have upward-facing flat red flowers with dark spots and reflexed tips to the petals in midsummer, and one or the other has white margins to the petals.

Late-blooming phlox, such as rose-lavender 'Ann', soft shell-pink 'Dresden China', 'Blue Ice', which opens palest pink and fades to white, or white-flowered 'Everest' with a rose eye, are possible garden partners. The broccoli-like rosy flowers of *Sedum spectabile;* pink spires of false dragonhead, *Physostegia virginiana;* mauve-lavender spikes of *Liatris spicata;* appropriate cultivars of bee-balm; and *Monarda didyma* such as 'Croftway Pink' suggest other possibilities.

These three divisions: Asiatic, Oriental, and Trumpet

At Hedgleigh Spring, the Swarthmore, Pennsylvania, garden of Charles Cresson, the soft yellow flowers of *Lilium* 'Edith' are tastefully combined with *Lychnis coronaria* and *Chrysanthemum parthenium*. (CHARLES O. CRESSON)

In light shade, a white-flowered Asiatic hybrid lily, together with hosta, feverfew, and fibrous-rooted begonias, creates a cool, refreshing display in the Berlin, Connecticut, garden of Pierre and Susan Bennerup.

Lilium 'Black Dragon' and *Phlox* 'Bright Eyes' create an attractive midsummer display in the author's garden.

Deceptively tangled together in the author's garden, *Lilium* 'Sans Souci' is protected from the wide-ranging roots of *Monarda,* which are confined in a buried container.

Hybrids provide the majority of lilies available today. These hardy plants with a sturdy constitution and excellent flowers are easily cultivated. Certain other groups offer possibilities as various as their parentage is different. Perhaps requiring more attention to their cultivation, certainly not as readily obtainable, they have a unique appeal for both the typical gardener and dedicated enthusiast.

I have difficulty comprehending why *Lilium martagon* is not in wider cultivation. Variable and adaptable, growing in sun or shade, this has the widest distribution of all species, from northern Mongolia, Turkestan, and Siberia through Russia and Europe to the Pyrenees, Portugal, and Spain. Clusius grew this, calling it *Lelieken van Cavarien,* having obtained specimens soon after its introduction into cultivation in 1596. It has naturalized in England, most notably in the College Garden at St. John's, Cambridge, where the bulbs are reported to grow so thickly in rough grass as to cast a pink haze over the scene when in bloom. The flowers appear in early to midsummer, as many as 20 or 30 to a stem, and are dull pink, purple, or white, with the tips of the petals tightly curved into a Turk's cap, named for the turban adopted by the sultan Muhammed I. Some find their scent pungent rather than fragrant. This lily is long-lived and easy to cultivate once established. Being one of those bulbs that prefers not to be disturbed, often it will flower poorly the year after planting, taking time to settle down. Plant deeply, as this species is stem rooting. Production from seed is slow, as germination is hypogeal, with a root produced the first season and a shoot the second year. Flowering will occur 5 to 7 years after sowing. The bulb is yellow. Several varieties exist, most notably var. *album,* with creamy-white unspotted flowers and paler green leaves and stem. Unlike many albino forms it is scarcely less vigorous than the type and it comes true from seed. The white flowers are particularly effective against a dark background, which can be provided by evergreen shrubs in an edge-of-woodland setting. Var. *cattaniae* has very dark maroon unspotted flowers, hairy buds and stems, and is even more vigorous than the type, reaching 6 feet tall. Var. *caucasicum* has dark red–spotted lilac-pink flowers that open from fuzzy buds.

Classification of lilies sets aside Division II for martagon hybrids. The Paisley Hybrids in a range and shades of yellow to orange, pink to lilac, tangerine, and red, are July flowering with 20 to 30 3- to 5-inch-diameter flowers with reflexed petals. *L.* x *dalhansonii* is a cross of var. *cattaniae* with *L. hansonii,* which has numerous deep maroon flowers spotted and flushed with orange at the center of the petals. Several clones have been selected. Especially notable is 'Mrs. R.O. Backhouse', with mauve-pink buds that open to red-spotted brownish-gold flowers. 'J.S. Dijt' is a handsomely purple-spotted pale creamy-yellow martagon hybrid developed from a var. *album/hansonii* cross.

Madonna lily, Lily of the Annunciation — the connection of *Lilium candidum* with religious symbolism is clear. Believed to have originated in the Balkans, it was carried by the Phoenicians into the western Mediterranean (Lebanon, Syria, and eastern Israel), from whence it spread into northern Europe. The Romans brought it to Britain, and after their departure in 409 A.D. and through the Middle Ages it was cultivated in monastery gardens. This is different from any other lily in that it produces basal leaves in autumn that remain through the winter. This characteristic also influences its cultivation. It should be planted very shallowly, even with the tip of the white-scaled bulb at the surface of the soil. As a result it is difficult to grow in cold winter regions.

The outward-facing, openly bowl-shaped, very fragrant flowers, from 5 up to 20, appear in June, golden pollen gleaming softly against the petals. Linnaeus named it *candidum,* which means not simply white but "of dazzling white," for the purity of its color. Older stocks of bulbs were often infected with a virus that weakened the plants and made them difficult to grow. Fresh bulbs are easily raised from seed because this species has epigeal germination, and the cotyledon quickly emerges from the soil. The most vigorous strain available today, Cascade Strain, has been produced in this manner. This lily is a superb border

Cultivated only by nature, an elegant wildling, *Lilium canadense,* blooms in a meadow.

At Hillside Gardens, the renowned nursery and display garden of Fred and Mary Ann McGourty in Norfolk, Connecticut, *Lilium regale,* shasta daisies, and delphinium provide a refreshing blue and white Delft display in July.

are arranged in whorls. It is a meadow, edge-of-woodland species. The bulb is unusual in that it will send out a 1- to 2-inch stolon, and a new bulb will form at the tip. Mice adore the bulbs, and deer eat the flowers with apparent relish, as I discovered when I went to photograph the flower and found only a beheaded stem. It is charming in combination with grasses and other meadow flowers such as black-eyed Susan, butterfly weed, and bee-balm.

An elegant bulb for moist meadows is another North American lily, *Lilium superbum.* Naturally growing from eastern Massachusetts to southern Indiana, Alabama, and northwestern Florida, the great colonies described earlier in this century by Mary Henry (an ardent Pennsylvania horticulturist/botanist who botanized by chauffeur-driven automobile) are vanishing, destroyed by the "progress" that drains swamps and wet meadows for construction of houses and highways and shopping malls. It is generally taller growing than *L. canadense,* but is more readily distinguished by the Turk's-cap flower, with strongly reflexed deep orange-yellow petals heavily spotted with maroon and having a green base. Growing as much as 9 feet tall, usually less, it can have as many as 40 flowers in late summer. The brittle, rhizomatous bulb forks, establishing large colonies fairly quickly. Even though it is stem-rooting, do not plant too deeply; 3 to 4 inches is sufficient. Given the stature of this lily, shrubs make a suitable choice of companion. While the flowering periods will not necessarily overlap, the lilies will add later color to follow the blooming time of the woody plants. Think of the possibilities: hydrangeas or azaleas, perhaps the white swamp azalea, *Rhododendron viscosum.*

The wood lily, *Lilium philadelphicum,* has cup-shaped, orange or deep red flowers speckled with purple-black spots that narrow sharply at the base, leaving obvious gaps between the petals. Usually flowering in midsummer, there is a single flower to a stem, perhaps two in the case of a more vigorous bulb. The stems, with whorls of leaves, grow about 2½ to 3 feet tall. Again, the bulb produces a short horizontal stolon, and new bulbs at the tip. This species is difficult to bring into cultivation, transplanting with difficulty. Despite the common name of wood lily, suggestive of shady places and loamy soils, this is a species of open scrubby woods or brush. It needs an acid pinewoods duff in a sandy, peaty sort of heath soil, usually in combination with lowbush blueberries and similar plants. The small bulb, about an inch in diameter, is formed anew each year adjacent to the previous year's. It is apparently winter wet, which may be the critical factor, with moisture leading to rot. Much better to enjoy it in the wild than dig "just one or two" to bring home. This species was brought to Europe relatively early, having been described in 1676 in Dodart's *Herbal.* He called it the dwarf lily of Acadie, a French colony in Nova Scotia. Sometime prior to 1757 it was sent by John Bartrum of Philadelphia to Phillip Miller, who grew it in the Chelsea Physic Garden in London. The finest colony I ever saw was growing under a power-line right-of-way, which was maintained by mowing rather than with herbicides. There were approximately 50 flowering plants growing under the transmission lines and around the pylons. It is native to upland sites, from Nova Scotia, Ontario, and Quebec extending its range southward to North Carolina.

Providing the advantage of summer flowers and winter hardiness, these genera extend the seasons of the gardener's world beyond the awakening year. Planted in autumn along with more familiar spring-blooming geophytes, they awaken in a more leisurely fashion, beginning their growth under more moderate conditions than snow and freezing temperatures. Their blossoming brings pleasure and continuing gratification to gardeners who plan ahead for the season of lengthening days.

6

Tender Bulbs for Summer Color

Dahlia, Canna, Caladium, Oxalis, Ipopomea, Gladiolus, Crocosmia, Tritonia, Freesia, Galtonia, Hymenocallis, Zantedeschia

THE DIFFERENCE between hardy and tender geophytes is a matter of geography, not underground structure. Plants have developed bulbs, corms, or tubers to help them survive hard times, whether winter cold or summer drought. Thus geophytes from regions with a mild climate and pronounced seasonal dry spells are killed by temperatures below their ability to survive, or wet conditions when they are dormant. In cold-climate gardens the more common varieties can be treated as annuals, allowed to die in winter and replaced yearly. This is feasible when their cost is moderate and availability high. Alternatively, with the advent of autumn, they can be lifted from the garden and stored through the winter to be replanted the next spring. Some, especially those in the Amaryllis family, are intolerant of an annual disturbance. But as generations of gardeners are aware, such familiar favorites as canna, caladium, dahlia, and gladiolus are amenable to a winter's rest indoors packed away in boxes.

Dahlia

For seasonal summer color, dahlias are an easy plant to grow. They can be raised from seed started indoors early in the year, with the dwarf Unwin and Coltness hybrids flowering that summer. Garden centers frequently offer them in six-packs, just like marigolds and zinnias. Should a particular seedling prove to be especially appealing, it can be dug in autumn and the tubers stored through winter for use the next spring. Dahlias are an excellent cut flower, but more than that, their bloom from midsummer until cut down by frost adds color to the late-season garden.

Dahlia tubers can be planted in the garden about two weeks before the last frost is expected. Examine the stored

Summer color for sale — dahlias, gladiolus, and lilies. (ILLUSTRATION COURTESY OF THE NETHERLANDS FLOWER BULB INFORMATION CENTER)

As colorful as an artist's palette, the dahlia trial fields near Lisse, Holland, display their rainbow hues.

At Sissinghurst, arguably England's most famous garden, the fiery colors of *Dahlia coccinea* and *Kniphofia* 'Brimstone' heat up the "hot" border.

The maroon streaks and splashes on this decorative dahlia accentuate the somber foliage of *Cotinus coggygria purpurea*.

The dark foliage of a canna, and dusty mauve-pink flowers of *Eupatorium purpureum*, create an attractive pairing in the damp soil along a meandering stream.

kills the top growth, dry in the sun for a few hours, and store in a cool, moderately dry area. They are usually packed in dry peat moss, vermiculite, or buckwheat hulls to prevent shriveling. Even more tender than dahlias, the rhizomes should not be planted outdoors until all danger of frost is past. They may be hardier than tradition suggests, as Henry Ross in Strongsville, Ohio, has successfully left *Canna generalis* 'Striata' in the ground through the first two winters of this decade. This part of the country, near Cleveland, is not particularly noted for balmy winters, so it is definitely a gamble, but the resulting enormous clumps are magnificent.

Coming as they do from the tropical regions of South America and Asia, and with one species, *Canna flaccida,* native from South Carolina to Florida, cannas demand a warm, sunny location with ample moisture in the garden. The branching fleshy rhizomes have a dark brown skin, and young bud-shoots are pale ivory. Plant them horizontally, about 4 to 6 inches deep. For the lushest growth, feed once a month with a complete fertilizer, and water well if natural rainfall is lacking. Cut back on nitrogen fertilizer in mid-July, and reduce watering toward the end of summer. This will signal the plant that a resting period is approaching. The easiest means of propagation is through division of the rhizomes in spring before they are replanted. As might be imagined of a plant commonly named Indian shot for its bullet-hard seeds, nicking the seed coat and soaking for 24 hours in tepid water will aid germination. (I put the seed and warm water in a thermos, which keeps the water from cooling down too quickly.) A recent introduction is *Canna* 'Tropical Rose', a pink-flowered dwarf that germinates more readily.

Parentage on most modern cultivars, selected for their flowers, features *C. flaccida.* Ample selection is available, in sizes ranging from 20 inches to over 4 feet tall. Unless otherwise noted, they have green leaves. The Seven Dwarf series is the shortest, with yellow, salmon, pink, red, or crimson flowers. Pfitzer's Hybrids are 30 inches tall, and include 'Pfitzer's Cherry Red', 'Pfitzer's Chinese Coral', 'Pfitzer's Primrose Yellow', 'Pfitzer's Salmon', and 'Pfitzer's Shell Pink'. This can be confusing, as there exists a 'Chinese Coral' developed by Herr Schmid, another breeder who introduced many canna hybrids. Other dwarf Pfitzer hybrids are 'Perkeo', with claret-rose flowers slightly striped with yellow in the throat, and 'Puck', with mimosa-yellow flowers. He also developed taller varieties: still popular is 4-foot-tall orange-red-flowered 'Stadt Fellbach', introduced in 1934. There are W. Pfitzer introductions starting in 1898. 'Paul Lorenz', with marigold-orange flowers on a cadmium-orange ground and brown leaves, was followed in 1901 by 'Franz Graf von Thun', with amaranth-red flowers shaded orange-yellow on the lower petals, and 'Luigi Beretta' with orient-red flowers and brown leaves. The last registered W. Pfitzer selection, 'Mazurka', with dull carmine flowers and brown leaves, was made in 1966. This would appear to be an extremely long career, perhaps instead it is a heritage kept in the family.

As attractive as many find the flowers on cannas, I prefer them as foliage plants. Their large, broad leaves, 10 to 18 inches long and 4 to 8 inches wide, serve as a contrast to other foliage — thread-fine cloud of asparagus; linear shape of ornamental grasses; or for a bold combination of textures on a Brobdingnagian scale, huge palmate leaves of castor bean, *Ricinus communis,* or enormous arrow-shaped foliage of elephant ears, *Colocasia esculenta.* A bronze-leaved canna such as 'Wyoming' creates an effective background for the swooning pink flowers of a crinum, with red zinnias or the hot orange flowers of *Cosmos* 'Diablo'. With more restraint, a round bed with purplish-red-leaved 'Wyoming', silver dusty miller, and a pink-flowered bronze-leafed fibrous-rooted begonia might appeal even to the Victorians. Growing 5 to 6 feet high, varieties such as bronze-purplish-leaved 'Roi Humbert' ('Red King Humbert') are a useful, attractive screen to block out an unwanted view in summer. Most likely a selection of *C. iridiflora,* which itself often grows over 8 feet tall, the tallest cultivar is 'Omega', reported to grow a towering 16 feet tall. There are some golden-leaved cannas, deliciously, thinly striped in green. 'Nirvana' grows a scant 18 to 20 inches tall and serves in my garden as a backdrop for the glaucous blue foliage of rue and yellow-flowered *Allium flavum.* Sometimes offered as 'Bengal Tiger', 'Bangkok Indian Shot', or 'Pretoria', *C. generalis* 'Striata' is taller at 4 to 5 feet. I saw this on a rainy day at Stonecrop, Frank and Ann Cabot's Cold Spring, New York, garden. In combination with, among others, golden hop vine, *Humulus lupulus* 'Aurea', and shaggy orange zinnias, the effect was as warm and sunny as can be imagined.

Caladium

Another tender tuberous plant grown for foliage effect is the familiar caladium. A relative of jack-in-the-pulpit, this South American genus has large heart- or arrow-shaped leaves variously colored with white, pink or red, and green, often translucent. Popular cultivars include pink 'Fannie Munson', red 'Postman Joyner', red-veined, green-laced white 'Arno Nehrling', and white 'Aaron' and 'June Bride', both with a green margin. The newer lance-leafed and strap-leafed cultivars often have an attractively ruffled edge and a pointed tip. 'White Wing', 'Lady of Fatima', and 'Jackie Suthers' are elegant whites with good substance, 'Pink Symphony' is a transparent green-veined pink, and 'Rosalie' is crimson-red with a green-tinted border and wide leaves. Growing wild in the tropical jungles of Brazil, with some species native to Colombia, Peru, Ecuador, and Guyana, they perform best under hot, humid conditions, protected from the wind. Those August nights when the air seems thick enough to swim in are ideal caladium weather. Excellent as permanent plantings in Florida and portions of the South and as seasonal additions to northern gardens, they perform poorly in the arid regions of the country.

The flattish, rounded, somewhat hairy tubers are available in early spring. In cold-climate gardens they cannot be planted outside until conditions are warm and settled, often early June in Connecticut. The tubers are started indoors at 70°F in March, planted in flats filled with a moisture-retentive potting mix. If planted as received, the tubers produce fewer, larger leaves. More, but smaller leaves will grow if the primary shoot is scooped out before planting (a thumbnail does just fine). Once growth starts humidity must be kept high. Feed with a dilute liquid fertilizer as soon as roots are well developed. When shoots appear they can be moved to individual containers, or planted three small tubers in a 6-inch pot. They need a soil high in organic matter, amended with compost, aged manure, or leaf mold. While they also require moist conditions, standing water will rot the tuber. In the garden plant tubers an inch or two below the soil surface, with an organic mulch to help retain moisture. Slugs also thrive under the mulch and dine on developing leaves, so some form of deterrent will be necessary — diatomaceous earth, slug bait, saucers of beer, or whatever local wisdom endorses as effective. Caladium are successful in shaded areas, but need some light to produce good color. Winter storage conditions should be warmer than for gladiolus and dahlias, 55°–60°F.

For the gardener and garden visitors, summer shade is more comfortable than full sun, but this is a time when such sites have few plants in flower. Caladium foliage is a colorful addition: 'Bleeding Heart' has a rose-colored central blotch edged with white, crimson veins, and a green margin, and is effective on its own, concealing dormant spring-blooming bulbs in a bed of myrtle or pachysandra. Adding caladium to other foliage plants and the few late-blooming perennials and annuals such as impatiens produces attractive results in the shady summer garden. The green-veined chalky white leaves of *Caladium* 'Candidum' or 'White Christmas' lighten a shady corner. Combined with *Hosta planaginea,* a glossy bright green–leaved species with fragrant white flowers in August, and white impatiens, the result is an attractive grouping that requires little maintenance. White, marbled green, and with substantial texture, 'Pothos' is charming in combination with the gray-green leaves splashed with white of *Hedera helix*

Foliage can be as attractive as any flower, amply demonstrated by the backlit leaves of *Canna* 'Pretoria'.

An elegant display of white *Caladium*, ever-so-softly flushed with pink at the center, together with pink and white impatiens, provides a gentle, peaceful display at Longwood Gardens, Kennett Square, Pennsylvania.

'Glacier' as a ground cover. The somber coppery leaves of *Heuchera americana* 'Palace Purple' will appear brighter when paired with a red caladium such as 'Frieda Hemple'. A few scarlet-red impatiens will enhance the planting even more. Transparent rose 'Lord Derby' is lovely with soft rose-pink impatiens and silver-leaved Japanese painted fern, *Athyrium goeringianum* 'Pictum'. Made for the shade, caladium are a boon in the woodland garden.

Oxalis

Another summer bulb for foliage interest is the purple-leaved form of *Oxalis regnellii*. Commonly offered as a houseplant, the 12-inch-tall shamrock-like leaves are a somber purple enlivened by a bright cerise blotch at the base of each segment. Clusters of small pale pink flowers float on long stems above the foliage. This geophyte forms both smooth fleshy roots and scaly tubers, which look somewhat like a small pinecone. It is a somewhat tender species in my garden, a blessing in disguise, as oxalis can be obnoxiously invasive plants. I simply dig the tubers in autumn, store them packed in rice hulls, and replant in the spring. Alternatively, grow them in a container to add color to a winter windowsill. They do well in shade, and I especially like them with silvery-leaved Japanese painted fern, *Athyrium goeringianum* 'Pictum', and lavender- or violet-flowered impatiens. Tolerant also of more sun if it is balanced with more moisture, it offers interesting possibilities in the front of the border.

Ipomoea

One houseplant we grew when I was a child was sweet potato: several toothpicks were inserted about one-quarter to one-third down from the end to make a spiky collar that rested on the rim of a glass jar partially filled with water. The ensuing vines with heart-shaped leaves would trail attractively from the kitchen windowsill. Today I still use a sweet potato vine for decorative effect, but it is the handsome black-leaved sweet potato, *Ipomoea batata* 'Blackie'. This has 6-inch-long palmately lobed leaves of an intense purplish black. I use it in the summer garden, most often as a container plant. I got my starts as cuttings, and they rooted very quickly in a sand-peat mix. When the weather was mild and settled they were planted in a large terra-cotta pot together with hot pink New Guinea impatiens and silver licorice plant, *Helichrysum petiolatum*. In September I lifted the large, white-skinned, white-fleshed tuber that had formed, and stored it over the winter like a dahlia.

Gladiolus

Hybrid gladiolus are understandably popular: easy to plant, beasy to grow, and by successive planting may be had in bloom for several months, from July until frost. The imposing stiff spikes are superlative for cutting, but I dislike modern hybrids for garden use, finding myself perplexed in attempts to create attractive combinations with other plants. Early hybrids and the species from which they were developed do not carry as many flowers as the garden forms, nor are they as thick stemmed and tall. I find them more satisfactory, graceful, and elegant in association with other perennials. *Gladiolus byzantinus* and *G. tristus* are the species most frequently found in modern catalogs. They, and the early hybrid forms of summer- and autumn-flowering gladiolus, including *GG. colvillei, childsi, lemoinei, anceinanus, nanus,* and *gandavensis,* are best planted in April or early May, taking into consideration the state of the weather and the locality. Plant 4 to 5 inches deep, or about three times their own depth. Be careful to set each corm so the pointed side is up. Choose a warm, open, sunny situation. As soon as the flowers have withered and the leaves begun to yellow the tops may be cut down to the ground and the corms lifted and dried in preparation for winter storage in a cool, airy, frost-proof location. They do not need to be packed away in peat moss or buckwheat hulls. One frequent recommendation is to store the corms in panty hose, sliding them down into the legs, and hanging the resulting lumpy contraption for good air circulation.

Companion plants might include rosemary, in milder climates, or, in colder locales, silvery-leaved lamb's ears, *Stachys lanata;* lavender, *Lavendula spicata;* or catmint, *Nepeta* x *fassenii.* The soft purple haze of Russian sage, *Perovskia atriplicifolia,* provides a pleasing backdrop, as does *Caryopteris* x *cladonensis,* especially if the gladiolus are planted so as to weave through the shrub, rather than clearly separated in the foreground. Medium-height ornamental grasses such as *Pennisetum alopecuroides;* poverty grass, *Andropogon scoparius;* single white shasta daisies; and the gladiolus create a meadowy cottage garden effect. Another grouping would combine gladiolus with hardy *Geranium sanguineum,* with its vivid pink flowers, and low-growing shrub roses such as 'The Fairy', with its clusters of small, double, soft pink flowers, or brighter, single-flowered 'Bonica'.

Gladiolus have fibrous-coated corms, sword-like leaves, and tall spikes of incurved or obliquely funnel-shaped flowers, all turned one way. The three upper segments are usually larger than the lower ones, but the latter are often beautifully spotted and blotched with contrasting colors. With the exception of *G. byzantinus* and *G. communis,* from Mediterranean Europe, most of the cultivated species are natives of South Africa extending from the Cape Province to the Transvaal and Natal. There are also numerous tropical African gladiolus, none of them yet in cultivation.

Gladiolus may flower in spring, summer, or fall, depending on the rainfall of the area in which they grow naturally. Whether a particular species comes from an area with summer rainfall or one with winter rainfall is an important concern for the gardener. Those from the southwestern Cape and the Mediterranean area grow during winter and generally flower in spring. Those from summer-rainfall areas of South Africa and tropical Africa are dormant in winter and green in summer, flowering during summer or autumn. They all need plenty of water while growing and dry conditions while dormant. If they are grown in regions where they would freeze or be wet while dormant, they should be lifted and stored at this time.

They need a light sandy soil with some protection from hot afternoon sun if they are grown in hot, dry climates. This is especially important for the spring-flowering species from the southwestern Cape. Summer-rainfall species may be grown as garden plants in cold regions where they need to be stored during the long, cold winters. Those that grow in winter and flower in spring will probably need container cultivation. Small cormlets are freely produced, reaching flowering size in two or three seasons. They are generally robust enough to be planted in the open when they measure about ½ inch across; the time it takes to reach this size will vary with the vigor and eventual size of the species. Seed germinates freely in two to four weeks.

The Greeks knew this plant, as did the Romans, gathering the native species for decorative purposes. (The grammarian Athenaeus records that gladioli were planted over the graves of virgins.) While approximately 55 percent of the 215 wild species come from South Africa, it was not until well along in the eighteenth century that any were introduced into Europe. Modern garden forms are principally derived from these South African species, not those from Europe and Asia Minor. *Gladiolus tristis,* a fragrant species, was grown in Europe about 1740, and another Cape species, *G. cardinalis,* was introduced in 1789. From these two the first garden hybrid was bred by an English nurseryman from Chelsea, London, in 1823. James Colville gained a type of immortality, for this and other early-blooming crosses are still known as colvillei hybrids; they are the oldest garden forms and are widely grown today. Together with the nanus hybrids, a name used for several varieties of hybrid gladiolus that have been developed from successive crossings of several species such as *GG. carneus, cardinalis, tristis,* and no doubt others, they are elegant additions to the garden.

They are characterized by having slender and somewhat flexible stems, two or three of which often spring

Near the author's shady terrace, *Caladium* 'Candidum', with *Hosta plantaginea* and white impatiens, seems cool even on the hottest summer days.

The flowers of *Tritona crocata* 'Orange Delight' provide a colorful focal point in this planting.

from one corm. Their rather small flowers resemble those of *G. colvillei,* having pointed segments, the three lower ones usually conspicuously blotched with a distinct color. These grow about 2 feet tall and most have showy crimson-purple flowers blotched with white, usually from May to July. The markings are a contribution from the waterfall gladiolus, or New Year lily, *G. cardinalis,* an unusually beautiful species with sprays of bright crimson flowers marked with white blotches on the lower segments that are outlined in darker crimson. At home in the southwestern Cape this summer-flowering species blooms in December/January, growing in the spray-wet rock near waterfalls. It is nearly evergreen, going dormant only briefly. Nanus hybrids are reasonably hardy in my part of Connecticut and the nearby New York–New Jersey area. A covering of pine boughs or old manure should be given in winter to protect against frost. Often the corms are offered for sale in spring. 'Amanda Mahy' is pale poppy red with a white blotch rimmed in carmine-violet; 'Elvira' is pale phlox pink with large turkey-red-bordered pale yellow blotches; 'Nymph' is whitish pink with a cream blotch edged in china rose. Often they are simply offered as *nanus* mixed. There are two fine white forms: *albus* has white segments and red stamens; 'The Bride' has white segments and stamens. Marsh afrikaner, *G. tristis,* the other parent, is a winter-growing, spring-blooming deciduous species that contributed the early period of bloom. Marked in brown on the outside, the large creamy-yellow flowers on a 12-inch-tall stem, sweetly scented in late afternoon and evening, are enchanting. It has been in cultivation for over 100 years and is possibly the best known of the wild gladiolus, as well as a parent of many modern hybrids. It grows well in California, needing moisture in winter and spring, and summer dormancy.

The Ghent gladiolus, *G. gandavensis,* originated in 1837 with H. S. Beddinhaus, gardener to the Duc d'Aremberg at Enghien, Belgium, who crossed *G. dalenii* (formerly known as *G. natalensis* or *G. psittacinus*) with *G. cardinalis.* The parrot gladiolus (from its now invalid name) has magnificent long, one-sided spikes of large bell-shaped flowers, 10 to 12 on a spike, rich scarlet, lined and spotted with yellow. The most common form of this species in cultivation is an easily grown late-summer, early-autumn-flowering species, which can adapt to spring flowering in mild climates with dry summers and wet winters, needing ample water during the growing season. The Ghent gladiolus reveals its parentage by its red and red-yellow coloring, and was introduced by van Houtte in 1841. In France, M. Souchet of Fontainbleu was another to take to the serious business of producing *gandavensis* hybrids. He utilized the hybrids resulting from the previous cross, and bred them with *G. blandus,* with large white flowers in June having red marking and a yellow tube, and *G. ramosus.* In 1852 many of them bloomed for the first time in his garden. The exquisite, delicate colors included various shades and mixtures of white, cream, violet, crimson, lilac, purple, maroon, salmon-red, rose, scarlet, yellow, orange, pink, and amaranth, variously striped and blotched. In Nancy, France, Victor Lemoine fertilized flowers of pale sulphur-yellow, purple-blotched *G. purpurea-auratus* with pollen from *G. gandavensis.* The resulting *lemoinei* hybrids were distinguished by a beautiful large golden yellow blotch bordered with purple, scarlet, or maroon. He then continued his work by crossing the best forms of these with a Cape species, *G. saundersi.* Distributed in 1889 the resulting strain, *nanceianus,* was sturdy and very hardy; even today it is still very popular in Europe. The colors are varied, brilliant, in many shades of color including carmine, rosy purple, sulphur, salmon, yellow, creamy white, and blood red, and heavily spotted. They are as hardy as the *gandavensis* section and more free flowering.

In 1882 Max Leichtlin of Baden-Baden had been working on hybrids between *G. gandavensis* and *G. saundersi,* a South African species with enormous triangular vivid crimson flowers with large white patches on the three lower segments, which are speckled with red. It blooms in midsummer, at which time it needs ample moisture, and is dormant in winter. The entire stock of these crosses was sold in France in 1882 and nine years later became the property of John Lewis Childs of New York. The *childsi* varieties, as they were then named, were the real beginning of garden gladiolus as we know them today. The branching flower stems are often over 2 feet long with individual blossoms 6 to 9 inches across and shaded with various colors: purple, scarlet, blue-gray, salmon, crimson, blush, rose, pink, yellow, and more, often beautifully blotched, speckled, and mottled in the throat.

Today, the early-summer-blooming Mediterranean species (native in Turkey) *Gladiolus byzantinus* is the most frequently offered wild species. It is a robust plant growing to about 2 feet tall, with a loose spike of 6 to 10 red flowers often shaded with a tinge of purple or reddish violet in June and July. Fairly hardy, it grows best in sandy soil in a sunny position.

If available, the more tender *G. tristis* is dainty and charming for gardens or containers, especially appealing for its strong, sweet fragrance at night. The perfume continues even when the flowers are cut. A native of the Cape Province, growing about 12 inches tall, in July it has funnel-shaped flowers 2 to 3 inches deep, with a cream to yellow ground color, the three upper segments of the perianth sometimes streaked with green or purple. Variety *concolor* has pale sulphur-yellow or creamy-white flowers.

The current name for the Abyssinian sword lily, or peacock lily, is *Gladiolus callianthus.* Catalogs, however, continue to list it as *Acidanthera bicolor* or *A. bicolor murielae.* Native to Ethiopia and East Africa, the most commonly cultivated form has white flowers handsomely marked with a triangular plum-purple blotch at the base of the lower petals, and a sweet, pleasing fragrance. Well-grown specimens reach 3 feet tall, but half that size is more common. Winter dormant, the inch-thick, somewhat pointed corms with a fibrous tunic should be planted in spring to bloom in July and August, with buds opening in succession and often continuing until frost, as late as October in mild climates. The sword-like leaves closely resemble those of gladiolus. They need a sunny site with well-drained, fertile soil, and regular, ample water in summer with some afternoon shade in hot, dry areas. Where the temperature remains at least 10°F above freezing in winter they may be left in the ground, provided they can be kept quite dry during this resting season. In California gardens they self-sow, but sparsely. In cold winter areas lift the corms after the foliage has ripened and store like gladiolus.

Crocosmia and Tritonia

Distinctions between *Tritonia, Crocosmia,* and *Montbretia* are likely to be perplexing to gardeners, as taxonomists have been rearranging these three genera, sometimes including an *Ixia* or *Acidanthera* species for good measure. While *Montbretia* is seen in catalogs, it is not a name in current use botanically; *Crocosmia* is now the valid genus. Catalogs generally will also refer to *Tritonia* as *Montbretia.* Native to South Africa, these members of the iris family grow from small corms and have gladiolus-like leaves and erect spikes of small flowers.

While it would be more correct to call them Tritonias, Montbretias "of catalogs" have graceful arching spikes of waxy blooms in shades varying from yellow to crimson. From a distance the flowers resemble those of a very small gladiolus. In California summer-flowering species are excellent plants for partially shaded places near trees and shrubs provided that the soil is rich, light, and well watered in summer. In all locations they are suitable for the herbaceous border. Once considered rather tender, the recommended practice was to dig them in autumn as the leaves turned yellow and store the corms over winter in a frost-free place. They are more subject to drying out than gladiolus, and if so handled should be packed in peat moss or some other similar material. Noted plantsman Fred McGourty has found them hardy at Hillside Gardens, in the foothills of the Berkshire Mountains in Norfolk, Connecticut. Others grow them in Boston with a winter mulch of salt hay, although severe winters will thin their numbers.

These are hardier than many other genera of geophytes from South Africa but will still need to be lifted in regions where the ground freezes deeply in winter. In cold winter regions their initial planting should take place in spring, while in mild winter regions they are better planted in autumn, setting the corms about 3 inches deep, more deeply in marginal climates. They like a rich soil high in organic matter with ample moisture during growth but not saturated conditions. These plants bloom from late July until frost and make a long-lasting cut flower. Some multiply so rapidly that the corms should be divided every year during the winter dormant period and replanted in early spring. This is another genus that will thrive and naturalize in suitable climates.

Tritonia crocata (*Ixia crocata*) is a fine species growing 6 to 15 inches tall, having a two-ranked spike of saffron, salmon, or orange-yellow 1½-inch-diameter cup-shaped flowers in June and July. Some authorities now include pale salmon-orange *T. hyalina* (*T. fenestrata*) in this species. Several cultivars are occasionally offered: 'Aurora' is medium orange with a pale yellow striped center; 'Isabella' is flesh pink washed with yellow; 'Princess Beatrix' is a brilliant fire red; 'Roseline' is shell pink with a darker center; 'Salmon King' is salmon-pink, while 'Salmon Queen' is salmon-orange; 'Tearose' is creamy white with a yellow center; and 'White Glory' is amber-tinted white.

Crocosmia aurea (*Tritonia aurea*) has bright golden-orange, star-like large flowers, hence the common name of falling stars. They bloom from late summer into early autumn, with 8 or more flowers to each portion of the branching 2- to 3-foot-tall stalk. They are native to summer-rainfall areas of South Africa and to tropical African forests and grow best with a little light shade. While largely superseded by the hybrids, this is a delightful plant in its own right, especially when grown en masse.

Crocosmia pottsii was once *Tritonia pottsii,* and before that it was *Montbretia pottsii,* a fine species from Natal growing 3 to 4 feet tall with sword-like leaves 1½ to 2 feet long and gracefully nodding spikes of deep bright orange to orange-yellow funnel-shaped flowers suffused with brick red. The importance of the two preceeding species lies in their descendant, *Crocosmia* x *crocosmiiflora,* bred by Victor Lemoine in 1879, who apparently found time to work with this genus as well as gladiolus. They may be cultivated like the former and are very easily grown. The common garden montbretia grows 2 to 3 feet tall and has masses of bright orange-scarlet funnel-shaped flowers on branching leafy stems in July into August, sometimes later. In mild climates they multiply very freely and the corms need to be lifted and separated every other year or the plants will deteriorate through overcrowding.

There are many splendid garden varieties, including: 'Citronella', with small, lemon-yellow flowers; 'Emily McKenzie', with large orange flowers with a chrysanthemum-red blotch in autumn; 'James Coey', with large vermilion-tinted orange-yellow flowers; 'Lady Wilson', with buttery, apricot-orange flowers; 'Lucifer', with large tomato-red flowers; 'Vulcan', with large, vivid burnt-orange flowers, of complex parentage and hardiest of all; and 'Solfatare', one of Lemoine's hybrids from 1886, with pale yellow flowers and bronze foliage, which you'll either love or think looks diseased.

Their period of bloom suggests combining them with other late perennials: kniphofias, ornamental grasses, soft lavender *Aster* x *frikarti* 'Monch' or 'Wunder von Stafa'; Russian sage, *Perovskia atriplicifolia;* and shrubs such as *Rosa rugosa,* with its attractive orange hips.

Less hardy than the other species and hybrids, *Crocosmia masonorum* is another relocation from *Tritonia.* Called goue swane, or golden swan, in Afrikaans, because of its arched, branching spike of striking, wide-open, golden-orange or orange-scarlet flowers, opening gradually from base to tip of the 2- to 3-foot-tall stalk. It blooms for several weeks in midsummer. This is a plant for semi-shaded conditions beneath trees or shrubs where it can receive morning sun and afternoon shade. The species does not multiply as freely as the others; in mild winter regions it is best left undisturbed for several years.

Freesia

Freesias, closely related to *Ixia,* have strongly, sweetly scented, trumpet-shaped, dainty colorful flowers about 2 inches long and arranged in an arching spike on a wiry stem. This is my favorite cut flower, and when we lived in Holland my husband claimed we would go broke from my purchases of it in the street market. I could not resist buying a bunch or two of the inexpensive flowers almost every time I went shopping. I cannot indulge myself now, as they are unfortunately more costly in this country. In most sections of the United States they are grown as greenhouse plants only, and corms offered for sale in cold climates in autumn must be container grown. Corms are now being offered in spring in some areas, to be planted for annual use in the summer garden. Freesias are purely South African in origin and very tender to frost.

The varieties now sold are hybrids of *Freesia alba* (previously incorrectly known as *F. refracta*) and other species, with white, cream, yellow, or pink flowers, sometimes flushed with purple and yellow, on stems that carry them above the foliage. Modern hybrids are sometimes not as fragrant as the wild type but are more spectacular, with larger flowers in brilliant shades of yellow, orange, pink, crimson, mauve, and purple on long stems up to 18 inches in height. Where winters are so mild that freesias are hardy, the small pointed corms, covered with a netted tunic, should be planted in autumn about 2 inches deep with the points upward in a light, well-drained soil. They will grow in full sun in southern California's foggy coastal districts but need partial shade in inland areas, where they must be protected from hot afternoon sun. As the plants tend to fall over with the weight of flowers, it is best to brace them with short, upright, twiggy branches placed between the corms at planting time, or interplant them with perennials and small shrubs as living supports. The same range of Mediterranean herbs suggested elsewhere will be effective, selecting a prostrate rosemary as the upright forms grow much too tall. Freesias need plenty of water while in active growth, dry conditions when dormant. Since they multiply rapidly and form new corms freely, clumps should not be left undivided longer than three years. Seed germinates within a month and seedlings generally bloom the second season. Some new hybrids will flower in eight months from seed. From 'Adagio' to 'Zwethlana', the International Checklist for Hyacinths and Miscellaneous Bulbs, published in 1991 by the Royal General Bulbgrowers' Association, lists over 40 pages of cultivars with their descriptions.

The oldest known cultivated species is *Freesia refracta,* which was first cultivated in Europe in the 1780s. This species and its varieties are great garden favorites. Typically, it has ovoid corms with a thickish fibrous or netted tunic, and produces five or six narrow leaves. The slender flexible stems grow 1 to 1½ feet high with several yellowish-white tubular, intensely sweet-scented flowers, sometimes striped or tinted with pale violet and usually spotted with orange at the base of the segments. There are several other species: *F. alba,* one parent of modern strains, has white flowers without the yellow basal blotch; *F. leichtlini* has large pale citron-yellow flowers blotched with yellow ocher; *F. corymbosa* (*F. tubergenii* is an earlier, invalid name) has soft yellow or rose-pink flowers and is a parent of the modern strains. *Freesia sparmannii* has pure white flowers sometimes tinged with blue outside, and is not at all fragrant.

Galtonia

For some reason not as widely grown today as at the turn of the century, summer hyacinth, *Galtonia candicans* (*Hyacinthus candicans*) is another attractive South African. Although it is from the mountains of Natal and Lesotho it has the Afrikaans name of Kaapse hiasint, or Cape hyacinth, in allusion to its sweet fragrance. Suitable as a permanent addition to the garden where temperatures do not fall much below 20°–25°F, they are not so tender as freesias. In colder areas the bulbs must be lifted and stored over the winter, which does not unduly discommode this member of the *Liliaceae.* I first saw this in the Berry Botanic Garden in Portland, Oregon, grouped with tawny grasses and the thistle-like flowers of *Eryngium* 'Miss Wilmott's Ghost'. Each flower about 1 to 2 inches long, the tiers of drooping white bells tipped with green on the three outer petals remain in my memory as a clean, clear image. At their best where summers are moist and rainy, they make effective border plants. One effective use of space would pair summer hyacinth with narcissus for early spring followed by herbaceous peonies in May. The peonies' tidy foliage would both conceal the spent leaves of the narcissus and accent the summer hyacinth when it flowered in summer.

This species, native to the Drakensberg Mountains, is thought by some to be the most beautiful, perhaps a pragmatic judgment as it is the only one likely to be available. It grows from 3 to 5 feet tall, with anywhere from 3 to 40 flowers, and stiff erect gray-green leaves, 30 inches long, in a tuft. The large bulbs, up to 5 inches in diameter, are planted in autumn just below the soil surface. Once established the plants should be left undisturbed for a few years, receiving a mulch of well-decayed manure in autumn. In colder regions plant in spring at the same time as gladiolus, 4 to 6 inches deep, but be sure drainage is adequate. They need a rich, well-drained soil in light shade inland, full sun with cooler summers or along the foggy West Coast, with ample water in spring and summer. In borderline areas mulch well and keep dry in winter. Offsets will be produced on established bulbs in the garden, more readily in mild climates and slowly in colder areas. These may be removed and replanted in the spring. Seed, which is produced freely, is a more reliable means of increase. Sown in late summer or early autumn, the shiny black seeds usually germinate within a month. Under protected conditions the seedlings will grow for a year or more before going dormant, and generally flower in the second or third season.

The other species, pale green *G. viridiflora* and *G. princeps* with pale creamy-green flowers, are more tender. The genus is named for Francis Galton, author of *A Narrative of an Explorer in South Africa.*

Hymenocallis

Summer daffodil, Peruvian daffodil, and spider lily are all common names for *Hymenocallis,* a genus of summer-blooming bulbs native to the southeastern United States, Mexico, Peru, and the West Indies. And just as there are several common names, so too have several scientific names been applied to these bulbs. *Hymenocallis narcissiflora* was known as *Ismene calathina,* and its first change was to *H. calathina.* Study revealed that the first valid description named the plant *Pancratium narcissiflorum,* and thus the currently valid name was arrived at by precedence. These changes are not an idle fancy, or fulfillment of some abstract quota. Taxonomic revisions are based on priority, a matter of what was published first. More often scientific study of the relationship between one plant and another engenders the changes. Different species of *Hymenocallis* have also been named *Pancratium.* This genus is native to the Mediterranean, but geography is not a sufficient basis on which to characterize genera. For example, *Arisaema* may be native to Japan or to the United States. In *Pancratium* the flowers are striped with green and the outer segments are shorter and stubbier. *Ismene,* now included in *Hymenocallis,* comes from the Americas, with elegantly curled tendril-like segments. Books attempt to keep the nomenclature current; catalogs will often list these bulbs as *Ismene.*

They are large, rather fleshy bulbs with a papery tunic, strap-like leaves, and white or yellow flowers in summer. The flowers are fragrant, grouped at the top of a thick stem that rises to 2½ feet from between long, thick leaves. Their name means "beautiful membrane" in reference to the membrane that connects the stamens, forming a staminal cup. The bulbs are fairly large and should be planted with their necks near the surface of the soil. Plant in May in rich, sandy soil, where they will be in sun for most of the day, 3 inches deep, 15 to 18 inches apart, with three to five bulbs in a group. Tolerant of full sun or light shade, *Hymenocallis* are easily grown, thriving in rich, well-drained soil with plenty of water in summer. Sometimes it is difficult to bring them to flower consistently, but success is more likely in a warm, sunny location. Water during the flowering period and while in active growth but keep dry while dormant. In northern gardens treat like *Hippeastrum,* with a dry resting period in soil over the winter. The spider lilies are elegant bulbs for containers.

Native to Peru, *Hymenocallis narcissiflora* is sweetly fragrant, with more intense perfume early in the morning and at dusk. The white flowers appear in summer, two to five on an 18-inch-tall stalk, growing rapidly and blooming quickly. Easy to cultivate, bulbs increase rapidly, and a new supply will be found each fall when the bulbs are dug for storage. Since it is found at fairly high elevations, up to 8,000 feet, it can tolerate colder conditions than other species and is hardy to temperatures close to freezing. This has been useful in hybridization. One cross was with another Peruvian species, *H. amamcaes,* which has deep yellow, very fragrant flowers. Their offspring, 'Sulphur Queen', has six flowers to an umbel, primrose yellow with a green star at the throat in June/July. Hybridizing with *H. speciosa,* an autumn/winter-flowering evergreen species from the West Indies with a large umbel of five to seven fragrant white

Annual Growth Cycle of *Hymenocallis narcissiflora*

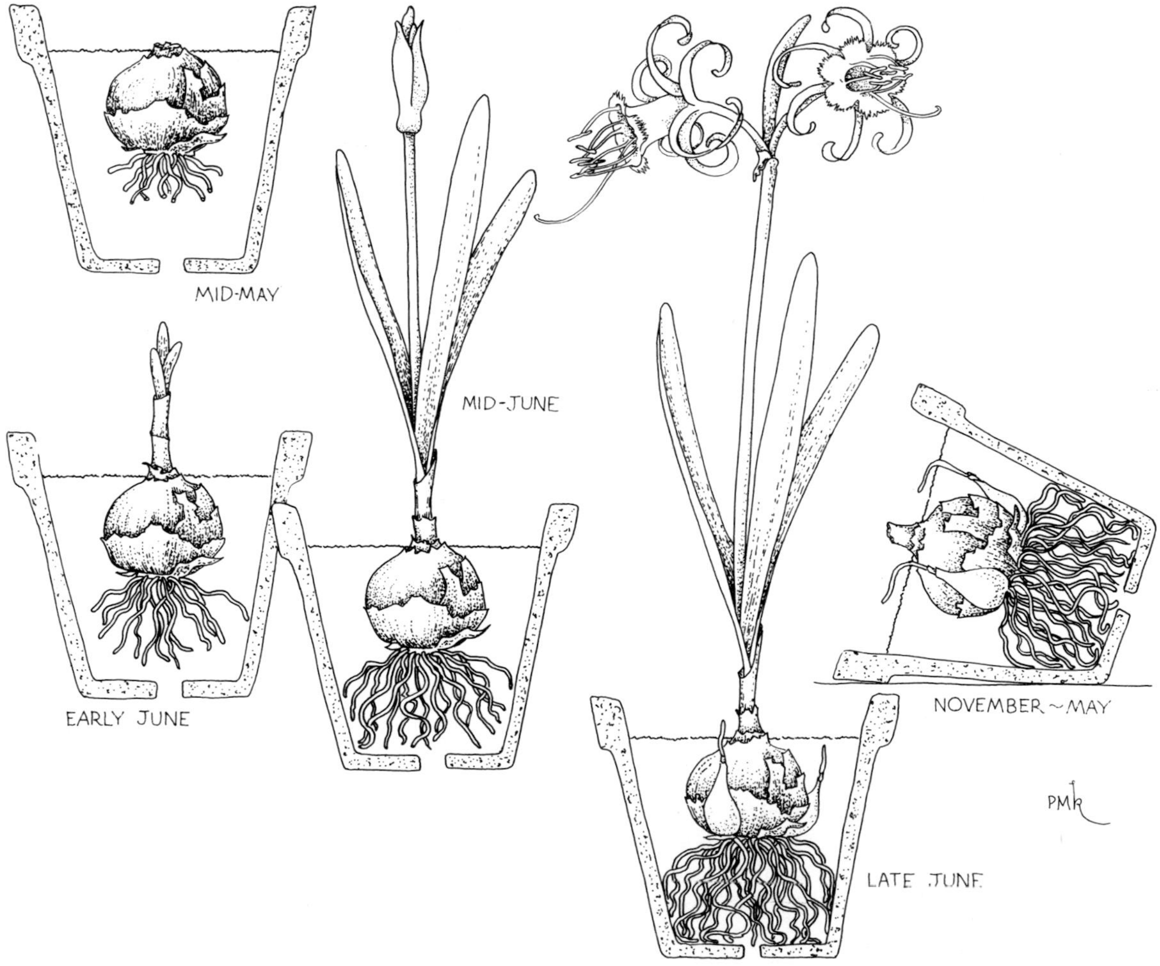

to greenish flowers, produced 'Advance' with large, pure white, intensely fragrant flowers in early summer. *H. festalis* is a cross of *H. narcissiflora* and *H. longipetala* with white flowers with a small defined green base. A further selection was named 'Zwanenburg' with large ivory-white flowers with long gracefully curved segments in a large umbel.

The Southern white spider lily, *Hymenocallis occidentalis,* is native to wooded swamps from Indiana and Missouri south to Texas, Florida, and North Carolina. At Piccadilly Farms, Sam and Carleen Jones's hosta and perennials nursery in Georgia, it grows amid a colony of ferns, blooming in August with several long-tentacled white flowers on 2-foot-tall stalks. It is attractive near ponds and similarly moist sites. For damp places, consider using it in combination with shrubs such as the swamp azalea, *Rhododendron viscosum.*

Zantedeschia

In confirmation that the grass is always greener on the other side of the fence, Americans adore a South African roadside ditch plant there given the epithet of "pig lily," which refers to porcupine and not porcine gastronomes. This weed is none other than the elegant calla lily, object of paintings by Georgia O'Keeffe and an expensive florist flower. Related to jack-in-the pulpit, *Arisaema triphyllum,* and a member of the Arum family, arum lily, pig lily, or calla lily, *Zantedeschia* species have been cultivated for over three centuries. All like good garden soil enriched with well-rotted compost and ample moisture when in active growth. In mild climates they may be left undisturbed to multiply into large clumps. Plant the tubers 4 to 6 inches deep, with spacing dependent on both the ultimate size of the plant and the size of the tubers. Their needs are very simple; the only attention they require is continual watering and consistently warm temperatures. Once growth begins the temperature must be kept steady, as erratic changes, especially a nighttime drop when the spathes are showing, will halt growth. For best flowering commercial growers select large tubers at the end of winter or in early spring, cutting them through like a potato and allowing one or two buds to each portion. Dust the cuts with powdered sulphur and allow to dry thoroughly before replanting. They are easily propagated this way or by offsets from the old tubers. For winter storage in cold climates, keep the thick, fleshy, more or less tuberous rootstocks in dry sand or vermiculite to prevent shriveling. If the crowns of the tubers can be kept free from frost some are almost hardy, and the variety 'Crowborough' is hardy in England, especially when grown in ponds.

There are six species of calla lilies, all native to South Africa and found in the Transvaal and extending from the western Cape as far north as Zambia in the east and across to Angola. The upright to somewhat spreading arrow-shaped or lance-shaped leaves vary from bright green to dark forest green to a yellowish green, plain or attractively spotted with white. The flowers themselves are inconspicuous, male and female borne on an erect cylindrical or club-like spadix enclosed by a large and ornamental funnel-shaped spathe, white, yellow, or rosy pink.

Most familiar as a cut flower, *Zantedeschia aethiopica* is a large-growing, 3-foot-tall species with large, green, arrow-shaped leaves. The flower stalks grow from 3 to 5 feet high, supporting a beautiful white overlapping funnel-like spathe that tapers at the tip like a pig's tail, enclosing a cylindrical yellow spadix at the center. Elegant for Florida gardens as a permanent feature in the landscape, it is evergreen if grown in permanently wet situations like the marshes of its homeland. There, in winter-rainfall areas it will be dormant in summer during the dry season. It grows best in swampy conditions, even in a pond, and creates an attractive waterside effect. If the water does not freeze to the level of the tubers, it will survive, even if the leaves are frozen. Strong sunlight will yellow the foliage, especially if the soil is not constantly moist; light shade is preferable. It is easy to force at almost any time of year, convenient for the cut flower industry. This species is mentioned in a listing of plants in the collection of the Leyden Botanic Garden of 1686. 'Green Goddess' has a spathe strongly flushed

The sumptuous flowers of *Zantedeschia aethiopica* extravagantly decorate this wet meadow in South Africa. (DR. ROBERT ORNDUFF)

Like some fanciful illustration in a medieval manuscript, the flowers of *Hymenocallis narcissiflora* are decorated with graceful arabesques.

with green and is considered relatively hardy (for an arum lily), thrives in semi-shady locations, and can be grown in large containers on a shady veranda. *Z. aethiopica* 'Devoniensis' is snow white and produces more flowers than the arum usually grown; both 'Childsiana' and 'Little Gem' are dwarf forms growing about 18 inches high.

Kleinvarkblom, or little pig flowers, *Z. albomarginata* ssp. *albomaculata* grows 18 inches to 2 feet tall, has rather narrow, arrow-shaped leaves 12 to 18 inches long and 2 to 3 inches wide, either plain green or decorated with translucent white spots and stripes. The flowers are similar to the preceding but smaller, with ivory-white, cream, pale yellow, or coral pink spathes with a vivid crimson-purple or black patch in the throat. It grows in summer and is winter dormant. Temperatures much below freezing will kill the tubers. 'Aurata' has spotted leaves and large yellow spathes from early to late summer; 'Sulphurea' has soft yellow flowers and a maroon blotch. 'Helen O'Connor' has coral pink spathes and comes true from seed. Ssp. *macrocarpa* has unspotted or sparsely spotted leaves and cream- or straw-colored spathes with a conspicuous purple blotch; ssp. *valida* has unspotted leaves and ivory- to cream-colored spathes with a purple blotch.

Yellow arum, *Z. elliottiana,* is a splendid species growing about 2 feet tall. The dark green leaves are heavily blotched with white, and it has pure yellow spathes of good size, wonderfully showy in the lightly shaded sites it prefers. This species needs good drainage, and a dry period when it is dormant. It will be harmed where temperatures fall below 25°F. There is some doubt as to whether this is a true species or a hybrid of garden origin as it is not known as a wild plant. Yellow arum is propagated by offsets, and is easily raised from seed. Sow seed as soon as it is ripe in summer, distributing it thinly in pots of rich sandy soil kept moist. It will begin to flower the third year.

Purple arum, *Z. rehmanni,* a popular species growing 12 to 18 inches tall, is easily distinguished from the others as the base of the leaf is not lobed but instead long and narrow, tapering at both ends like a spear. They are plain green, occasionally spotted with light green or white. The spathe may be pale pink or even pure white, but the best forms include deep rosy pink or reddish pink with a purple tinge, blooming from early summer to midsummer. Useful in a lightly shaded site, this species tolerates drier soils than most arums and is dormant in winter but is best with plenty of water while in active growth.

Yes, they are more expensive than a six-pack of zinnias or marigolds, but these tender geophytes offer elegant, exciting possibilities for the summer garden. Gardeners fortunate enough to live in milder climates can have them as permanent landscape components. For those of us who face the challenge of winter there exists the option to lift and store them through the cold times in order to resurrect them the following year.

7

Unfamiliar Tender Bulbs for the Summer Garden

Cyrtanthus, Vallota, Veltheimia, Lachenalia, Rhodohypoxis, Crinum, Clivia, Eucomis, Babiana, Watsonia, Ixia, Sparaxis, Chlidanthus

GEOPHYTES are found just about everywhere except the polar regions. However, more grow wild in areas with Mediterranean-type climates — regions with mild temperatures (although not necessarily frost-free), summer droughts, and winter rainfall — than in any other areas. Perhaps not so well-known, these tender bulbs definitely deserve wider use. There are five areas that fit these parameters: the Mediterranean rim, the Cape region of South Africa, southwestern and south Australia, central and southern California, and central Chile. Naturally enough, geophytes evolved to cope with these wet/dry conditions. The mountains and coastal regions of the Mediterranean rim: Morocco, Corsica and Sardinia, southern France, Greece, the Balkans, Mediterranean Turkey, the coasts and islands of the Aegean, Lebanon and Syria, Anatolia, and northern Iran are home to *Narcissus, Crocus, Galanthus, Colchicum, Tulipa, Scilla, Puschkinia,* and *Fritillaria,* to list only some of the bulbs that grace our gardens.

The Cape region of South Africa is the smallest of the six floristic provinces in the world and arguably the richest, with over 8,550 indigenous plant species in a 33,000-square-mile area roughly one percent the size of the United States. Mildest of the Mediterranean climates, the region from Cape Town to around Port Elizabeth has winter rainfall and dry summers. The midsummer months of December and January are completely dry, and the winter months of May to August are the wettest. Many of the geophytes flower in the austral spring of August, September, October. (Add six months to approximate the equivalent season in the United States.) Cape Town's average minimum temperature is 37°F, and the average maximum is 95°F. Annual precipitation averages approximately 25 inches. Nearby, Table Mountain affords a moderating effect with summer mists, much as occurs in California along the coast near San Francisco. The area is brilliantly sunny.

Following European colonization, the thorny aromatic scrubby fynbos spread as a result of habitat disturbance. Comparable habitats are called chaparral in California, maquis in the Mediterranean rim area, mallee in Australia. Profusely carpeted with brilliant spring flowers, a rich bulbous layer grows beneath the shrubs. Flowering and seed production of the woody plants is frequently triggered by fire. The soil is generally poor and of acid pH.

From this small region come superb geophytes, many of them lamentably scarce in ordinary gardens. Often, they are thought to require high temperatures during their resting period. The need is not so much for incineration as for parching, as it is water while they are resting that quickly rots and spoils these geophytes. *Lachenalia,* for example, can be spoiled by even a few days of heavy rain after they have gone dormant. Where grown, these tender geophytes are often suggested for container cultivation. Some are suitable for seasonal use, with annual lifting and storage over cold winter weather in the same manner as the geophytes discussed in the previous chapter. And they are far better for use in the comparable Mediterranean climate of California than daffodils and tulips, with their need for simulated winter through precooling. When summer drought has brought most growth to a halt, acclimated as they are to a dry summer and a mild, wet winter, the flowers of these Cape bulbs are naturally suited to add color to a parched landscape. Some of these summer- and early-fall-blooming bulbs refuse to wait and begin their growth with the stored reserves of moisture contained within the bulb. *Amaryllis belladonna, Brunsvigia orientalis,* and *Nerine sarniensis* produce flowers first, and delay leaf growth until the rains are likely to have begun. Semi-tropical geophytes from the eastern Cape forests and Natal are suitable for the southern states approaching Florida. In general the bulbs will, over time, adapt so that normally spring-blooming species will flower in the spring, all other conditions being satisfactory. Where rigorous winters are the norm, species that flower in spring in South Africa can be planted in spring to flower in summer, lifted, and stored over winter.

In the late fifteenth century the Portuguese were searching for a route to India, gradually working their way down the African coast. Finally in 1497 Vasco da Gama made it around the Cape of Good Hope to Calicut on India's western coast. Only 44 of the 170 who sailed with him survived to return to Lisbon when the ship sailed home more than two years later. Thus when the Dutch East Indies Company established a permanent base at the Cape, in 1652, it was as a stopping place for supplies and fresh water. A thriving colony developed, and these men became the first non-Africans to discover the botanical wonders of the region. These new and curious plants of the Cape became fashionable in European gardens and glasshouses. Today they can be used as permanent plantings to enrich mild-climate gardens, and for seasonal color in colder regions.

Cyrtanthus

One of the most fascinating groups in the Amaryllis family is *Cyrtanthus.* With sweetly scented, brightly colored, more or less tubular, slightly curved flowers grouped in a drooping cluster at the top of a hollow stalk, they are attractive in gardens where winters are mild and sunny, and also as florists' flowers. Some species, especially the deciduous ones, are difficult if not impossible to grow, but it is puzzling that even the easily cultivated evergreen species are rarely seen in gardens. Most *Cyrtanthus* are actually summer growing, from areas with summer rainfall, and are not Cape geophytes. In Afrikaans those species that are summer growing are often called brandlelie or vuurlelie, fire lilies, as they burst into bloom after the grasslands burn, forming brilliant scarlet patches in the blackened veld. This would suggest their adaptability to the chaparral canyons of Los Angeles with a similar fire-dependent ecology.

In general they are cultivated the same way as the more familiar *Amaryllis belladonna,* with a rich, light, free-draining soil containing well-rotted compost in a warm,

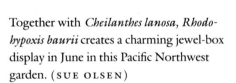

Together with *Cheilanthes lanosa, Rhodohypoxis baurii* creates a charming jewel-box display in June in this Pacific Northwest garden. (SUE OLSEN)

Fire lilies indeed, these *Cyrtanthus* are blooming in this burned-over African veld scant weeks after the flames passed through. (DR. ROBERT ORNDUFF) lightly shaded situation. In the wild some species such as *C. obliquus* grow with a portion of the tunicate bulb out of the ground. In cultivation they are usually planted with their necks at soil level and from 2 to 6 inches apart, according to their size. The bulbs usually lose their narrow, strap-shaped, sometimes grass-like leaves in winter, but some are almost evergreen, while a few are deciduous in summer. Give them plenty of water during active growth, but naturally during the dormant period they require less moisture. Evergreen species such as *C. obliquus* and *C. carneus* require some water year-round. Offsets form rapidly with the smaller-flowered species but more slowly with the larger kinds. Propagate by detaching offsets at the time of replanting or repotting. It is best to leave the plants undisturbed in the ground, but when they become too thick clumps may be divided. They also make excellent pot plants, easily brought indoors for winter storage in cold climates. Seed germinates in about a month and blooms in the third season.

From the eastern Cape and Natal, the Ifafa Lily, *Cyrtanthus mackenii,* is the best-known species in cultivation and is often grown for cut flower use. The typical species has narrow, funnel-shaped, ivory-white flowers in umbels of 6 to 10 somewhat drooping on a slender, hollow, foot-high stem during winter and spring months. Var. *cooperi* has cream or yellow flowers, and there are two forms with pink or apricot flowers. All are strongly and sweetly scented. They bloom in midwinter or early spring, depending on the warmth of the climate, usually before the 2 to 6 linear foot-long leaves that appear together with or immediately after the flowers. There is only a brief dormant period from the beginning of winter, and the bulbs should not be kept out of the ground later than the end of winter. Found wild near the Ifafa River on the Natal coast it will flower well in the garden if given adequate moisture in summer, growing in partial shade as well as sun. Red Ifafa Lily, *C. obrienii,* from Natal is almost identical but has no scent and the flowers are not quite as long. It appears intermediate between the fire lily, *C. angustifolius,* of the southern and southwestern Cape and *C. macowani.* The linear leaves appear with the flowers that are bright scarlet in color, 1½ inches long, about 8 being borne in an umbel. It blooms in early spring, leaves appear either during or just after the flowering period, and it is dormant in winter. *C. macowani* grows wild at an elevation of 5,000 feet in the eastern provinces of Cape Colony. It has ovoid bulbs about 1 inch in diameter, and 1 to 3 linear leaves 6 to 12 inches long. From 6 to 8 bright scarlet, narrowly funnel-shaped flowers about 1½ inches long are borne on scapes about 12 inches high. Small red fire lily, *C. parviflorus,* has similar red flowers, only they are constricted at the mouth. It flowers erratically at intervals in summer or autumn. The leaves appear together with flowers in early summer, and it is deciduous for a brief period in winter. Light shade or sun are suitable. This species comes from the mountains of the eastern Cape and Natal.

Knysna lily, *C. obliquus* (*Crinum obliquum*), is a rare, spectacular plant that has been overcollected in the wild. It has been in cultivation since 1774, grown as a cool greenhouse plant in Europe for over 200 years. The large ovoid bulbs are 3 to 4 inches in diameter and should be planted with at least half the bulb exposed above ground. The erect hollow stem grows 12 inches high, with a drooping cluster of 6 to 12 large, funnel-shaped flowers at the top in April and May. Each is about 3 inches long, yellow at the base, changing to orange-red, tipped with bright green. About a dozen strap-shaped leaves 1½ to 2 feet long are produced after the flowers. They are nearly evergreen, dying down for a brief period in winter. It grows in sun along the coast or with partial, especially midday shade in hotter, more inland regions, and likes moisture. This might have possibilities for more open grassland areas with adequate moisture, such as the bluffs around Mendocino, California.

Cyrtanthus angustifolius (*Crinum angustifolium*) was introduced from the southwestern and southern Cape in 1774. It has ovoid bulbs 1 to 2 inches in diameter, bearing 2 or 3 linear leaves 1 to 1½ feet long. The bright scarlet-red, pendulous, unscented flowers appear in late autumn, from 4 to 10 in an umbel on top of a peduncle about 1 foot tall. Variety *grandiflorus* has larger flowers, 2½ to 3 inches long, and *striatus* has bright red flowers with yellow ribs.

Originally *Cyrtanthus hybridus* was thought to be a bigeneric garden hybrid between *C. sanguineus* and *Vallota purpurea,* most resembling the latter in general appearance. The flowers are clear orange-scarlet or bright carmine, the tube being sharply curved in front and almost sharply dilated at the throat.

But to some taxonomists Vallota no longer exists, having had as many monikers as a swindling con man. The intricate taxonomic revisions began as *Crinum speciosum* transmigrated through *Amaryllis speciosa, A. purpurea, Vallota purpurea,* and *V. speciosa.* It was renamed *Cyrtanthus purpureus* in 1963 before a hopefully final resolution as *Cyrtanthus elatus* in 1986. This lovely bulb will most likely be found in catalogs as *Vallota speciosa.*

Native to the Knysna forest on the Indian Ocean side of South Africa, bulbs reached England early in the nineteenth century. They were washed ashore from a Dutch ship wrecked off the Yorkshire coast near Scarborough. Thus the common name of Scarborough lily. It has a narcissus-like bulb with a brownish tunic and fleshy roots. In cold winter regions it should be grown crowding the roots in small pots, placing the bulbs with their neck at soil level, with a sandy compost. In warmer regions where the bulbs can be a permanent addition to gardens, grow with about one-quarter of the large ovoid bulb exposed. The amaryllis-like, strap-shaped bright green leaves are virtually evergreen and require abundant water while in growth. From 6 to 9 funnel-shaped flowers are carried on a hollow stem 2 to 3 feet high. The most common color is a glowing coral or salmon red. In addition to lighter and darker pink forms, there is a soft pink, with the name var. *delicata,* and a pure white. Flowering season is from midsummer to autumn. One year I found some bulbs at a nursery in late March. I potted them up and had one bulb bloom rather precipitously, scarcely a month later, in early May. The others more sedately waited until late May to flower. It is often watering after a dry period that most effectively governs the flowering of wet/dry cycle geophytes, as warm/cold sequences regulate tulips and daffodils. When the bulbs are well established they throw up their brilliant flowers every year. Offsets are formed freely and are an easy means of increase.

Veltheimia

Veltheimia is a real favorite of mine, easy to cultivate, with modest, subtly attractive flowers. Early in the new year the potted bulb sends up a dense spike of numerous small pendant tubular flowers, variable but always in shades of pink, tipped with green. This is a small genus with only two species, both growing in winter. *V. bracteata* should be planted with the bulb at or just below the level of the soil. Named forest lily, in mild-climate gardens it is useful as a shade-tolerant species. Those forms native to regions of the eastern Cape with year-round though scanty rainfall are almost evergreen, with only a brief dormant period in midsummer. The leaves grow in a rosette, glossy, medium to dark green with an undulating edge. Then in January or February from the center of the rosette appears an 18-inch stem with 30, 40, or more flowers. It does make offsets, at a rather leisurely pace, which can be removed after the bulb has gone dormant. The black seeds, developing one inside each large, buff-tan, winged, tissue-paper-like seed case, are another means of increase. Young bulbs will sometimes begin to flower in their third season. Mature leaves can be removed from established plants and inserted into a sandy mix where they will form bulblets at their base. *V. capensis* is native to the drier regions of southern Namibia, Namaqualand, the western Cape, and Little Karroo. It has a longer summer dormant period. This species grows with at least a third or more of the bulb out of the ground. Many layers of old, dry tunics protect it from desiccation while dormant. It is such an easy bulb to grow in containers for winter bloom that it is difficult to explain its scarcity in favor of the gaudy, fussier *Hippeastrum* hybrids.

Lachenalia

The same might be said concerning the Cape cowslips, *Lachenalia,* a genus of about 40 species of South African geophytes closely related to *Hyacinthus* and *Scilla.* Little grown at present, they have a long history. The genus was named in 1784 after Werner de la Chenal, professor and eminent botanical authority in Basel, Switzerland.

When grown in pans or hanging baskets lachenalia are elegant, relatively easy as winter-flowering houseplants once popular with Victorian gardeners. In late summer or early autumn plant five or six of the small fleshy bulbs in a 6-inch pot. Set the bulbs in a pocket of pure sand just below the surface of a light and extremely well-drained soil mix, not more than an inch deep. Drainage must be excellent at all times. Water well after potting and then keep barely moist until growth begins, after which they should be watered on a regular basis. Keep dry again when the leaves have begun to wither after flowering. It is important to provide regular watering while in growth and then afterward dry off promptly or the soft bulbs will rot. In South African garden centers and nurseries they are sold in small plastic-mesh packages, stapled to a color display card, much the same as we see gladiolus. Available in April/May, in 1993 a package of 25 *Lachenalia pearsonii* was priced at 14 rand 95, about five U.S. dollars.

Intolerant of frost, they are excellent for a rock garden in mild climates. Garden cultivation is problematical if other plants in the area will need water while the lachenalia are dormant. Moisture-conserving perennials such as low-growing agaves and aloes, dwarf yuccas, and small cacti will be attractive while the bulbs are dormant and require little supplemental watering. Shrubby herbs from the Mediterranean area — lavender, rosemary, sage, artemisia — would also be useful. Annuals and perennials adapted to the same climactic limitations would add additional color. Such Cape species as star of the veldt, *Dimorphotheca* spp.; monarch of the veldt, *Venidium fastuosum;* dill-leaf ursinia, *Ursinia anethoides;* sunshine daisy, *Gamolepis tagetes;* and *Gazania rigens,* all with daisy-like flowers mostly in shades of yellow, golden yellow, and soft orange; and ice plants, *Mesembryanthemum* spp., in brilliant pink, red, white, and lavender, in addition to yellow, would be suitable. As well, such North American dryland annuals as California poppy, *Eschscholtzia californica;* California bluebells, *Phacelia campanularia;* annual lupines; tidy tips, *Layia campestris;* baby blue eyes, *Nemophila menziesii,* would grow and flower, perhaps establishing themselves as permanent additions to the garden as self-sowing colonies.

The tubular flowers of lachenalias are crowded on a fleshy stem that varies from 6 to 12 inches long. Depending on the species their color can be golden yellow, coral red, crimson, and variegated, while others are glaucous blue, purple, and delicate opalescent colors. Usually there are two leaves to a bulb, sometimes handsomely marked with chocolate or maroon spots. Small bulblets form freely; seed does not set well in cultivation.

Lachenalia bulbifera (*L. pendula*) is a fine showy species remarkable for its pendulous, orange-red to deep crimson tubular flowers tipped with emerald green and purple on thick, fleshy stems about 12 inches tall in February. It has been used as a cut flower. The bulbs are relatively large, and it has deep green lance-shaped leaves sometimes faintly mottled with brown.

L. aloides is another excellent species. It has broad, fleshy green leaves about 12 inches long, mottled with dull purple. Typically, it has from 12 to 20 tubular flowers banded bright yellow with a bright red base and a green tip, on stems growing 6 to 12 inches tall. It is variable in color in the wild, and several varieties have been named. Var. *quadricolor* (*L. tricolor*) has beet red-purple tips on reddish-orange-, yellow-, and green-banded flowers; var. *aurea* is a uniform clear golden yellow; 'Pearsonii', larger at 12 to 15 inches, was raised in New Zealand and appears to be an improved form that has bright orange-red flowers edged with claret-red; 'Nelsonii' is named for the Reverend John G. Nelson, who raised the first hybrid lachenalia in 1878. It has a stout 12-inch-tall scape and rich golden yellow flowers slightly tinged with green and edged claret red. I like to arrange 'Pearsonii' with other potted plants such as an apricot gazania, or single French marigolds with russet-stained orange flowers, attractive with the lachenalia's chocolate-spotted leaves and fine flower spike.

Called the opal lachenalia, *L. orchoides* var. *glaucina* has somewhat fragrant flowers, 30 or more, in deep blue or pale purple fading to mauve and lighter shades at the tip, on a 12-inch stem. Fairy lachenalia, *L. mutabilis,* is a variable species. The form I grew had a 7-inch stalk covered with flowers of a pale iridescent bluish mauve tipped with reddish brown. *L. violacea* has a 7-inch stem crowded with small ½-inch greenish or bluish flowers tinged with violet and green.

Rhodohypoxis

Another dainty South African charmer for a rock garden in mild climates with dry winters is *Rhodohypoxis.* For those of us in colder areas, it is quite satisfactory as a container plant. It has a tiny, ½-inch-diameter corm-like root, usually with a few persistent roots. The short, stiff, linear leaves have attractive silvery hairs, and the flowers on the most commonly available species, *R. baurii,* vary from white to deep pink to red. I obtained my first plants from an English nursery in Haslemere, England, in 1973; and in the winter of 1992/93 they were offered in the White Flower Farm holiday gift catalog. In Seattle, Washington, they are sold in supermarkets with other houseplants! They are well suited to cultivation in a shallow bulb pan, using a well-drained sandy/peaty mixture. Water thoroughly once, when planting, and then wait until growth appears before watering again. Their hardiness is no doubt critically influenced by winter moisture. Native to the Drakensberg Mountains, it occurs in short turf at 4,000 feet elevation, so it must be able to endure some frost. It is winter wet that is its nemesis. Geoffrey Charlesworth, a skilled rock gardener in Massachusetts, grows these in pots, which he sinks in the gravel of the rock garden for the summer. The little corms flower beautifully, and it is simple to lift the pots, keeping them dry over winter. At Sir John Thuron's garden in Pennsylvania I saw rhodohypoxis growing in crevices in stone steps. In such a site drainage would be sharp, and the massive stones would buffer winter temperatures.

Crinum

Very different, statuesque, with bulbs the size of footballs, *Crinum* are imposing plants in the landscapes of Florida and the southeastern United States, regions with mild winters and ample moisture. A far-flung genus, with species native to tropical Southeast Asia, tropical America, Australia, Polynesia, and southern and eastern Africa, including Mozambique, and Namibia, only some of the 100 or so species are in cultivation. A few outstanding species from South Africa are the easiest to obtain and have the most horticultural merit. Popular in the southeastern United States, Florida, and California, their imposing flower stalks reach 2, 3, or even 4 feet high. The large, sweetly fragrant lily-like flowers may be distinguished from *Amaryllis belladonna* by their longer perianth tube, which adds a graceful drooping character to the display.

They are easy to cultivate and should be left undisturbed for many years, as they are difficult to dig up and often need a season to settle down again and flower after disturbance. In the garden they need a rich, fertile soil with ample moisture, in a sunny site with some shade through the hottest part of the day. When out of bloom the foliage is ornamental. Since they are evergreen, or nearly so, they have no need for an extended dry resting period. However, the coarse foliage of crinums becomes impressively shabby in autumn when it enters its brief dormancy, and the bulbs are best planted somewhere in the middle of the border where the ungracefully aging foliage can be concealed behind perennials or shrubs. The bulbs, which are quite tender, should be planted with the neck aboveground and then left undisturbed. In areas where temperatures regularly fall below 32°F, crinum should only be grown in large containers, to prevent disturbance of the fleshy roots when they are brought inside for sheltered winter storage.

Crinum are easily propagated by detaching the offsets, which are freely produced in some species. They also can be reproduced by means of the seeds formed in large fleshy fruits that follow the flowers. Place seed, just barely covered or on the surface of a moist, sandy mix. A short, fleshy radicle is soon produced, sometimes while the seed is still on the plant. Flowering will often begin the third or fourth season.

Bush lily, *Crinum moorei,* is the most familiar garden species. A fine species native to Natal and the Cape Province, it has a graceful nodding head of 6 to 10 clear soft pink vanilla-scented flowers in late summer or early autumn. Each individual trumpet-shaped flower is about 4 inches long, and they are grouped at the top of a sturdy 3-foot stem. This species is more or less evergreen, dropping its 2- to 3-foot-long bright green leaves for a brief period immediately after or even during flowering and forming a new rosette of fresh leaves soon afterward. It has very large, ovoid, long-necked bulbs that are remarkable for producing stolons or runners. This is a woodland plant from the eastern Cape that will grow in dense or partial shade as well as in more open conditions. It is a good companion plant to *Agapanthus orientalis,* which flowers at the same time under similar conditions. Bronze fennel, *Foeniculum vulgare* 'Bronze', with its dense mass of fine-textured purple-bronze foliage, makes an attractive companion, as does the moisture-loving Joe Pye weed, *Eupatorium purpureum,* or a canna with purple-red foliage.

The Orange River lily, *Crinum bulbispermum* (*C. longifolium*), has a large head of trumpet-shaped flowers in spring. These may be pink or white, characterized by a rose-red stripe running down the center of each petal. Each long-tubed flower is about 4 inches long, with 15 or so grouped at the top of a sturdy, 2- to 3-foot-tall stalk. The long, bluish-green leaves rise in a fountain from the ground in spring and summer, dying away in winter. It will grow in full sun if in damp soil, but thrives in any well-watered situation. It can survive limited freezing in winter, and has proved hardy in the milder districts in England. This suggests that a sheltered site and deep airy winter mulch might permit it to survive Philadelphia/New York City/Long Island (on the bay shore) winters. Wild along the Orange River in South Africa, it was introduced to Europe in 1752.

The fine hybrid, *Crinum* x *powellii,* a cross of *C. bulbispermum* and *C. moorei,* is a very popular choice for the garden. About 8 large flowers, similar to *C. moorei* but larger and varying in color from white to deep rose-pink, appear in midsummer on a flattened gray-green peduncle about 2 feet tall. There is a pure white, 'Album'; 'Intermedium' has pale pink flowers; 'Haarlemense' is soft pink; and 'Krelagei' is deep rose pink; while 'Roseum' is a dwarf, deep pink-flowered form. The bright green, pointed, sword-shaped leaves, 3 to 4 feet long and 3 to 4 inches broad, are like that of *C. bulbispermum.* It has roundish, short-necked bulbs.

There are several hybrids of mixed parentage, many involving *C. moorei.* 'Cecil Houdyshel' is a fine, desirable pale lilac-pink, white at the base, with a long period of bloom, and hardier than many others; 'J.C. Harvey' is an old form with pink, long-lasting flowers widely distributed in the South perhaps through its ability to form 10 or more offsets each year; 'Maiden's Blush' is worth the long, three-year wait until it establishes itself, as it then will produce up to 20 fragrant pink flowers on each stem. Louis Bosanquet, a Florida breeder, awarded his best plants family names: 'Louis Bosanquet' produces numerous scapes of pink flowers, and a classic red, 'Ellen Bosanquet', exhibits fragrant, wide-open flowers in early summer. This was used to develop 'Elizabeth Traub', also with large red flowers on a 6-foot-tall stem. Two fine white-flowered crinums developed by Luther Burbank, perhaps better known for his work with plums, are 'Burbankii' and 'White Queen'.

Also called veld lily, the milk-and-wine lily, *Crinum fimbriatulum,* has 4 to 6 beautiful lily-like milk-white flowers with a delicate pink stripe down the outside center of each petal from mid-August until late October. In the wild

I envy southern gardeners the ease with which they grow milk-and-wine lily, *Crinum fimbriatulum,* with elegantly nodding flowers.

This exquisite illustration of *Crinum pedunculatum* comes from Bury's *A selection of Hexandrian plants, belonging to the natural order of Amaryllidae and Liliaceae,* published 1831–34. (ILLUSTRATION FROM THE LIBRARY OF THE NEW YORK BOTANICAL GARDEN) it is found in moist places near rivers, or in small depressions in the grassland where moisture gathers, or in marshy meadows. This is another popular species, long cultivated in gardens of the southeastern United States.

Native to the eastern Cape of South Africa the water crinum, *Crinum campanulatum,* actually grows in marshes and ponds that dry up in winter. It is a beautiful plant for water gardens, with 6 to 8 bell-shaped flowers, smaller than those of most other species, clustered at the top of a slender 18-inch-tall stem. Appearing in late spring or early summer they are a lovely pink with a red stripe down the center of each petal. There is also a white form. It has small ovoid bulbs with slender, deeply channeled, arching leaves, 3 to 4 feet long, ½- to 1-inch broad, which disappear while the plant is dormant in winter. When pot-grown it can be lifted from the pool for a three-month resting period and replaced in the water in early spring. It should not be covered by more than 3 to 4 inches of water. The water level should be low and conditions warm if it is to be left in the pool over winter, but it is better with a short resting period. A combination of cold and wet will quickly rot the bulbs.

The sable crinum, *Crinum macowani,* is similar to the foregoing species with a wide-open trumpet and distinctive semicircular black anthers. The flowers are white or pink with red stripes down the center of each petal, up to 20 on a 36-inch-tall stem. Uncommon in cultivation, it grows wild in the eastern Transvaal, flowering in late spring or early summer and going dormant in winter.

With the intimidating common name of Asiatic poison lily, *Crinum asiaticum* is a spectacular plant. Widely distributed throughout tropical Asia, it was introduced to Europe in 1732. Flowering chiefly in summer, it has strong 2-foot-tall stems that bear a dense head of about 20 beautiful fragrant pure white flowers tinted green in the throat, each about 3 to 4 inches long with narrow petals. Var. *procerum* has larger flowers tinged with red. The bulbs are 4 to 5 inches in diameter with necks 6 to 9 inches long, bearing masses of bright green tapering leaves 3 to 4 feet long and 3 to 4 inches broad in a rosette. The long thick leaves are more or less evergreen in mild climates, dying off for a short period in winter. It thrives in a subtropical climate, suffering damage if winter temperatures fall below 40°F.

Crinum americanum is native to the southern United States, found in swamps and marshes from Florida to Texas. Flowering periodically from spring to fall, it has 3 to 6 creamy-white flowers on an 18- to 36-inch-high stem. The short-necked ovoid bulbs are 3 to 4 inches in diameter, with arching strap-shaped leaves 2 to 3 feet long and 1½ to 2 inches wide. *C. cruentum* is a Mexican species with large, short-necked stolon-bearing bulbs and dark glossy green leaves 3 to 4 feet long and 2 to 3 inches broad. The stout peduncle, about 3 feet tall, bears 6 to 8 bright pink flowers in summer.

Widely distributed over tropical America and in cultivation since about 1784, *C. erubescens* is a variable species. The short-necked ovoid bulbs are 3 to 4 inches in diameter and give rise to numerous thin, strap-shaped arching leaves 2 to 3 feet long and 2 to 3 inches broad. From 4 to 12 flowers are borne on the top of a peduncle 2 feet or more tall. The whitish flowers are washed with claret-purple on the outside while the filaments are bright red.

Clivia

Useful in a lightly shaded site and growing as easily as it does in its native woods in Natal, South Africa, *Clivia* is an outstanding plant popular in California gardens, where it flourishes in rich sandy soil high in organic matter. They are elegant when massed under trees that will provide light shade, combined with ferns and other lacy-textured foliage plants. The numerous broad, deep green, strap-like leaves are arranged in two rows (distichously), forming a neat ornamental evergreen clump. Very tender, they turn brown at the lightest frost. A small genus of imperfect bulbs, the underground portion consists only of leaf bases and very stout roots. In colder regions it is favored as a container plant, flowering well if under-potted with restricted root space. Today South African garden centers and popular home and garden magazines refer to this as St. John's lily. The older common name of Kaffir lily has fallen into disfavor, as the epithet is as opprobrious an expression there as "nigger" would be in the United States.

Give ample water while in active growth in spring and summer, and only enough to keep the plant from shriveling when resting in winter. They are extremely drought resistant during the resting period in winter and at that time only need watering once a month. Long-lived, they may be left in one location for an extended period of time but also can readily be lifted and divided to increase the number of plants. New divisions will take a year or two to settle down and begin flowering again. Whether planting new plants or separating established ones, care must be taken to avoid damage to the fleshy, thickly matted roots.

New plants can also be raised from seed, which should be sown in summer while still red and fleshy. Place on the soil surface and keep moist and shaded. It will germinate in about a month, and immature plants should be kept in a seed pot until large enough to plant out in the garden in a year or two.

Clivia miniata is the only species widely cultivated today, and is reminiscent of agapanthus, with umbels of 12 to 20 more or less erect, funnel-shaped, scentless flowers borne on top of a stout stem. The flowers appear in spring, in September if south of the equator in their African home, and during April into summer in the northern hemisphere. Each individual trumpet-shaped flower is about 3 inches long, and they can vary in color from pale orange with a yellowish throat to a glowing reddish orange. The fruits are also attractive — large red berries about the size of a small olive. There is also a rare variety, *C. miniata* var. *citrina,* which has clear pale creamy-yellow flowers tinted with orange at the base. Var. *striata* is grown for its foliage, as the leaves are freely striped with white, handsome in contrast to the dark green.

Now hardly seen, *Clivia nobilis* was the first species discovered in the Cape colony of South Africa. It was named by John Lindley for the Clive family, who were benefactors of horticultural exploration during the period known as the golden age of plant discovery. Rarely grown, its smaller size would appear to make it more suitable for pot culture. It has narrow, dark green, leathery leaves. The bright red and green funnel-shaped flowers, tipped with green, appear in May or June on a stalk about a foot high.

Eucomis

Unique, attractive in flower and in fruit, it is small wonder that pineapple lily, *Eucomis,* is so popular with flower arrangers. Reminiscent of the crown imperial with a tuft of leaves above the flower spike, hundreds of small, usually greenish, 6-petaled flowers crowd together to form a thick spike near the top of a sturdy stem, truly suggestive of a pineapple. The name comes from the Greek word *eukomes,* beautiful-haired, and refers to the tufted crown above the flower spike. Where hardy they are popular in gardens, and may be grown in colder climates with an annual lifting and storage of the large tunicate bulbs over winter. Surely worthy of more general cultivation, they are most attractive when several are grown together. In one flower bed I combine them with purple-leaved *Perilla,* emphasizing the delicate purple edge of each green *Eucomis* flower. *Eucomis* is a small genus, containing about ten species from the eastern Cape and Natal, with three of the larger, more robust species generally in cultivation. Flowering occurs at the end of summer or early in autumn with an extended attractive display provided since the flowers turn green as they age, remaining starry and open while the ovary slowly enlarges and turns bright green.

Where year-round temperatures remain above freezing in the daytime they can be left in the ground. They like a sunny site with rich, gritty, and well-drained soil and ample water while in active growth in the summer. In milder districts plant with the bulbs just below soil level. Additional protection in marginal areas is provided by planting the bulbs deeply so as to have about 6 inches of soil above the top of the bulbs. The bulbs have a long dormant period of 5 to 6 months and may be allowed to dry out completely in the soil. (Do not water during the dormant period if the bulbs are growing in containers.) Growth appears later in spring than most other geophytes, and this is an advantage as spring frosts are thus unlikely to harm the new foliage. When doing well allow the bulbs to remain undisturbed for some years, but give a good top-dressing each year in spring when the shoots have appeared above the soil. If the flower spike becomes thinner it is a sign that the bulbs have become overcrowded and will benefit from separation. The plants are easily increased by offsets removed from the old bulbs. Because pineapple lilies flower late in the season, seeds do not always have time to mature. Ripe seed can be sown in rich gritty soil in pots under glass. The seedlings need careful attention for the first couple of years, and reach flowering size when about four years old.

Eucomis bicolor is a handsome species from Natal, where it grows wild along streams in damp grasslands. The rather odiferous, pale greenish-yellow flowers, conspicuously marked with a distinct purple edge, appear in August in dense racemes. 'Alba' is a selection made by van Tubergen that has greenish-white flowers.

The species we today know as *Eucomis autumnalis* ssp. *autumnalis* used to be called *E. undulata* and *E. clavata*. It grows to 2 feet tall with wavy-edged, fresh green leaves half folded down the center and growing in an upright tuft. The flowers are greenish yellow, green, or white, aging to green.

Eucomis comosa (originally named *E. punctata*) is one of the prettiest, with a dense spike of sweetly fragrant, greenish-white, pink, or purple flowers. The yellow-anthered stamens and the deep violet ovary in the center of the flower make it distinctive and attractive. This is usually the earliest species to flower, in late July or early August. As they age and ripen the ovaries become wine-colored. The 2½-foot stems are spotted with purple at the base, and the green leaves are sometimes shaded with purple or are purple spotted. 'Striata' is heavily striped with purple on the underside of the leaves.

E. pole-evansii, from the Transvaal, is huge, with flower spikes growing to 6 feet tall, the top 24 inches covered with green flowers. The leaves, 24 inches long and 6 inches wide, are finely crisped along the margins. It likes more swampy conditions in summer than any of the other species.

Babiana

Collectively called "babiaantje" in Dutch and "babejaantjie" in Afrikaans (diminutives for "baboon," as the apes eat these corms) *Babiana* were among the earliest of the Cape bulbs introduced to Europe. The corms are known to be edible, and early Cape colonists reportedly boiled and ate them, perhaps taught to do so by the indigenous tribes. This genus has densely matted tunics on the corms, short, stiffish, pleated, hairy leaves, and funnel-shaped flowers in dense spikes. Blooming in spring and early summer, they are available in rich, dark shades of blue, mauve, and crimson as well as cream and white. The small six-petaled flowers are more or less cup-shaped, some with long tubes, and have a tendency to close toward evening or in damp weather. They are tender and cannot be grown year-round in gardens where the temperature falls below 20°F. Pot cultivation is difficult because of the depth at which they prefer to bury themselves. In mild winter regions they should be planted in autumn; in an open sunny situation along the California coastal fog belt; but with afternoon shade in drier inland areas. In the experience of Dr. Goldblatt, B. A. Krukuff Curator of African Botany at the Missouri Botanical Garden, planting the corms 2 inches deep is usually okay, although some growers in California prefer to plant them at least 6 inches deep in light loam with good drainage, and often they will pull themselves down another 3 or 4 inches. While in growth they need ample water, but they must be kept dry when they are dormant in winter. Fresh seed germinates easily. Use deep pots, sow in late summer or early autumn, barely covering the seed. Flowering will begin in two to three years. Offsets form along the thin un-

Eucomis bicolor is worth the nuisance of digging each fall and storage each winter, in summer rewarding the attentive gardener with an exhibition of delicately purple-edged green flowers.

This close-up of *Watsonia pillansii* clearly shows its attractive spike of pink flowers, reminiscent of gladiolus. (DR. PETER GOLDBLATT)

derground stems, as well as next to the mother corm.

Upright babiana, *Babiana stricta,* grows about 12 inches tall, with a loose spike of four to eight flowers, sometimes slightly fragrant, in May. Variable, the color can be dark purple, deep royal blue, mauve, or (though rarely) pale cream. Var. *sulphurea* has scented, creamy, or pale yellow flowers. Named forms introduced from Holland include dwarf 6- to 8-inch tall 'Blue Gem', a dark campanula violet with purple flecks, and several 12- to 16-inch-tall varieties including 'Purple Sensation', a very fine variety with luminous bright purple flowers, blotched yellow and violet on the outer petals; 'Purple Star', a dark cyclamen purple with white stripes in the throat; 'Tubergen's Blue', with methyl-violet flowers blotched with white at the base of the inner petals edged in darker purple; and 16- to 18-inch-tall 'Zwanenburg Glory', dark sea lavender outside, with the inner petals marked with large white blotches.

Low-growing, 6- to 8-inch-tall wine-cup babiana, *Babiana rubro-cyanea,* has 5 to 10 flowers on a stem in spring. Deep aster-violet with a dark crimson zone at the base, sometimes completely purple, it is a very attractive species. It needs moisture in winter and spring, and should be kept drier for the rest of the year.

Blue babiana, *Babiana disticha,* sometimes called *B. plicata,* grows 6 to 12 inches tall with sweetly hyacinth-scented yellow-throated violet to pale blue flowers in May or June.

Katjetie (kitten), crimson babiana, *B. villosa,* has 6 or 7 brilliant crimson- or claret-colored flowers with thick blackish anthers gracefully arranged on a 15-inch-tall stem in September. It needs summer-dry conditions, and moisture only while in growth.

Watsonia

Very similar in appearance to gladiolus, with fibrous-coated corms, sword-shaped leaves, and tall spikes of tubular bell-shaped flowers, watsonia is a genus of beautiful plants native to high-rainfall areas in the mountains of South Africa. Some, such as *Watsonia aletroides,* are found on the plains of the southwestern Cape. Adaptable, some grow so well in New Zealand that they have become naturalized. One Australian book recommends destroying any surplus corms "as this South African bulb [sic] has escaped into the hills and mountains in certain parts of Australia and become a pest." In regions with temperatures below freezing, however, it is safer to grow them in frames or greenhouses. As far as gardeners are concerned the complication is whether a particular species is deciduous, divided again into those that are summer dormant, growing in winter and flowering in spring and early summer; or winter dormant, growing in summer and flowering in midsummer and autumn; or evergreen, to be planted in spring to flower in late summer or early autumn and left undisturbed. Most evergreen kinds can survive light frosts to about 25°F. Winter deciduous kinds are similarly hardy, and winter-growing, spring-flowering deciduous kinds are tender to frost. Evergreen watsonias need watering throughout the year, and will not flower well unless they receive plenty of water for at least three months before the flowering period; it is almost impossible to overwater them. Many species are native to the mountains near Knysna, where they receive about 100 inches of rain a year, and a few species come from the eastern Cape and Natal mountains.

The corms vary in size and should be planted at twice their depth and 6 to 9 inches apart, depending on the ultimate size of the plants. The soil must be well drained and rich in compost. During growth they need ample water but should be stored dry when dormant. Best to lift and store the corms of deciduous species unless their resting period coincides with the regional rainless season. They all like full sun along the southern California coast, and afternoon shade in spring and summer if grown in a hot inland area. Propagation is easy, as the corms multiply extremely vigorously. Divide deciduous species every year or every other year while they are dormant. Evergreen species can be divided every four to five years, after the flowering period. Seed germinates in about one month and will generally flower the third season — perhaps the second season for dwarf species. Summer dormant species should be sown in autumn; winter dormant and evergreen species should be sown in spring.

Deciduous species include several that flower in late spring or early summer and are dormant in summer. Corms must be planted in autumn and the plants kept moist in winter and until after the flowering period. Many are tender to frost. Summer-flowering deciduous species are not as showy as the other types but are hardier and can be grown in cold winter areas where the corms are lifted and stored during the winter dormant period.

Native to the southern Cape Province, *Watsonia aletroides* is unusual in that it has tubular flowers like an aloe, which droop down in a 12-inch spike at the end of a 2-foot stem in June and July. They are tomato-red to salmon-coral in color and bloom in early spring, with deciduous, narrow, sword-like foliage about 18 inches high. Winter growing, it may be used as a border plant where conditions are suitable.

W. borbonica (*W. pyramidata, W. ardernei*) is a deciduous winter-growing species that blooms in late spring to early summer with large white flowers on a 3-foot stem. It is one of the few watsonias that has a white-flowered variety, and has been used as a parent of large-flowered hybrids. Popular in gardens, this species is thought to be extinct in the wild. Also known as *W. rosea,* it has clear mauvish-pink, 2-inch-wide flowers, which form a graceful spike at the top of 4- to 5-foot-tall stems. It has been used effectively on highway plantings in the Cape Province, where it blooms in October. Hybrid forms of this species have even larger flowers in delicate shades of mauve and pink.

Watsonia pillansii (formerly known as *W. beatricis*) is an outstanding species with about 36 flowers on the spike, with almost half open at a time. They bloom in midsummer. Each flower measures about 2 inches across and the stem grows to about 3 feet tall. The type has rich apricot flowers, but numerous hybrids have been developed, including salmons, reds, yellows, and shades of orange. This evergreen species is found growing in damp areas.

Watsonia densiflora from Natal and the eastern Cape Province is a fine species with narrow stiffish leaves 1½ to 2 feet tall. Each stalk has a core of brown bracts from which the cyclamen-pink flowers appear in a double-sided crowded spike in June. There are about 22 flowers, which all open at the same time. There is a pure white form as well as a burgundy one that is not as showy. This is a deciduous, summer-growing species that flowers in June/July. Needing rich moist soil, this species refuses to bloom in poor or dry soil.

Tall-growing *W. marginata* is a remarkably pretty plant with 5- to 6-foot-tall stalks bearing about 30 flowers with at least half open at one time. They are cup-shaped like *Ixia,* clear lilac, and marked at the center with magenta and white. The distinctive, somewhat leathery lance-shaped leaves, 2 to 2½ feet long, are bluish green with pronounced yellowish-brown edges. This is a deciduous, winter-growing species.

Ixia

Corn lily, from the Afrikaans "'kalossie," *Ixia* have thin wiry stems varying from a few inches to 3 feet in height, which stand up to the wind with no ill effect. The dense clusters of starry flowers are bright and varied in color, including scarlet, pink, mauve, purple, cyclamen, yellow, white, and turquoise. The flowers open late in the morning and close at the end of the afternoon but remain decorative, as they are richly colored outside. They need midday sun or the flowers may not open. In moist coastal situations they may be grown in full sun but need shade in hot, dry inland locations, especially in the afternoon. They are easy to grow in ordinary, light, well-drained soil. In milder climates the small, smooth, or fibrous-coated corms, up to an inch wide, should be planted in autumn to grow through winter and spring. Water well during winter and spring when the erect, strongly veined, sword-shaped leaves are in growth, but withhold water when the foliage turns yellow. It is best to lift the corms and store them during the summer months when they are dormant, as they rot easily if the summer is wet. In northern gardens they may be handled like gladiolus, planted in early spring to flower in midsummer. Plant them about 2 to 3 inches deep and 2 inches apart in groups of at least two dozen for effect. After flowering is over and the leaves have withered, the corms should be kept dry and in a dormant state. Propagate by offsets, which form easily and flower the second season. Seed germinates

A grassy hillside on the Cape of South Africa displays an intricate show of native wildflowers — warm orange-flowered *Watsonia aletroides* and the delicate-blue flowers of *Aristea spiralis*. (DR. PETER GOLDBLATT)

in a month and flowers the third season. *Ixia* is closely related to *Babiana, Sparaxis,* and *Tritonia,* but it differs structurally in botanical details. They are elegant plants of fairly easy growth but are unfortunately not hardy except in the very mildest parts of the country. Exclusively from South Africa, there are about 45 species, but only a few are in cultivation.

Yellow Ixia, *Ixia maculata,* has a dense showy spike of bowl-shaped flowers in early spring (late February through March), which vary from 1 to 2 inches wide (de-

At the opposite side of the year from spring, *Crocus speciosus* displays its autumn flowers above a carpet of *Cerastium tomentosum*.

As though frost and snow have already returned to the garden of Christopher Lloyd at Great Dixter, the tulip-like blooms of *Colchicum speciosum* 'Album' raise their white chalices above a hoary carpet of *Artemisia canescens*. (C. COLSTON BURRELL)

sieboldii, whose arching stems of mauve-pink flowers overlap in blooming sequence with the crocus. At the very edge of woodland I have it interplanted with *Ophiopogon planiscapus* 'Nigrescans', whose deep black leaves are an elegant foil for the lavender chalices of the crocus. When the thin grass-like leaves appear in spring they are not a problem, even where it grows in profusion. They grow and fade without harming nearby plants as the coarse foliage of colchicum might. This has been in cultivation long enough that several selections are available. Also September flowering are 'Albus', which has white flowers with a yellow throat and pointed petals, and 'Artabir', with light blue flowers with darker veining. 'Oxonian' is particularly attractive, with very large, deep violet-blue flowers, darker veining, and a deep purple throat. Flowers appear in October, as do those of pale lavender-violet 'Aitchsonii'. Yellow-throated, aniline-blue 'Cassiope' flowers in October and November and is also one of the more generally available species.

Crocus cancellatus, with its yellow-throated, pale to mid-lilac-blue flowers veined with violet, usually flowers by the end of October. The tunic around the corm is very conspicuously, coarsely netted in this species. It is native to southern Turkey, western Syria, Lebanon, and northern Israel, and, as might be expected, requires a warm, dry resting period in summer. This species is readily procurable, as is *C. goulimyi,* discovered in 1954 in southern Greece by Dr. C. N. Goulimis, and named for him. The flowers appear in October/November, a pale to deep lilac-purple, darker on the outside with a white throat. A pure white form, 'Albus', was named by Michael Hoog in 1972.

Crocus kotschyanus (*C. zonatus*), from central and southern Turkey, northwestern Syria, and central and southern Lebanon, has pale to mid-bluish-lilac flowers with conspicuous darker veins in September/October. Their color is so soft that the effect is like a pale wisp of smoke floating close to the ground. The throat is whitish with a pair of yellow blotches like a chevron at the base of each petal. Flower shoots grow parallel to the surface of the flattish corm, so it is best to plant them at an angle to ensure that flowers reach the surface. New cormlets are produced in abundance. Leaves appear after the flowers fade. *C. kotschyanus* var. *leucopharynx* lacks the yellow markings in the throat, and flowers in September.

A European species found wild in northwestern Italy and southeastern France, *Crocus medius* is a pretty species flowering in September to November. The flowers are lilac to deep purple, feathered with purple at the base, and extending into the white throat. The forked style is scarlet-red and makes a brilliant contrast to the petals.

From the Balkans and northwest Turkey, *Crocus pulchellus* is similar to *C. speciosus* and blooms in September to November, with the bulk of its clear pale to mid-bluish-lilac flowers with a deep yellow throat appearing in October. Its form 'Zephyr' has large flowers, pearl-gray outside and white inside with an orange throat, in September/October, and 'Sylvia Cobb' has pure white flowers in September.

A change from the lavender and lilac already mentioned, *Crocus ochroleucus* has small creamy-white flowers with a pale to deep yellow throat. It flowers quite late, blooming for me in late October, early November. The flowers appeared deceptively frail and delicate, but easily withstood the season's rough weather, attractive as they blossomed through the hoary mat of *Thymus serpyllum lanuginosus.* The first flowers appear before the leaves, which appear together with the next group of blossoms. With good drainage during the period of summer dormancy this has been reasonably persistent. It is a tough species, able to grow anywhere if it is given a hot, dry summer location as suggested by its native habitat in southwestern Syria, Lebanon, and northern Israel.

Gardeners with culinary interests may be aware of the saffron crocus, *Crocus sativus.* It is the red stigma of this crocus that is the source of the costly spice. The enormous expense reflects the fact that it is difficult to grow and tedious to harvest. Each flower has three pistils, which must be plucked by hand. It takes approximately 4,300 flowers to produce one ounce. A 1/10 ounce vial of Spanish saffron will include about 50 deep red stamens, enough for one ordinary paella serving 10 people. The dried threads should be infused for 20 minutes or so in broth before using them in the recipe for paella, in milk or cream for a custard, or in Cornish saffron buns.

Widely cultivated around the Mediterranean, saffron was an important element of Phoenician trade. Introduced to Spain by the Arabs, in La Mancha the saffron crocuses are still picked around Santa Teresa's Day in mid-October. In the eighth century one of those serendipitous combinations occurred, the melding of saffron, rice, and seafood into paella. It was Rome that introduced the spice to Britain, and its cultivation continued after the Romans' departure. During the Middle Ages it was sought after not only for its supposed medicinal attributes (plague, madness, melancholia, and toothache were just a few conditions it would cure) and culinary properties, but as a source of yellow dye in manuscript illumination (a pinch of saffron was infused with glair, an egg-white glue, to produce a transparent yellow glaze sometimes used as a substitute for gold, and often mixed with blue color to give a good green) and cosmetics, especially as a hair dye.

The cultivated variety is a sterile plant not found in the wild. This is one crocus that does not seem to like my garden. Plump corms do well the first season, producing their conspicuously veined lilac-purple flowers and vivid blood-red, branched pistil lolling out of the flower, and then dwindle and decline rapidly in subsequent years. I once saw a boxful of unsold corms in bloom at a nursery and was tempted to pluck the pistils to salvage *something* from the waste. I decided discretion was a better course to follow; it was an herb nursery and perhaps they had harvest plans of their own.

The above are the most routinely available species of autumn-flowering crocus. There are other fine ones well worth the search.

A favorite of mine is dainty *Crocus longiflorus*, one of the few that produces flower and foliage together. The gently rounded flowers are a soft lilac purple with a yellow throat, appearing in late October through November. The flowers have a sweet, violet-like odor, but are so close to the ground and the weather so chill that the fragrance may be hard to detect. Kneel, cup your hands around the plump little egg-cup of a flower, and gently puff a warm breath into the space. Then inhale and enjoy. This species multiplies freely by offsets, and each spring I dig and separate a clump to extend my planting more rapidly.

Another choice species is winter-blooming *Crocus laevigatus* 'Fontenayi', from Greece, with attractive yellow-throated lilac flowers feathered with purplish brown. It starts blooming in late November and continues almost all winter into February. It is one of the most indestructable of the crocus, even though it presents both flower and foliage together. Early in the morning or on a cloudy day the tightly furled buds are buff, and like camouflage the feathering makes them difficult to see against a gravel mulch. Even thin watery winter sunlight is enough, and the flowers open wide to show their purple heart.

One I have not yet chanced outside is beautiful white November-blooming *Crocus niveus.* It had been on my wish list ever since I'd read a description of it in 1970, but the corms never seemed to appear in any catalog. When I was in England in 1990 my friend Philippa Wills took me to visit Mike Salmon's Monocot Nursery. It was obviously the right choice for my entertainment from the moment we drove up and I saw the beds of colchicum in bloom. As we were chatting I happened to mention my longing for this particular crocus. With a gentle smile around the stem of his pipe Mr. Salmon reached under the greenhouse bench, picked up a paper bag, and selected five corms, which he presented to me, saying that he thought "they would make up to a nice potful." As it flowers so late in the year and would be difficult to replace I am content to keep it in the security of the alpine house (walk-in cold frame).

Colchicum

Confusingly called autumn crocus or meadow saffron, colchicum are one of the most popular of the autumn-

Annual Growth Cycle of *Colchicum speciosum*

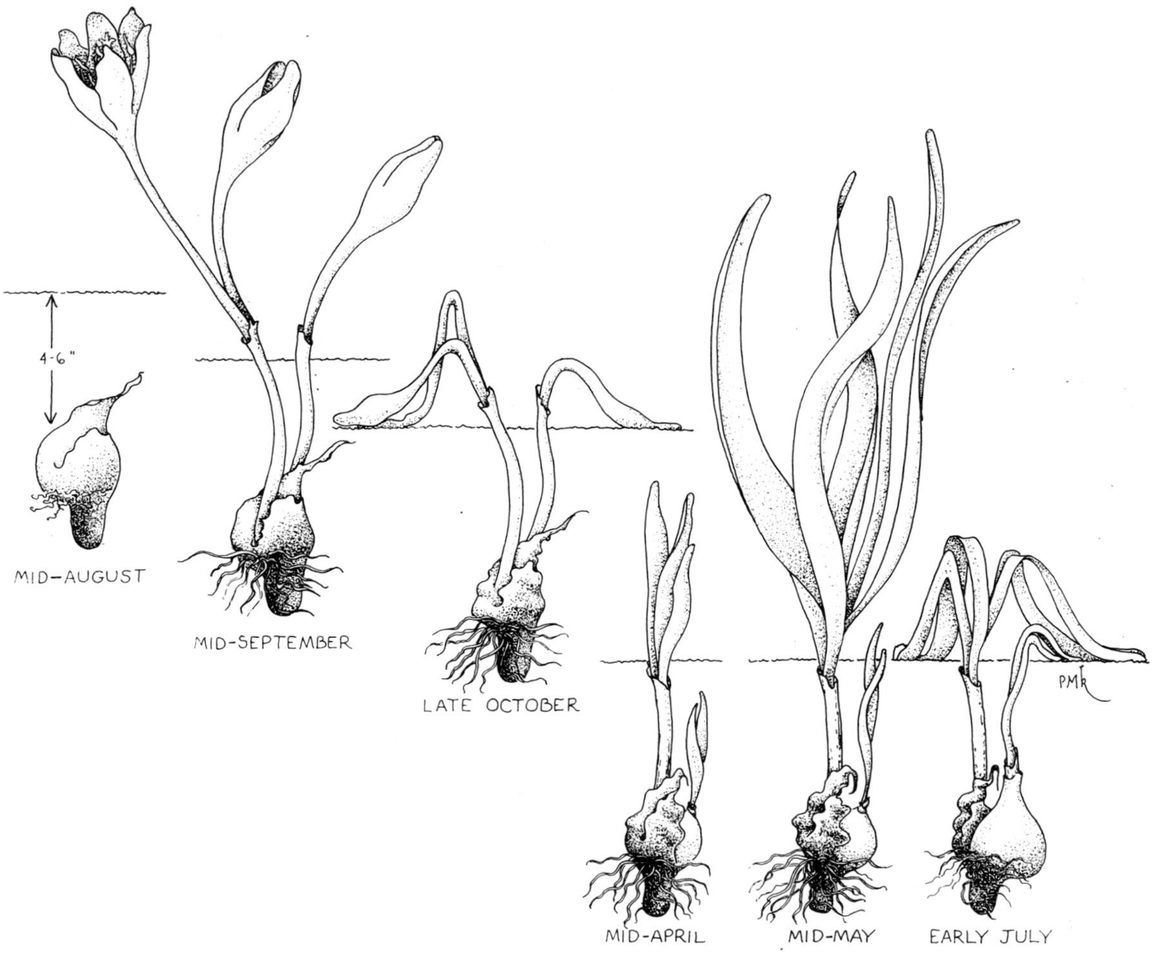

flowering bulbs. Sometimes it has been named 'Filis ante Patrem' ("the son before the father") for the cycle of seeds in the spring, flowers in the autumn. Their goblet-like flowers appear in September and October, swooning to loll seductively on the ground once they are pollinated. Color is generally a soft mauve-lilac, either self-colored or checkered, depending on the species, and white forms are sometimes found. The flowers may readily be distinguished from crocus by more than size, as colchicum have six stamens, crocus only three. Corms of colchicum have an irregular shape, convex on one side and flattened on the other with a tongue-like projection at the base, the whole business wrapped in a papery chestnut-brown tunic. Shoots are produced on the side. Crocus have symmetrical corms with an annulate or reticulate tunic, and the shoots emerge from the top. Colchicum have coarse, broad, bright green strap-like foliage in the spring, which persists until mid-June when it turns yellow and collapses all over its neighbors. Crocus leaves are thin, grass-like, with a central white line, withering to inconspicuous brown remnants.

Colchicum speciosum is the most frequently offered species. Native to the Caucasus region, northern Turkey, and Iran, it has large corms, 4 inches in length and 2 inches thick at the widest part. They should be planted as early as possible, in late summer or early autumn, setting the corms 4 to 6 inches deep. A lightly shaded site is preferable; however, colchicum will also grow in a sunny location if given midday shade. Avoid planting near short, small, or delicate herbaceous plants, since the foliage, produced in spring, is so coarse. Combinations with shrubs, trees, and vigorous perennials will provide the most satisfactory results. The flowers, shaped like a cottage tulip, are a pale ivory color when they first appear, arousing greedy thoughts of albino forms. The color gradually deepens to lilac or a deep rosy purple, with yellow stamens. Fresh flowers continue to appear for a couple of weeks with as many as four flowers produced from each shoot, extending the flowering period. They can reach 10 to 12 inches high before pollination, after which they swoon. There is an exquisite white, *C. speciosum* 'Album', which I grow with *Hosta* 'Francee', enjoying the white variegation on the edge of its leaves with the albino flower. Several fine deeper-colored forms also exist, the most available of which is 'Atrorubens', petunia-purple with a white center. Some authorities feel that 'Bournmuelleri', with rosy-pink flowers and a white throat, is within the range of variation; others accord it specific rank as *C. bournmuelleri*. The perianth tube does remain soft green, not aging to purple as happens with the other colored forms.

Autumn colchicum, naked boys, *C. autumnale* has smaller, rosy-lilac flowers with rather starry segments about 2 inches long, one to six in each shoot, growing 4 to 6 inches high. Sometimes they exhibit a faint checkering, or tessellation. It begins blooming in August, earlier than the preceeding species, and continues flowering from late summer into autumn. Native across southern, western, and central Europe to Russia, it was introduced into cultivation in 1561. In England it grows wild in wet meadows. There is an attractive white, 'Album'; a double, 'Pleniflorum'; and a ravishingly beautiful double white, 'Alboplenum'. This is the source of the drug colchicine, a poisonous alkaloid used in the treatment of gout. It is also used in plant breeding as it induces the doubling of chromosomes, producing tetraploids.

Colchicum cilicium has numerous pale rosy lilac flowers, upward of 20 in succession, beginning in September and thus providing weatherproof flowers for an extended period. It seeds freely. In this species the leaves appear soon after the flowers fade, rather than waiting for spring. The rather massive foliage, four or six leaves to each corm, are more than a foot long and 3 to 4 inches wide. It is sometimes suggested that *C. byzantinum* is a form or hybrid of this. I side with the splitters rather than the lumpers, since *C. byzantinum* has paler flowers a month earlier in August, and is usually finishing as *C. cilicium* begins. Also, it waits until spring to produce its foliage, and the leaves are more strongly ribbed and even broader.

I am much attracted to the species with tessellated flowers, finding the markings a handsome addition. One such is *C. variegatum*, from Greece and southwestern Turkey. It is strongly checkered, with darker tessellations on a deep red-purple or violet-purple ground, occasionally paler at the base, in September/October. Similar, and more frequently offered, is *C. aggripinum*, which displays moderate lilac-purple checkering on a pinkish-lilac ground in August/September. This species multiplies freely and is easily grown in a sunny site. It is possibly of garden origin, a hybrid of *C. variegatum* and *C. autumnale*. Named in honor of E. A. Bowles, *C. bowlesianum* has large flowers, strongly checkered in purplish violet on a rosy-purple ground, sometimes white at the base, in October. This species from Greece is hardy but slow to increase.

A number of hybrids exist, with parentage involving *CC. autumnale, bournmuelleri, bowlesianum, giganteum, speciosum,* and others. 'Autumn Queen' has tessellated flowers, deep purple on a white ground; 'The Giant' has violet flowers with a white base; 'Lilac Wonder' is rosy lilac; and 'Violet Queen' is imperial purple. 'Water Lily' has

Annual Growth Cycle of *Cyclamen hederifolium*

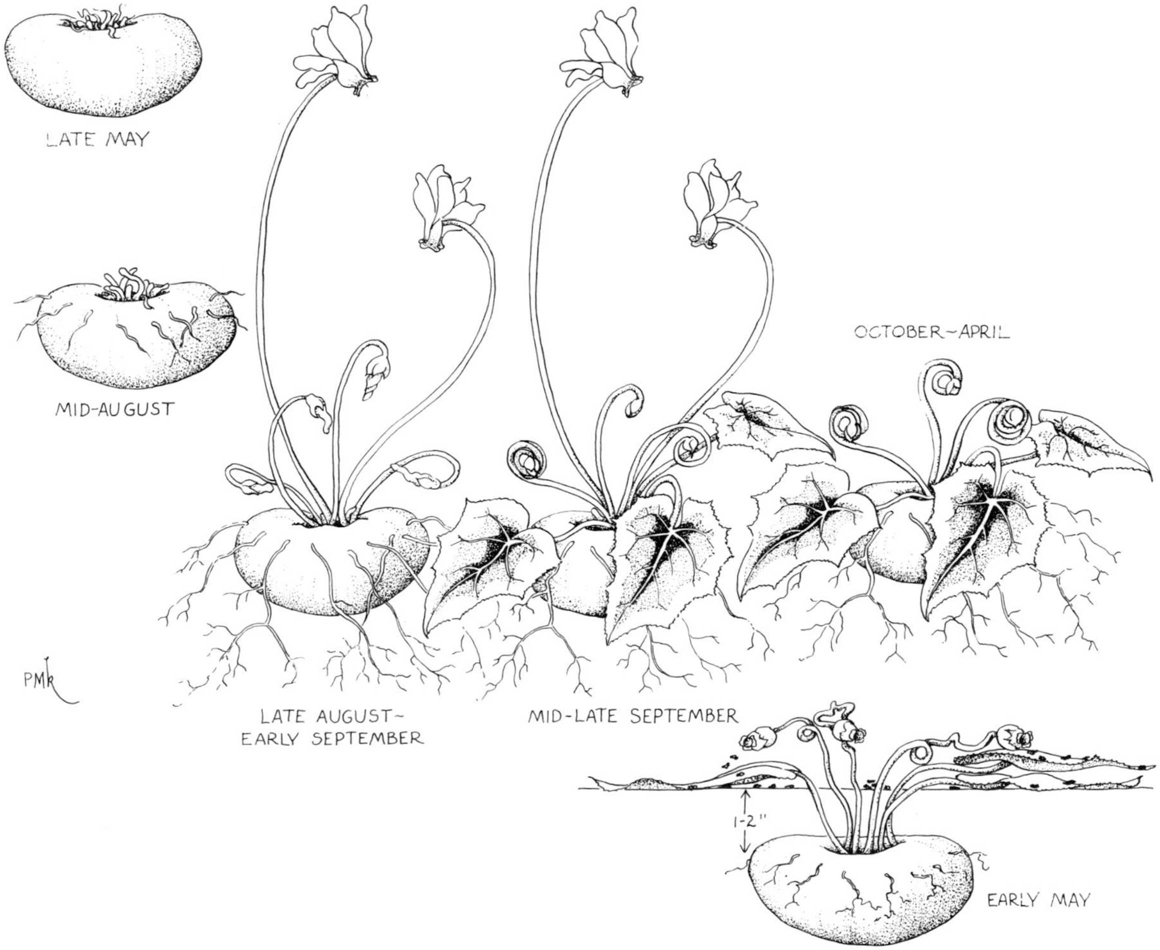

rather blowsy fully double mauve-colored flowers, which act as blotting paper when it rains, and even fall over of their own weight.

One offbeat colchicum from Afghanistan, northern India, and central Asia is spring-blooming, yellow-flowered *C. luteum.* It is difficult to obtain, and not all that easy to grow. One year the deer ate them. I hope I will be pardoned for wishing they at least had a tummy ache from alkaloids in the leaves and flowers they ingested.

Cyclamen

Very different from crocus and colchicum in every way is the ivy-leaved cyclamen, *Cyclamen hederifolium,* which used to be known as *C. neapolitanum.* The flowers appear first, in late August and early September, dancing on naked stems like diminutive badminton shuttlecocks or some flock of dainty miniature butterflies, pale to medium pink, or white. The leaves appear later in September, remain through the winter, and only fade into summer dormancy in late May or early June. The foliage is attractive for nearly ten months of the year, certainly a good return for the space it occupies. No two tubers produce identical leaves, which may be ivy-like or shaped like an arrowhead. Each also exhibits an individual pattern of silver, cream, or gray markings on a dark green ground; occasionally a plain green form occurs.

The ivy-leaved cyclamen, native of Corsica, Sardinia, Italy, Sicily, the Balkans, Greece and the Aegean Islands, and western Turkey, is perhaps the easiest and hardiest species to grow in gardens. It requires a soil rich in humus, moist but well drained, in dappled shade. This species roots from the rounded sides of the tuber and should be planted shallowly, only an inch or two deep, mulched with leaf litter. In England and Holland I have seen the tubers completely exposed, but our winters are more severe, our summers hotter. The tubers neither split nor make offsets, only growing larger to an eventual 4 inches in diameter, producing more flowers each year, with a mature tuber having 50 or more flowers. Generally seed is freely produced and should be gathered and sown under protected conditions. (Ants carry the seed away, and mice, voles, and chipmunks find the first-year tubers irresistible, decimating the numbers reaching blooming size.) This is an easy means of propagation, with many young plants flowering in their second year, and a sure way to avoid plants that have been collected in the wild.

Since it begins its flowering unaccompanied by foliage, I prefer to find a partner for it. One excellent annual is the inch plant, or wandering Jew, *Zebrina pendula,* with leaves striped greenish silver and violet-purple above, entirely violet-purple on the underside. This is common as a houseplant, especially in hanging baskets. It makes an excellent annual ground cover for shady gardens. If set out in the garden in late May or early June it quickly fills bare space, and in late summer forms a neat backdrop to the cyclamen's flowers before dying away with the hard frost. A more permanent ground cover is provided by *Ajuga reptans* 'Burgundy Glow', with burgundy, creamy white, and green foliage. Only light shade, please, or the color will be poor.

Allium

There are other hardy geophytes to explore for autumn color. Queen Olga's snowdrop, *Galanthus nivalis regina-olgae,* is offered at regal prices, flowers without its leaves, and departs this world (or at least my garden) before spring. A more reliable addition is *Allium thunbergii,* a dainty onion from Japan that is popular with rock gardeners. This forms inconspicuous grass-like tussocks 4 to 6 inches tall that remain throughout the summer. Buds begin to form in September, and it flowers in early October, producing dainty umbels of rose-purple flowers. There is some confusion over names, and the dwarf plants sold as *A. splendens* variety *kurilense* are more likely *A. thunbergii.* One cultivar is offered, under the name 'Ozawa'. The flowers are attractive with *Sedum sieboldii* or fall crocus such as *C. speciosus,* or thrusting through a mat of *Thymus serpyllum.* The spent seed heads remain attractive long into the winter. There is a white form that is no less vigorous than the purple. Neither is invasive, and I increase this geophyte by separation of the clumps in spring after growth begins.

Begonia grandis

Appearing as though it belonged in a milder climate, the hardy begonia, *Begonia grandis* (*B. evansiana*), flowers reliably for me each September in my woodland garden. While it maintains itself, it does not reproduce as vigorously as in the milder climate of Long Island, suggesting that Connecticut is perhaps approaching its limit of hardiness.

At Hedgleigh Spring, his garden in Pennsylvania, Charles Cresson enjoys the flowers of *Colchicum byzantinum* and *Lespedeza,* proof that autumn is not the end of gardening. (CHARLES O. CRESSON)

The amber waves of *Pennisetum alopecuroides* nod over *Allium thunbergii* 'Ozawa' for an attractive combination of ornamental grass and a hardy autumn-flowering bulb. (PHOTOSYNTHESIS)

Like some exotic denizen of the deep, the stamens of *Lycoris radiata* appear to writhe in front of a caladium. (CHARLES O. CRESSON)

Native to China, Japan, and Malaysia, it survives winters in cold regions with the assistance of a thick mulch. Late in spring the tuberous rootstock sends up fleshy, leafy stems that will reach about 15 to 24 inches at maturity. The leaves are typically asymmetrical, lopsided begonia leaves, about 6 inches long and 4 inches wide at the broadest part, flushed red underneath. In late summer it produces clusters of pink flowers continuing until cut down by frost. Reproduction is by means of aerial bulblets formed in the leaf axils; these do not mature before the onset of cold weather in my garden. Though tall, it does not make a dense screen, and I find it suitable at the edge of beds in combination with ferns, astilbe, and other lacy-leaved plants. Epimedium also makes a good partner, flowering and maturing its foliage before the hardy begonia makes an appearance. This is generally offered as potted, growing plants in late spring or early summer. Plant with as little disturbance to the root ball as possible, and set at the same depth as, or a little deeper than, it was growing in the pot. A moderate to lightly shaded site, with rich soil high in organic matter, moist but well drained, is most suitable.

Lycoris

Japanese magic lily, resurrection lily, rain lily—these common names describe the manner in which *Lycoris* species flower suddenly after late summer and early autumn, most often after a deep soaking. Up rocket the bloom spikes from the bare soil much as *Nerine* and *Brunsvigia* do, reaching full height in a week or so and then beginning to bloom. The flowers are in umbels and last as long as ten to twelve days, depending on the weather. There are about eight species, all native to Japan and China. For garden purposes they may be separated into two groups: those from regions with cold winters, which delay their leaf growth until January or later; and those from areas with warmer winters, which make leaf growth promptly after flowering and stay in growth all winter. In both instances the leaves die back in spring and there is a summer dormant period. The roots remain active even during leaf dormancy. Unlike the South African geophytes such as *Brunsvigia* and *Nerine* that prefer a deep drought, *Lycoris* still require some moisture even in summer. During leaf growth all *Lycoris* prefer an abundant supply of water, and the soil should be kept constantly moist. Propagation is by division, which reduces flowering for at least a year, or by seed. From seed to bloom takes about five years or longer. The seed, resembling large black BB shot, should be sown ½ inch deep. Some produce leaves immediately, some wait a year.

Lycoris squamigera, formerly known as *Amaryllis hallii,* is probably the most widely known lycoris in the United States. The delightfully fragrant flowers are a pale rose or smooth, satiny pastel pink. This is the hardiest of the magic lilies, producing its fan of smooth, gray-green daffodil-like foliage in spring and flowering satisfactorily in the Northeast and abundantly in the Southeast. There is even one report of it blooming in West Yellowstone, Montana, where perhaps deep snow cover insulated it from the bitter temperatures. It seems to require some chilling to encourage flowering, and is a shy bloomer where winter temperatures are high. Areas with temperatures reaching winter lows of 20°F, such as northern California, Oregon, and Washington would also be suitable. It does not bloom, or does so only rarely, along the Gulf Coast, in Florida, or in the Los Angeles area.

Magic lilies are in the Amaryllis family, typically resent disturbance, and are unlikely to flower the first season after planting. The bulbs resemble those of large daffodils but may have plump fleshy roots attached. In those instances I soak the roots for a couple of hours in a dilute liquid fertilizer before planting. Plant four to six bulbs in a group, 4 to 6 inches deep. Early summer, the period between flowering and leaf growth, would be ideal if only the bulbs were available at that time. In colder climates my preference is for spring planting, to allow roots the longest possible growing period before winter. When undisturbed they develop large clumps, and Bob Wilder of Raleigh, North Carolina, patiently mows around one such established planting, which appears each summer in the middle of his lawn. A long-abandoned planting on the grounds of the Shaw Arboretum in Gray Summit, Missouri, flowers profusely along the forest edge in late August. With their preference for at least midday shade, and acceptance of light dappled shade, *Lycoris squamigera* combines well with hosta, their tall stems of pink lily-like flowers being most appealing when they materialize in late summer. In a perennial border they are attractive with ornamental grasses, especially those that prefer some moisture such as *Calamagrostis* x *acutiflora* 'Karl Foerster', with upright growth pattern and attractive inflorescences from June through September, or variegated purple moor grass, *Molina caerulea* ssp. *caerulea* 'Variegata', with long blades variegated green and yellow, and small dark panicles of seed. Showier flowering plants with which to combine it include balloon flower, *Platycodon mariesii,* with slate-blue, five-pointed flowers; the pink daisies of prairie coneflower, *Echinacea purpurea;* and later-blooming varieties of phlox.

Although I have never seen it, from descriptions, *L. sprengeri* sounds very similar, rather like a junior version of *L. squamigera*. Its flowers are smaller, more of a purplish rose with a bluish tint on the tips of the petals. The foliage appears in the spring and flowers in mid- to late summer. At 20 inches tall it is only one-half to two-thirds the height of the magic lily.

The following geophytes will provide autumn color in milder regions.

Lycoris species that produce their leaves in autumn are more tender than *L. squamigera*. They prosper in the Southeast, doing well in coastal areas where the coldest winter temperatures are not lower than 20°–25° F. Two or three nights of colder weather might not be detrimental, but a climate without winter warm spells and with consistently low winter temperatures would likely be fatal. Any autumn-leaved lycoris should do well in warmer southern California, while the spring-leaved species do better in cooler northern California, Oregon, and Washington. Bulbs of autumn-leaved species should be planted with the nose near soil level. At the time of blooming bulbs can be in partial shade, but when the foliage is up it should be in sun for part of the day. Sun until midafternoon with light shade for the rest of the day is suitable for most species growing in the almost frost-free conditions of southern California. With their need for summer moisture, they are best grown in flower beds along with herbaceous annuals and perennials that get year-round watering and cultivation.

Southern red spider lily from Japan and China, *Lycoris radiata,* grows in the millions in the Southeast and is considered marginal in colder climates. I think it is more cold-tolerant than generally suspected, but still not as reliable as the earlier-blooming magic lily. There is no question that it is most floriferous in Georgia, Alabama, and other states with mild winters. In the cooler Piedmont region of North Carolina, winters are usually characterized by alternate freezing and thawing, often with the ground freezing at night and thawing the next day. There is not the deep, hard, all-winter freezing experienced by northern gardeners.

Spider lily grows to perfection where the winter temperature does not drop below 20°F. In colder climates, even if the bulbs are not damaged, the leaves are burned by cold weather and few flowers are produced the following summer. Planting in a sheltered site may provide a suitable micro-climate: red spider lily flowered reliably most years planted against the south wall of a house in Indianapolis, where the temperatures go below 0°F. in winter. The narrow dark green leaves with a paler central stripe appear in late September in my garden, and in late December I cover them with evergreen boughs to provide some modicum of protection. If the winter is not unduly harsh I will be rewarded with a scattering of flowers the following September. The numerous flowers have narrow rose-red, deep red petals that are strongly reflexed, curling back toward the 15-inch-tall stem. The stamens protrude like the antennae of some exotic shrimp.

White spider lily, *L. albiflora,* has similarly shaped creamy-white flowers, sometimes pinkish cream, in late summer or early autumn. The foliage also grows in the fall. It may be a form of red spider lily. It flowers well in southern California, beginning in early September and lasting for several weeks.

The other species of lycoris are too tender for colder climates except as container plants, producing their green strap-like leaves in winter under protected conditions indoors, and can be brought outside to a terrace or patio for their late-summer, early-autumn flowering period. *Lycoris sanguinea* is a charming little plant with unscented orange-red, apricot-orange flowers whose petals are only slightly recurved, and which blooms in July and August on stalks 12 inches tall. After heavy rains sporadic flower scapes are produced for two months after the first flush of bloom. Native to Japan and Korea, where it is found in woodland, its flowers scorch unless given high shade. Tender, it would be suitable in southeastern gardens, and regions with similar climate.

One September my husband and I were in Davis, California. Checking into the University Best Western motel, my attention became riveted on a small bouquet of flowers on the counter. They were golden spider lilies, St. Augustine lily, or hurricane lily, *Lycoris aurea.* From South China and Burma, this is the tenderest lycoris species. It is not hardy above the lower southeastern states, south Texas, and central and southern California, flowering admirably in the Los Angeles area as long as it gets water all year long, and blooming into November. It is said to have naturalized in gardens on the west Florida coast. Though there is no leaf growth in summer and the bulbs are seemingly dormant, this bulb needs constant moisture to bloom. The flowers are large, of good substance, and a rich golden yellow, canteloupe orange, with slightly recurved tips and ruffled edges. Coming from Burma and Taiwan, its susceptibility to cold is readily understandable. Hurricane lily is hopeless outdoors in all except the balmiest regions but is a good pot plant for the cold greenhouse.

* * *

Quite a few colorful, fall-flowering geophytes from South Africa and the Mediterranean region are accustomed to a dry summer and a mild, wet winter. Some, especially those earliest into bloom, refuse to wait for rain, and early naked lady varieties will often start flowering before the end of July, using moisture stored in the bulb to initiate growth. By the middle of August a garden of these tender bulbs would be in full bloom, continuing on into September, October, and even November in some instances.

Amaryllis belladonna

Familiar to anyone who visits California in September is *Amaryllis belladonna,* naked lady. With only one species in the genus, this native of the southwestern Cape was introduced to cultivation in 1712. From 6 to 12 sweetly scented, clear pink, lily-like flowers are borne on top of a solid, 12- to 18-inch-tall stem in August/September. Forms have been selected with modifications of the basic color, resulting in large umbels of flowers ranging from deep rose red through pink shades on to pure white forms. Each flower measures about 5 inches long, and is about 3 inches across at the fully open mouth. It flowers without any leaves showing, while *Crinum moorei* (with which it might be confused) has a large tuft of leaves at flowering time and unscented flowers. In Africa, naked ladies shoot out of the ground quite rapidly in February or March, whereas on the other side of the equator, in California and Connecticut, it blooms in August or September. Seven to 9 strap-shaped, dull green leaves, 12 to 18 inches long and about 1-inch broad, quickly emerge when flowering is nearly over and remain green through the winter, dying down and drying off in summer. *Lycoris squamigera,* from Japan, has this same habit, resembles *A. belladonna,* but has no scent and no variation of color. Amaryllis is a rather primitive bulb, and the flower stalk is borne at the side, between the scales, rather than centrally between the current season's leaves, as in *Narcissus.* If drainage is good the bulbs may be left in the ground even in areas with summer rainfall. On the Cape coast it grows in full sun but needs light shade in hot inland districts. It is hardy in the warmer parts of England, and one September I saw at Wisley a lovely display of *Amaryllis belladonna* flowering together with the feathery pink plumes of *Tamarisk.* It can be grown outdoors in Australia and New Zealand, and flowers magnificently in southern California. Long-lived in Mediterranean climates, I saw some in the Pioneer cemetery in Calistoga, flowering on the grave of a 17-month-old child buried in 1876. An empty lot in Mendocino was an exquisite combination of sere tawny grasses, naked ladies, and crocosmia. I have flowered this regularly in a protected position in my Connecticut garden once it became established, but I am definitely pushing at the limits of hardiness, and one severe winter will finish it.

The early-flowering naked lady varieties such as van Tubergen's 'Johannesburg', with light rose pink, white-throated flowers with a yellowish base; 'Cape Town', with deep rose-red flowers; 'Barberton', with uniform dark rose-pink flowers; and 'Leydenburg', with pink flowers having a large white center, will often start blooming before the end of July. By the middle of August the large umbels of amaryllis-like flowers range from deep rose-red through pink shades on to the white forms such as 'Hathor', tinged with ivory at the base of the petals. Later van Tubergen varieties such as the deep carmine-red, white-centered 'Durban', rosy-colored 'Windhoek', also with a white center, and 'Jagersfontein', with its deep pink flowers and a yellowish interior, extend the period of bloom, with 'Stellenbosch', a uniform pink, usually not in full flower until September.

Naked lady flourishes in warm, sunny, well-drained sites sheltered from the wind. In mild winter areas the bulbs should be planted with the neck at soil level. In colder regions the bulb must be planted more deeply, with about 9 inches of rich, sandy, loamy soil above the bulb, and a winter mulch. This is one bulb that resents disturbance. The first season after planting, the large ovoid bulbs, 3 to 4 inches in diameter, may not even send up leaves while it sulks underground thinking things over.

Hybrids between *A. belladonna* and *Crinum moorei* have been produced, and given the name of x *Amarcrinum howardii,* or x *Crinodonna.* As might be suspected from the parentage, this is a tender bulb that flowers in autumn with clear pink flowers.

Brunsvigia

Another stately bulb is *Brunsvigia,* with large rounded flower heads as much as 2 feet in diameter but usually half that size at the top of a stout 18-inch-long stem. Usually red or rose red in color, the numerous long-stalked flowers are each about 2½ inches long and shaped like a giant *Nerine,* with gracefully turned back segments. They flower in summer and autumn, usually starting late in July. When the flowers shrivel and die the remnants enlarge and dry to form an ornamental spiked ball that rolls away in the wind. The long, strap-like leaves appear after the flowers fade, beginning growth with the first fall rains. When the leaves wither, withhold water for the dry dormant period.

It is difficult to transplant established plants, since the bulb is rather large, frequently 12 inches long to twice that size in well-developed mature specimens. Once established they should be left alone, as it takes them several seasons to flower after being moved. In mild winter areas plant in an open situation with a sandy, peaty, well-drained soil with the neck of the bulb at soil level. If they are to be grown in borderline situations where temperatures might drop to 30°F, plant deeply so that the neck of the bulb is 6 inches or more beneath the surface for frost protection. Then, for additional protection, mulch in winter and cover with a pane of glass or plastic to help keep them dry. While they need dry conditions when dormant, ample water is necessary when they are in growth. Offsets form slowly, nor is seed freely produced – often only one or two on each flower head. Seeds produce a root the first year, a leaf the second year, and will flower in 5 or 6 years.

In an amusing visual pun, the fishing-pole-like wands of *Dierama pulcherrimum* arch over this ornamental pool. (PHOTOSYNTHESIS)

At Kew, in England, a beautiful September show is provided by grouping *Amaryllis belladona purpurea grandiflora* with the wispy pink flowers of *Tamarisk pentandra*.

There are several species of *Brunsvigia,* with *B. josephinae,* named for the Empress Josephine, perhaps the best-known species. The genus is named for the House of Brunswick: Ryk Tulbagh, governor of the Cape Province in the eighteenth century, sent bulbs to the Duke of Braunschweig, in Germany. In the wild it is common on the grassy veld of the northeastern Cape. The bulbs are 5 to 6 inches in diameter and produce bright coral-red flowers 2½ to 3 inches long in large umbels of 20 to 30 or more flowers on an 18-inch-high scape. The gray-green, strap-shaped leaves are 2 to 3 feet long and 1½ to 2 inches wide. Brunsvigia grow well in gardens under any conditions except deep shade. The leaves start growing with the first fall rains and suffer some damage during very cold winters.

Brunsvigia is closely related to *Amaryllis, Nerine, Lycoris, Crinum, Vallota,* and *Cyrtanthus.* This suggests the possibility of some interesting bi-generic hybrids, and indeed, in the autumn of 1892 C. G. van Tubergen pollinated *B. josephinae* with the pollen of *Amaryllis belladonna.* Seed was freely formed and 16 years later, in September 1908, two of the strongest resulting bulbs, now named x *Brunsdonna tubergenii,* produced flower spikes. The color of these hybrids was a clear deep-rose, suffused with carmine, and a single spike produced 22 flowers. In addition, the hybrid produces offsets freely. This is a very useful characteristic, since *Brunsvigia josephinae* itself is a poor seed producer; seedlings take 7 to 12 years to reach flowering size, and offsets are not freely produced, an amalgam of characteristics that makes increase a slow process.

Nerine

Yet another relative of *Amaryllis* and *Brunsvigia* is *Nerine,* named for the sea nymphs, or Nereids, of Greek mythology. They flower in autumn and have a winter growing season. The leaves, produced in winter, are very susceptible to frost damage. A few species are nearly evergreen, but the commonly available species have a summer resting period. When the leaves have withered in April or May the bulbs should be given a dry resting period, and absolutely no water should be given from May to August. Most species multiply freely and grow very easily, but it is essential to know their active season in order to achieve success.

Some species, especially the smaller ones, will flower regularly every year. A few of the larger kinds are more irregular in their display. The flowers are produced in a compact head at the top of a slender stalk, varying in size according to the different species. They begin to appear in June and from then onward until October and November. Each flower is on a separate stem and has six narrow segments gracefully rolled back to reveal the stamens. Leaves are long and narrow, varying from grass-like to ribbon-like. In some species they appear with, and in others after, the flowers. There are about 31 exclusively South African species, with one that is found in Rhodesia. Most come from summer rainfall areas. Plant the bulbs with their necks at or above soil level and 2 to 3 inches apart. The soil should be light, loamy, and well drained. Most prefer full sun but will grow in lightly shaded situations, especially inland from the coastal regions of California. The grassy-leaved species can tolerate more sun than those with broader leaves.

They are easily propagated by offsets from the older bulbs, detached after the flowers have faded. The smaller species will reestablish themselves freely, larger ones may take a year to recover. Sometimes confused with *Lycoris,* which has black seeds, all true *Nerine* have green seeds. Fresh seed germinates so freely that a radicle often appears before the fleshy seed is even planted. Sow promptly in spring, pressing onto the soil surface. Keep moist and shaded until germination occurs. The seedlings will pull themselves down as they grow. Flowering will generally occur in the third season.

A popular Cape bulb both for the garden and as a cut flower, *Nerine sarniensis,* red nerine, or Guernsey lily, was once thought to be native to the Channel Isles in Great Britain, and a reference from 1911 mentions that it had been cultivated there for 200 years. It is, in fact, native to the mountains of the Cape Province. In 1659, bulbs washed up on the island of Guernsey from a Dutch East India ship that had foundered and shipwrecked in the English Channel while en route to the Netherlands from the Cape. The ovoid bulbs are 1½ to 2 inches in diameter, and each stem has from 10 to 20 flowers. They are about 1½ inches across, a brilliant scarlet, with the most remarkable iridescent sparkle, as if the petals were overlaid with diamond dust. The flower head is full and compact, about 4 inches across, and the stamens are colored and erect but not nearly so long as in *Lycoris radiata* (which is quite similar in color but lacks the shimmer). It flowers at the end of summer or early in autumn, usually in September, with the 12- to 18-inch-long flower stems emerging rapidly out of the ground. The leaf tips often show together with the flowers or follow immediately afterward, remaining green throughout winter and spring and becoming dormant again during summer. They need a sandy soil with good drainage, remaining dry while dormant in summer. In mild winter areas they should be planted with the neck of the bulb above the soil. In time they will form large clumps, often with the bulbs exposed. Separation is necessary only for propagation; they bloom best when root-bound and congested. Companion plants to disguise the lack of bulb foliage at flowering time might include ornamental grasses, whose sere blades act as a neutral foil to the pink flowers; small shrubs; or evergreen succulents such as the smaller agaves.

Often the Guernsey lily is grown as a pot plant. Since they do not mind crowding, 5 to 7 can be planted in a 6-inch pot, but remember that the bulbs do need room to develop. As container plants they do best with cooler temperatures, about 59°F with good ventilation, to keep foliage in good condition for as long as possible. When dormant they can be stored at 68°–73°F. Crosses between *Nerine sarniensis* and *N. flexuosa,* again by van Tubergen, have produced hybrids in a clear sparkling cyclamen or pale pink. 'Ancilla' is a scintillating carmine-red with pink shades that won a first-class certificate from the Royal General Bulbgrowers' Association in 1965. 'Elvira', neyron-rose (an intense shade of pink) with somewhat darker veining; and 'Bettina', neyron-rose with pink shading, both received their first-class certificate in 1968. They flower in late October and November.

Nerine bowdenii, sometimes called the pink agapanthus, is closely related and very similar in appearance to *N. flexuosa*. Both are autumn flowering, and have a rounded flower head 6 inches across. The individual bright Persian-rose to cyclamen-pink flowers measure 2½ inches in length, on stems 18 inches high. The robust, glossy, green, thickish leaves are over 12 inches long and up to 1 inch wide and grow through spring and summer, disappearing shortly before or during the flowering period in autumn. In winter the bulb must be kept dry. This species flowers erratically, but the bulbs multiply well, so an established patch will produce numerous flowers. It is grown outdoors in England, but, though hardier than other species of nerine, garden cultivation can be achieved only in the mild winter areas of the United States. From 6 to 12 flowers are borne in an umbel on scapes about 18 inches high. They are very large and of a pale pink color with a darker line down the center of the recurved segments, which are 2½ to 3 inches long. There are some named forms: 'Cape Town' is rhodamine-pink with darker veins; 'Pink Triumph' is bluish-pink with a darker streak down the center of the petals; and 'Alba' is white with a faint pink flush appearing along the margins with age. A cross between *Amaryllis belladonna* and *Nerine bowdenii* made in early 1940 resulted in yet a third bi-generic hybrid, x *Amarine.* This manmade hybrid has lovely deep pink flowers on 2- to 2½-foot-high stems, appearing in late September and October.

Nerine filifolia, grass-leaved nerine, is the most commonly grown of the smaller species. Growing only 10 to 15 inches high, with fine-textured, nearly evergreen leaves, it soon multiplies to form a thick mat of soft, grassy foliage. The charming small flowers with narrow, crinkled petals are then so numerous as to make a sheet of bright cyclamen pink in the garden. Since this species is nearly evergreen in places where it receives adequate moisture summer and winter, it does not require a prolonged rest period. For this reason, and its dainty size, it is popular as a container plant.

Nerine undulata, often known in gardens as *N. crispa,* winter nerine, has dainty pale pink flowers with wavy, undulate margins. The flowers, 8 to 12 on a 12- to 18-inch-tall stem, appear in autumn. The leaves appear after the flowers, and are ribbon-like, up to 18 inches long and ½ inch wide. They disappear briefly, for about 3 weeks in midsummer. It will grow in sun or shade and likes a regular water supply. This species is native to the Kalahari and coastal regions of South Africa.

Dierama

Wand flower or fairy bells—just one look at the tall arching spike with pendant clusters of flowers trembling in the least breeze will explain the reason behind these common names for *Dierama.* Few plants are as graceful. The stem emerges well above the clump of tall, narrow, grass-like leaves, pulled into a willowy arch by the weight of numerous bell-like flowers in pale pinks, purples, crimson, or white that open continuously for about a month. They are South African bulbs from the cool mountain areas of the Drakensberg and other eastern mountains, and are also found near the eastern coast of the country. Some botanists believe that there are only three or four species with many variations, while others recognize about 22 species. Many color forms have been selected from the two available species, *Dierama pendulum* and *D. pulcherrimum.* Evergreen or nearly so, they need plenty of water during spring, summer, and autumn but need not be watered at all in winter. Without sufficient water in the growing season they will not flower well. Along the California coast or in places with humid, foggy conditions an open sunny position is most suitable. Where the climate is hot and dry, partial shade, especially in the afternoon, is recommended. The narrow sword-like leaves sometimes remain evergreen in winter, but should be cut away in spring if they do not turn brown and shed by themselves. The corms should be planted about 2 inches deep and 6 inches apart, soon forming clumps that are best left undisturbed for at least five years or until the flowers deteriorate in quality. The clumps may be separated in early spring, or after flowering, but they will not always bloom the first year after transplanting. New corms form each year. When transplanting you can pull off the old woody corms remaining beneath the new ones, but do not remove the fibrous covering of the swollen rootstock. Seed may be sown thinly in pots in spring, and will germinate in a month. The seedlings should be kept in the pots for at least two seasons, when they can be tipped out and planted into the ground without disturbing the young plants. While tall, the arching stem and light airy effect permit its location in the midst of other lower growing plants.

Grasklokie (grass bell) or harebell, *Dierama pendulum,* was discovered in 1781 in the eastern Cape Province and is widely cultivated in the milder parts of England. The leaves grow up to 3 feet and the wiry stem may reach from 5 to 7 feet. It bears a series of drooping spikes, with cup-shaped, inch-long flowers with gracefully turned-back tips in delicate pink or mauve in summer. This evergreen species likes moisture throughout the year but will go brown during cold, dry winters.

The other usually available species, *D. pulcherrimum,* is less hardy than *D. pendulum.* It has bright purple or blood-red flowers in late summer, early autumn (September/October). At 6 to 7 feet high it is taller, and the leaves are longer and slightly larger, than *D. pendulum.* Several color forms named for birds have been raised in England. 'Heron' is wine-red, 'Kingfisher' pale pinkish purple, 'Skylark' purple-violet, and 'Windhover' a bright rose pink. It needs good rich loam and plenty of moisture throughout the year.

Hybrids between the two species have been given classical and Shakespearean names: 'Ceres' is a pale blue-violet, 'Oberon' carmine-purple, 'Puck' a light rose pink, and 'Titania' a light pink. At 4 to 5 feet tall they are intermediate in height between the two parents.

Polianthes tuberosa

Intensely, overpoweringly fragrant, tuberose, *Polianthes tuberosa,* is late into flower and tender to frost, a precarious situation in colder gardens. One friend of mine grows the bulbs in a plastic pot buried to the rim in the border. Those years with a lingering summer gracefully coasting into fall will see the white flowers in the garden. If a frost threatens, the entire container can easily be relocated to a sun porch to bloom under protected conditions. They would spend the winter indoors in any event, as the dormant bulbs cannot survive anything more than intermittent light frosts. In colder regions bulbs are spring planted when night temperatures are mild and settled, 50°F and above. If this does not occur until June, extend the growing season by starting the bulbs indoors. Bulbs split after flowering and need a second season of growth before they flower anew. It is the juvenile offsets, resembling small, pointed cigars, that will bloom the next season. New bulbs can be planted for a couple of years to establish sufficient mature bulbs to flower each year. A sunny site with rich soil and ample moisture once in growth provides the most favorable conditions.

Less commonly grown today, this native of Mexico has been in cultivation for over 400 years, was cultivated by Clusius in 1594, and was still popular with the Victorians. Oddly enough, it is not found in the wild, nor are any other species. I find 'Mexican Single' more attractive, with its 3 to 4 tall spikes of single white flowers, than stockier, 2-foot-tall 'The Pearl'. The latter, with double flowers, is the most frequently offered form. Suggested as an excellent cut flower, the heavy perfume is often cloying within the confines of a room.

Zephyranthes

Storm lilies, zephyr flower, flower of the west wind are romantic names for a genus of dwarf bulbs native to the southeasten United States and the warmer parts of South America — Colombia, Guatemala, Mexico. Variable in their timing, they bloom suddenly after summer and autumn rains. The speed with which the flowers appear is astonishing: A Mrs. Morris Clint, writing in the journal *Herbertia/Plant Life* in January 1956, reported that "the first green shoots appeared and watering was initiated. Light rain the night following first shoots, three flowerbuds the next morning." There is a single flower to a stem, 6 to 10 inches tall, depending on the species. Some have lily-like tubular flowers. Others, especially the smaller kinds, have blooms that resemble crocus and are often confused with a similar, closely related genus, *Habranthus. Zephyranthes* have upward-facing flowers with stamens of equal length, while *Habranthus* holds its flowers at an angle and has stamens of unequal length. With a brown tunic and rounded, relatively long-necked bulbs, they resemble those of snowdrops, *Galanthus.* Plant 2 to 4 inches deep, in groups of ten or more. Leaves are narrow and strap-shaped, and appear with or after the flowers. Provide a rich, fairly sandy loam with a little leaf mold or well-decayed manure added in a sunny or lightly shaded position, keeping moist in summer, dry while dormant in winter. They are tender, and sensitive to winter wet. In regions with dry winters and temperatures of 20°F and above they can be left in the garden. In colder gardens they can be handled like gladiolus (but they are not as cheerful about disturbance). Their dainty size suggests their placement at the front of the border or in a rock garden, and especially as container plants. If pot-grown the bulbs can be left crowded, as they resent disturbance. Increase by offsets or seed.

From Argentina and Uruguay comes the autumn-flowering swamp lily, *Zephyranthes candida.* The white, upward-facing crocus-like flowers, sometimes flushed pink on the reverse, are so abundant in the marshes along the La Plata River in September and October that it has been suggested that the river is named for them. The narrow, rush-like, fleshy leaves are evergreen. It has naturalized in the Southeast in a few coastal regions, and is easily distinguishable both by shape and by its season of bloom from the native species, *Z. atamasco,* which is spring flowering.

Zephyranthes citrina is a golden-yellow-flowered species originally from British Guiana, in South America, and naturalized in the Caribbean, especially Trinidad. It has sweetly fragrant 2-inch-long flowers on a 10-inch stem in late summer or early autumn. *Z. candida* x *Z. citrina* has produced 'Ajax', a primrose-yellow, June-flowering hybrid.

Zephyranthes rosea has rosy-pink small flowers, about an inch long, on a 6-inch stalk in early autumn. Native to the West Indies and Guatemala, it is surprisingly hardy, tolerating winter low temperatures of 25°F if planted against a building foundation or low wall as is common practice in England. The narrow strap-like leaves appear with the flowers.

Included here with its kin, the swamp lily, *Zephyranthes atamasco* is a fine spring-blooming species from damp woods and fields of Virginia, Florida, Alabama, and Mississippi. With somewhat the look of a lily and pure white flowers it is sometimes called Easter lily, as it blooms in April or May, rarely June. Each scentless, 3-inch-long flower is carried singly on an 8- to 10-inch stalk, tinted with pink or purple while in bud and aging to pink, especially after pollination. The shiny green, narrow, grooved, grass-like leaves appear with the flowers, forming loose clumps. Naturally occurring in swales, ditches, and other damp sites, they need a location with adequate moisture and at least a few hours a day of direct sunlight. In an open woodland, mass to create an attractive display in a damp site beneath Carolina silverbell, *Halesia caroliniana,* or its close, more shrub-like relative, the American snowdrop tree, *H. diptera;* with native violets; wild bleeding heart, *Dicentra eximia,* with pink locket-like flowers; lavender-flowered biennial scorpion weed, *Phacelia bipinnatifida;* confederate violet, *Viola papilionacea;* and small ferns.

Pink storm lily, *Zephyranthes grandiflora,* is the most popular species. It has large, 3- to 4-inch rose-pink, purplish-pink flowers on an 8- to 10-inch stem. The strap-shaped leaves are about ½ inch wide and about 12 to 15 inches long. This Central American plant flowers in early summer and has naturalized in the West Indies and many countries with mild climates. It is frequently confused with *Habranthus robustus,* of similar appearance.

Remember that if these autumn-blooming varieties are scattered throughout the garden the effect will be diffuse and spotty. In colder climates select one area for your autumn garden, a site where the lingering golden sunshine will warm these last flowers and where fallen leaves will not bury smaller geophytes. Herbaceous perennials with seasonal interest, dwarf asters, *Solidago* 'Golden Fleece', *Sedum sieboldii,* small and mid-sized ornamental grasses, and flowering cabbage will add to the diversity of this special encore to the gardening year. In milder regions the autumn rains renew the growth held in abeyance in summer droughts. In either instance they are the counterpoise to spring.

Appendix 1

PLANTING, CULTIVATION, AND PROPAGATION TECHNIQUES

In *The Secret Garden,* by Frances Hodgson Burnett, published in 1909, little Mary discovers some sharp little green points pushing through weeds and grass in a Yorkshire garden. With a piece of wood she clears out around them. Later that day she asks the young housemaid Martha what "those white roots that look like onions" might be. "They're bulbs," Martha tells her. "Lots o' spring flowers grow from 'em. Th' very little ones are snowdrops an' crocuses an' the big ones are narcissuses an' jonquils and daffydowndillys. Th' biggest of all is lilies. . . ." Mary asks, "Do bulbs live a long time? Would they live years and years if no one helped them?" And for me, Martha's reply explains part of the charm of bulbs. "They're things as helps themselves, that's why poor folks can afford to have 'em. If you don't trouble 'em, most of 'em'll work away underground for a lifetime an' spread out an' have little 'uns."

Those aspects are part of the appeal of bulbs: their magical reemergence in spring from their winter rest and subsequent growth without fuss or bother is the essence of their popularity. However, adequate care given to their initial planting, followed by a modicum of attention, will produce the most satisfactory results.

Planting

Bulbs (in the generic sense) are more resistant to desiccation than fibrous-rooted perennials. You would not expect to leave bare root specimens of asters or phlox, ferns, or ornamental grasses sitting around for weeks on end until you got around to planting them. But we do it with geophytes. Astonishingly enough, often we get away with it and they obligingly grow and flower. However, in the natural course of events it was never intended that geophytes leap forth from the earth, lay around on the surface for a while, and then burrow back underground again. Just because they are underground and out of sight in autumn, it does not mean that they are not growing. If, one autumn, you dug up daffodils planted the previous year, you would find that they were growing roots. New geophytes should have the same opportunity to establish themselves. So it behooves the ardent gardener to see that newly purchased geophytes are planted as expeditiously as possible. It is possible to set priorities and organize a planting sequence if, like me, you acquire more than can be dealt with quickly. Tubers, as was mentioned, go to the head of the queue. Small bulbs have proportionally more surface to volume than do larger ones, so they should also be planted sooner rather than later. Bulbs that lack a tunic, as do lilies and *Fritillaria meleagris*, guinea hen flower, become flabby more quickly than tunicate bulbs and also need prompt interment. Bulbs awaiting planting should be kept in paper rather than plastic bags. In plastic, small amounts of moisture will collect and the bulbs can get moldy. Refrigeration is not necessary if there is a cool area such as a garage where they can wait. If they must be refrigerated, keep them in a vegetable bin. Do not let it be a case of out of sight, gone and forgotten. And do not mistake daffodils for onions, as they are poisonous.

Unless the soil is very soft and the geophytes are small and few in number, I prefer a shovel to a trowel. The longer handle means better leverage, less fatigue, and a more thorough preparation of the planting area. In addition, a shovel allows you to prepare the area for a group rather than having to dig individual holes. I find this often allows better placement. I do not like the tools that look like a tin can with both ends cut out, attached to a handle. In Connecticut I am likely to ram it into a rock, which might be pried out with a shovel. If the soil is loose and sandy it pours back out as the tool is lifted. Also, you have a fixed-diameter hole, nonadjustable for little crocus, midsize tulips, or large lilies.

Fertilization

It is important to understand the habit of growth of different geophytes in order to perceive the most suitable way to fertilize them. One major difference is between those that grow in summer and those that are planted in the autumn, flower in the spring, and promptly go dormant. The former can be treated much as any other perennial. Because the latter are growing most actively while the soil is cool they need different treatment. Nutrients are available to plants through the action of microorganisms in the soil. They are active when soil temperature is above 50°F. Spring-flowering species are drawing on those reserves contained in their underground larder, and these nutrients must be replenished for healthy bloom the following year. The elements most closely associated with root and stem growth are phosphorus and potash. (Nitrogen is important for leaf growth.) These two elements do not move much through the soil, so it is necessary to place them beneath the bulbs where they will be most available to the roots. This can best be done at planting time. Bonemeal is often touted as a great fertilizer for bulbs, but I do not like it. First, it is very slow acting. Also, bones are scraped and steamed before they are ground into fertilizer, so the nutrient level is lower than it was in the past when meat scraps and marrow were part of the meal. Second, every skunk in my suburban neighborhood comes by to dig up the geophytes, looking for the bones they smell buried. The geophytes are not eaten, but it quickly becomes boring replanting the same ones several times when there are other new ones waiting their turn.

I use chemically treated forms of phosphorus and potash, muriate of potash, and superphosphate. The nutrients are more readily available to the plants, but in this form they can burn the roots just as road salt does. Dig the planting hole, mix the quantity of fertilizer as recommended on the bag with the soil at the bottom of the hole, and then add a thin layer of unimproved soil to cover the granules before planting the bulbs. Both muriate of potash and superphosphate are available as single-element fertilizers in bags ranging in size from five pounds up. Both are hygroscopic and will absorb moisture from the air. Purchase only the amount you need each season, as leftovers will cake into a single hard mass before the next planting season.

Many of the early-blooming woodland geophytes do not need any supplementary feeding in following years if they are growing in good soil. Where I feel it is necessary I use a liquid fertilizer with an analysis of 10-30-20 (lower nitrogen, higher phosphorus and potash), making two or three applications at half the recommended strength. Nutrients are immediately available to the plants, but of short duration. The first feed is when the leaves are up and fully expanded, the second is immediately after flowering is over. If specific geophytes seem to need more nutrition, and I am operating in a highly organized manner that spring, I will give a third feeding (still at half strength) two weeks after flowering is finished. The nutrients can be absorbed by the leaves (foliar feeding) as well as by the roots. Application can be made from a watering can, pouring it on the leaves and nearby ground.

Planting depth is relative, and depends on the size of the bulb, corm, or tuber. More specific directions for individual species will be found accompanying their description in the text. (ILLUSTRATION COURTESY OF THE NETHERLANDS FLOWER BULB INFORMATION CENTER)

With the ground prepared, these tulips, hyacinths, and crocus have been laid out with a rough approximation of their relative placement. It will be a few minutes' work to properly space and then plant them. (ILLUSTRATION COURTESY OF THE NETHERLANDS FLOWER BULB INFORMATION CENTER)

It is also important that these spring-flowering geophytes be given every opportunity to manufacture these food reserves. They must be very efficient photosynthesizers, for their growing period is only scant months, and that at a time when the days are only beginning to lengthen. Many are dormant by early June, or even sooner. So it is absolutely prohibited to cut, fold, braid, spindle, or rubber-band bulb foliage. The neat tidy little bundle reduces the efficiency of the foliage and reduces the underground reserves stored for next year's bloom. The ideal is to wait until the foliage has begun to wither and turn yellow, at which time it can be cut away. If you absolutely cannot bear to wait that long, then within six weeks after flowering the bulb will have stored most of the food and the foliage can be removed.

Propagation

Plant propagation takes two forms: sexual, where new plants are raised from seed, and asexual, where a part of the plant is used to create new ones that are identical to the original. Seed produces plants that vary one from the other. If you are raising species this is relatively unimportant. If you are growing named forms ('White Triumphator' tulips, for example), then seedlings no longer have the cultivar name. Several geophytes self-sow in my garden. Each spring *Eranthis hiemalis* regularly produces seedlings around the original tubers, which will reach flowering size in another year or two. I collect the seed of trillium, cleaning them of the surrounding pulp as I stand in the garden and pressing the seed into the soil around the parent plant. Much slower than the winter aconite, it will be two years before the first spade-shaped leaf appears, and four or five more before the young plant reaches flowering size. Since the immature plants are in a colony with blooming-size specimens, I know where, and what, they are. Also, this method requires less effort on my part than tending seed pots would require. But what if you don't have the plants to start with? Seed can be a simple means of obtaining geophytes otherwise unavailable.

In general, raising geophytes from seed is simple, only requiring some patience to reach the resultant blooming stage. Some will flower in two or three years, other geophytes take from four to six years to reach flowering size. Sow seed and in several years you'll have new geophytes to add to your garden. If you sow nothing, in several years you'll still have nothing.

Sow about 25 seeds to a 4-inch pot. Use deep pots rather than seed pans, as geophytes tend to move down, pulled by their contractile roots. I prefer a light, sterile soil mix of half commercial potting soil, half synthetic soil (peat moss, perlite, and vermiculite) with some sand added. Be sure to label! Keep the pots moist but not sodden. When germination occurs, begin watering with a dilute liquid fertilizer every other week while the geophytes are in active growth. Monocots send up a single, grass-like leaf, dicots send up a pair of leaves. For larger geophytes, or those with slower growth, after the second year's growth, shift the whole potful to the next-larger pot as soon as the leaves are showing well at the start of the growing season. Pricking out or separating the tiny bulbs, corms, or tubers after the first year is actually harmful, as handling will set them back, and often if their growth is checked the seedlings will die. Transfer them to the next-sized pot without disturbing the contents. After the second or third season they should be planted in the open ground. If you are concerned that they might inadvertently be disturbed in the course of routine garden maintenance, set them out in a nursery area. Plant them in a row, water and fertilize, and give them a year in the ground before they move to their permanent location.

Seeds often require some special circumstance to overcome dormancy and germinate. This might be as simple as watering, which dissolves a chemical inhibitor in the seed coat. Or it might be a period of chilling to simulate winter. Or very small, fine seed might need exposure to light, failing to germinate if covered with soil. Some seed, such as *Sanguinaria canadensis, Trillium* species, and members of the *Ranunculaceae* need to be sown fresh. Others can be stored until it is convenient to sow them, maintaining viability best if they are kept cool, dark, and dry in the interim. I find a clean screw-cap glass jar with either a small packet of silica gel or a tablespoon of powdered milk contained in a facial tissue to absorb moisture, stored in the refrigerator, is ideal. I keep the seed in paper packets with name, date, and source penciled in.

When seed germinates it follows one of two patterns. In epigeal germination the cotyledon leaves appear at the same time as the roots emerge. This is the most familiar pattern for many geophytes, including some lilies. In other plants such as peonies and certain other lilies, though roots are growing belowground the cotyledons do not emerge aboveground, so nothing appears to be happening the first season. The second season sees leaf growth. This is called hypogeal germination.

Those geophytes that naturally propagate vegetatively are easy to multiply. Often daffodils form congested clumps that flower poorly because they are overcrowded. When I dig them in late spring as the foliage withers and yellows, there are many more bulbs than the number originally planted. This natural increase provides additional plants to separate and use elsewhere in the garden. In some instances, as with lilies, extra bulbs can be induced to form through special handling. Or the bulbs, tubers, or rhizomes can be cut apart to create additional plants.

Daffodils, crocus, gladiolus, and lilies are four examples of geophytes that frequently make offsets that can be detached from the mother bulb or corm. This type of increase is fairly obvious and occurs naturally without any effort on the gardener's part. The offsets on daffodils will remain attached to the mother bulb at the basal plate for several years. In crocus, crocosmia, acidanthera, and gladiolus, miniature corms, called cormels, develop from the basal plate of new corms, forming between the old corm and the new one. Shallow planting generally encourages cormel production, fewer being produced when corms are more deeply planted. Cormels are easily separated from the flowering-size corm, but require another year or two before they reach flowering size. They will reach flowering size more quickly if they are removed from the parent corm and grown on in a nursery area. Small gladiolus cormels especially can become somewhat dried out over winter storage, and are slow to come into growth in spring. In spring they can be soaked in cool water for one or two days, changing the water periodically. Then store them in damp peat moss until the first roots appear before planting. Or, store them over winter in barely damp peat moss to keep them plump and prevent hardening. *Lilium regale* naturally forms two to four daughter bulbs above the mother bulb's base, the old bulb disintegrating in the process. *Lilium canadense* and *L. superbum* form lateral bulblets from their rhizome-like bulb. It is when we desire more than develops unaided, or in instances where it does not readily occur, that intervention is necessary.

Offsets that form around the basal plate of hyacinths can be used for increase, producing identical plants to those with which you began. Only a few offsets are produced, and there are techniques to expedite matters. Hyacinths will produce larger numbers of offsets if their basal plate is damaged, either by scoring or scooping. Dig the bulbs after their foliage has died back, and wash them clean of soil. Either cut an X into the plate, or scoop it with a melon baller. A scored bulb produces about two dozen bulblets, which reach flowering size in three to four years, while a scooped bulb produces between two and three times as many bulblets, which take an additional year to reach flowering size. The cut must be deep enough to go through the basal plate. Dust the wound with a fungicide and place the bulb, right-side up, in a pot of dry sandy soil to allow the bulbs to form callus tissue. Commercial growers then keep the bulbs in a darkened area at 70°F for a couple of weeks, gradually raising the temperature by 15°–20°F. Over the next two to three months the bulbs are stored at a high humidity. Large numbers of bulblets form around the wound. In autumn these mother bulbs are planted out. The bulblets grow luxuriant foliage in the spring, and generally the mother bulb expires and disintegrates. When the bulblets' leaves yellow off, they should be dug, separated, and planted in rows in a nursery area, reaching flowering size in about four years. *Scilla* can be treated in the same way.

Some lilies form stem bulblets, below soil level as in *Lilium longiflorum*. The number can be increased by special handling. Underground stem bulblets form through the summer. The 30-day period between mid-August and mid-September is the best time to harvest them. Twist the stem out of the bulb, and either stand them upright like a small haystack if there are many, or heel them in a trench if there are few. Keep the stems damp by periodic sprinkling if upright, or a light covering of sandy soil or peat moss if horizontal. In mid-October, when the bulblets have hardened off, they should be planted in a nursery area. In two years they will be of sufficient size to bloom in the garden. Some lilies, such as *LL. bulbiferum, lancifolium,* and *sargentiae,* form aerial bulblets (called bulbils) in the leaf axils. The number will increase if the flower buds are pinched off as soon as they form. This process, called dis-budding, sacrifices one year's flowering to gain more bulbs. Some lilies that do not naturally form bulbils can be induced to do so by dis-budding and then a week or ten days later cutting back the stem and leaves by half. *LL. candidum, chalcedonicum, hollandicum, maculatum,* and *testaceum* respond favorably to such handling. Aerial bulbils, more correctly called tubercules, are produced in the leaf axils on *Begonia grandis.* In mild winter regions they can be planted promptly. Where cold winters are the norm (but within the range of hardiness for this tuber) the tubercles should be stored over the winter in a refrigerator, packed in barely damp peat moss in a plastic bag or container, for spring planting.

Lilies can be increased by scaling. I often use this method in autumn, as newly purchased lily bulbs frequently arrive accompanied by several detached scales that have fallen off in transit, and I feel quite thrifty in making use of them. This is a technique that can be executed in autumn, or after the bulbs have flowered in midsummer. Dig up the bulbs and remove several individual scales from the outside of the bulb. Be careful not to remove so many as to weaken the bulb itself, no more than the two outer layers of scales. Dust them with a fungicide powder, and then put them in a plastic bag with several times their volume of a barely damp peat moss/sand mixture. Close the bag and leave it at room temperature (65°–70°F) for about six weeks. Anywhere from three to five bulblets will form at the base of each scale, but leaf growth will not occur until after a chilling period. Refrigerate the bag for two months, after which the individual bulblets can be detached from the scales (depending on growing conditions in the garden), potted up, and grown under growlights, in a greenhouse, or outdoors. In autumn new bulblets are planted in a nursery row, and the following spring they can be planted in the garden. Alternatively, if done in summer the scales can be planted directly in a nursery row in a light sandy soil, set upright, and covered with only a couple of inches of soil. Or, again in summer, the scales can be stuck in a pot of sandy soil, placing them vertically and with the upper half of the scale exposed. In about three to six weeks small bulblets will form at the base of the scales. Transplant to a nursery row without separating individual bulblets, grow on for a year, and then separate and replant.

A somewhat similar technique is used especially for *Narcissus,* and *Cooperia, Hippeastrum, Hymenocallis, Lycoris,* and *Nerine* can be increased by a process called "twin scaling." Cut the bulb in half, the halves in half, into successively smaller wedges, creating eight to ten sections. Be careful to see that a piece of the basal plate remains with each segment. Detach these segments into pieces containing three or four scale segments and a piece of basal plate. Each is capable of forming new bulblets between the scales, on the basal plate. Place them vertically in a pot filled with a 50/50 mix of peat moss and sand, allowing the tips to show above the surface. Gentle bottom heat often helps things along. New bulblets form within a few weeks, at which point they should be moved to a pot or flats with a soil-based mix. Generally this technique is used to work up large stocks of a new variety.

Multiplication of lilies is also possible through stem and leaf cuttings. This is done in summer, shortly after flowering. Stem cuttings produce small bulblets in the leaf axil, as will leaf cuttings that are taken with a small heel of the old stem. These techniques require a moist, humid atmosphere such as a mist system or a shaded, plastic enclosed box to prevent the drying out of leaf and stem. The small bulblets must be handled with care, as described above. A somewhat different technique using leaf cuttings is used with *Muscari, Hyacinthus, Veltheimia,* and *Lachenalia.* A complete leaf is cut from the bulb while just mature, vigorous, and still green. It can be cut into two or three pieces horizontally. Each piece is placed, oriented as it was growing, in a sand/peat moss rooting medium with the bottom several inches below the surface. Keep moist; a high humidity along with bottom heat is desirable. In two weeks to a month, small bulblets will form on the bottom of the leaf, at which time they can be planted in soil.

Dahlias can be multiplied by stem cuttings, just like a coleus. When new shoots begin to grow in the spring, with a sharp knife or new single-edge razor blade take cuttings with three or four pairs of leaves. Remove the lower two pairs of leaves close to the stem, dust with rooting hormone, and set the cutting up to the remaining leaves into a pot filled with a sand/peat moss mix. Dampen lightly and cover with a plastic bag. New roots will quickly form, and the cuttings can be hardened off and planted in the garden to flower that summer. Tubers will form underground that can be lifted and stored over winter for the following growing season. The black-leaved sweet potato, *Ipomoea batata* 'Blackie', also roots readily from stem cuttings taken in spring.

Most home gardeners are not interested in producing huge numbers of additional geophytes. But the magical process of producing new plants from seed or cloning a few from an existing one is part of the adventure waiting down the garden path for those who are willing to try.

Appendix 2

SOURCES

Each autumn garden centers and nurseries across the country become a magnet toward which every gardener gravitates as to a lodestone, attracted by the bins, boxes, and bags of tulips, daffodils, hyacinths, crocus, snowdrops, and more. In spring a smaller display provides convenient access to dahlias, cannas, calla lilies, true lilies, and a few other geophytes. At some point the enthusiastic gardener/horticulturist will say, "Is that all there is?" and need to turn to mail-order sources. The following list does not claim to provide every possible source, nor (agreeable as it might have been) have I ordered from each firm. It is intended to provide suggestions of sources for unusual geophytes, and of specialty suppliers offering a wider range of specific kinds. Remember, printing catalogs and mailing them is an expensive proposition these days, and it is polite to send a couple of dollars with your request for one.

General

Jacques Amand
P.O. Box 59001
Potomac, Maryland 20859
North American office of a British firm offering a wide range of unusual geophytes. Color illustrated catalog.

Avon Bulbs
Burnt House Farm
Mid Lambrook
South Petherton, Somerset TA13 5HE
England
Specialists offering a wide range of unusual small geophytes, a few hybrid tulips or daffodils. Color illustrated catalog. Will ship to the United States.

Broadleigh Gardens
Barr House, Bishops Hull
Taunton, Somerset TA4 1AE
England
Separate spring and autumn catalogs for a wide range of unusual geophytes, some familiar garden hybrids. Color illustrated catalog. Will ship to the United States.

Cambridge Bulbs
40 Whittelsford Road
Newton, Cambridge CB2 5PH
England
Catalog of bulbs, corms, and tubers (primarily species, many "for the specialist") issued in spring, with a supplement list in summer. Will ship to the United States.

Cruickshank's: The Garden Guild
1015 Mount Pleasant Road
Toronto, Ontario M4P 2M1
Canada
Separate spring and autumn catalogs offering a good selection of familiar geophytes with a few less common genera. Color illustrated catalog. Will ship to the United States.

Dutch Gardens
P.O. Box 200
Adelphia, New Jersey 07710

Separate spring and autumn catalogs offering a good selection of well-known geophytes. Color illustrated catalog.

The Daffodil Mart
Rt. 3, Box 794
Gloucester, Virginia 23061
As might be expected, an especially broad selection of daffodils, and also a good selection of other geophytes. No color illustrations.

GardenImport
P.O. Box 760
Thornhill, Ontario L3T 4A5
Canada
Separate spring and fall catalogs, with a good selection of spring-flowering geophytes in the latter, and some harder to find goodies in the spring list such as four different crinums, Eucomis bicolor, Nerine bowdeni.

Hoog & Dix Export
Heemsteedse Dreef 175,
2101 KD Heemstede
Holland
Excellent selection of uncommon geophytes, mostly species. Does export to the United States, but their minimum order is 500 guilders. Shipping, phytosanitary certificate extra.

McClure & Zimmerman
108 W. Winnebago
P.O. Box 368
Friesland, Wisconsin 53935
Good selection of tulips, daffodils, crocus, alliums, and other familiar geophytes; great selection of colchicum and fall-blooming crocus; and a nice selection of less common types such as Lycoris, Veltheimia, Zantedeschia

John Scheepers, Inc
P.O. Box 700
Bantam, Connecticut 06750
Typical selection of spring-flowering geophytes, good selection of tender summer-blooming varieties such as Eucomis bicolor, Galtonia candicans, Ismene (Hymenocallis) narcissiflora *and 'Sulfur Queen',* Gladiolus *x* colvillei, Nerine bowdenii, Zephyranthes robusta, *as well as dahlias, a few lilies, hybrid gladiolus.*

Van Engelen Inc
Stillbrook Farm
313 Maple Street
Litchfield, Connecticut 06759
Wholesale. Good selection of familiar geophytes with some unusual offerings. No color illustrations.

White Flower Farm
The Garden Book: Autumn Edition
Litchfield, Connecticut 06759-0050
Noted mail-order supplier of fibrous-rooted perennials, with a good selection of familiar geophytes in the autumn color-illustrated catalog. Tender geophytes and lilies in the spring color-illustrated catalog.

Caladiums

Caladium World
P.O. Box 629
Sebring, Florida 33871-0629
Color folder. Minimum order 25 tubers, not less than 5 tubers of any one variety.

Spaulding Bulb Farm
1811 Howey Road
Sebring, Florida 33872
Folder with a descriptive list of 68 different caladiums. Minimum order 50 tubers, not less than 5 tubers of any one variety.

Cannas

Brudy's Exotics
P.O. Box 820874
Houston, Texas 77282-0874
Black-and-white catalog on newsprint listing nearly two dozen named cannas, and a range of tropical plants.

Kelley's Plant World
10266 E. Princeton
Sanger, California 93657
List of almost one hundred cannas, familiar and rare, inexpensive and pricey.

Wheel-View Farm
212 Reynolds Road
Shelburne, Massachusetts 01370
One-page list of a half-dozen cannas and a couple of other geophytes.

Dahlias

Connell's
10216 40th Avenue East
Tacoma, Washington 98446
Color illustrated catalog.

Dahlias by Phil Traff
10717 SR 162
Puyallup, Washington 98374
Descriptive brochure listing a wide range of cultivars. No illustrations.

Swan Island Dahlias
P.O. Box 700
Canby, Oregon 97013
Large descriptive list in color catalog.

Gladiolus

The Waushara Gardens
N 5491 5th Drive
Plainfield, Wisconsin 54966
More varieties of modern hybrid gladiolus than you ever dreamed existed, both as named varieties and collections for the farmer's market cut flower booth.

Lilies

Ambergate Gardens
8015 Krey Avenue
Waconia, Minnesota 55387
Primarily perennials, with a modest selection of martagon lilies.

B & D Lilies
330 "P" Street
Port Townsend, Washington 98368
Excellent selection of oriental and asiatic lilies, and also a nice selection of species lilies. Color illustrated catalog.

Rex Bulb Farms
P.O. Box 774
Port Townsend, Washington 98368
Asiatic, trumpet, and aurelian, oriental hybrid lilies, as well as a few species. Color illustrated catalog.

Oddments

Cape Seed and Bulb
Box 4063, Idasvalley
Stellenbosch, Cape
Republic of South Africa 7609
Free catalog.

The Onion Man
30 Mt. Lebanon Street
Pepperell, Massachusetts 01463
Mark McDonough is an alliaceous champion, for as well as offering seeds and bulbs he publishes G.A.R.L.I.C., a newsletter of alliums and related liliaceous plants.

Holbrook Farm & Nursery
115 Lance Road
P.O. Box 368
Fletcher, North Carolina 28732-0368
Allium, Crinum powellii *'Album'*, Crocosmia *x 'Lucifer'*, Zephyranthes candida, *and lots of fibrous-rooted perennials.*

Native Gardens
5737 Fisher Lane
Greenback, Tennessee 37742
Hymenocallis caroliniana, Zephyranthes atamasco, *native plants for sun and shade.*

Niche Gardens
1111 Dawson Road
Chapel Hill, North Carolina 27516
Lilium formosanum, Zantedeschia rehmannii, *native and exotic plants.*

Protea Farms of California
P.O. Box 1806
Fallbrook, California 92088
Clivia nobilis, Clivia miniata, Clivia cyrtanthiflora.

Prairie Nursery
P.O. Box 306
Westfield, Wisconsin 53964
Allium cernuum, Lilium superbum, *grassland plants.*

Robinett Bulb Farm
P.O. Box 1306
Sebastopol, California 95473-1306
A fine list of West Coast native geophytes issued each August, sometimes as plants, often only as seed. Excellent selection of erythronium, fritillaria, lilies.

Rust-en-Vrede Nursery
P.O. Box 231, Constantia
Republic of South Africa 7848
Free catalog.

Siskiyou Rare Plant Nursery
2825 Cummings Road
Medford, Oregon 97501
Arisaema, Erythronium, Rhodohypoxis, Trillium, Uvularia *in fall catalog, alpine and rock-garden plants.*

Sunburst Flower Bulbs
P.O. Box 183
Howard Place 7450
Republic of South Africa
Fascinating list of indigenous South African geophytes including eight species of lachenalia, several ixia, moraea, gladiolus, and others. Color illustrations. Prices in dollars include air mail shipping. Minimum order $20.

We-Du Nurseries
Rt. 5, Box 724
Marion, North Carolina 28752
Alliums, Arisaema, Cyclamen, Erythronium umbilicatum, Sanguinaria canadensis, Trillium, Uvularia, Lachenalia pustulata, Nerine filifolia, *American and Asiatic native plants.*

Index

Page numbers in **boldface** *type refer to illustrations.*

Abyssinian sword lily. *See Acidanthera*
Acidanthera, xvi, 102
aconite, winter. *See Eranthis*
Agardh, J. G., xv
Agriculture, U.S. Department of, 66
Allen, James, 6, 19
Allium, x, xiii, xiv, xv, xvi, 74–79
acuminatum, 75
aflatunense, 76
albopilosum, 76
beesianum, 75
cernuum, 75
christophii, 75, 76, **78**
cyaneum, 75
flavum, 75, **77,** 96
giganteum, 74, 76, **78**
karataviense, 75, 77
macleanii, 76
moly, 74, 75
rosenbachianum, 76
schoenoprasum, 75, 77
schubertii, 76
scordoprasum, 75
sphaerocephalon, 76
thunbergii, 136, **137**
tricoccum, 79
Amaryllis, xvi, 5, 36, 90, 111, 143
belladonna, xiv, 111, 116, 140–141, **142,** 143, 144
hallii. See Lycoris Squamigera
taxonomic changes, xv, 114, 138
Anemone, xv, 22, 24–25
apennina, 25, **40,** 41
blanda, xiv, 25, 68
intermedia, 22, 24
nemorosa, 22, 24
quinquefolia, 24
ranunculoides, 24
annulate, defined, xiv
Apios americana, x, 71
Araceae, xv
Arisaema, xv, 61–62, **63,** 71, 105
dracontium, 62
triphyllum, viii, 56, 57, **60,** 61–62, 73, 107
Arnold Arboretum (Boston), 63
Arnott, Samuel, 6
arum lily. *See Zantedeschia*
Atkins, James, 6

Babiana, 121–123, 125
disticha, 123
rubro-cyanea, 123
stricta, 122
villosa, 123
Balansa, Benedict, 8
Barnes, Stan and Helen, 25
Barr, Peter, 39
Bartrum, John, 89
basal plate, defined, xiii
Beckman, Johann, 44, 46
Beddinhaus, H. S., 101
Begonia grandis, 136, 138, 152
bellwort. *See Uvularia*
Bentham, George, xv
Berry Botanic Garden (Oregon), 76, 105
Bessler, Basil, 39
Bijl, Jan, 76
birthroot. *See Trillium*
bloodroot. *See Sanguinaria canadensis*
bluebells. *See Hyacinthoides*
Bluemel, Kurt and Hannah, 76
Boissier, Pierre Edmond, 19
Bosanquet, Louis, 117
Botschantzeva, Z. P., 51
Bowles, Edward Augustus, 4, 14, 16, 134
Briggs, Margaret, 31
Brimeura amethystina, 26
Brodiaea, xv
Brooklyn Botanic Garden, 13, 38
Bruinsma, B. F., xii
Brunsvigia, 138, 141, 143
josephinae, 141, 143
orientalis, 111
Bulbocodium, xvi
"bulbous plants," viii, xiii–xvi
bulbs, bulbils, bulblets, defined, xiii–xiv
Bulbs from Seed (Griffiths), 66
Burbank, Luther, 117
Burrell, C. Coleston, 4

Cabot, Frank and Ann, 96
Caladium, 55, 96–98
'Candidum', 55, 96, **100**
calla lily. *See Zantedeschia*
Calochortus, xv
Camassia, xv, **23,** 27
cusickii, 27
leichtlinii, 27
quamash, 27
Cambridge University, 30, 85
Canna, 93, **94,** 95–96, **97**
flaccida, 95
generalis, 95, 96
iridiflora, 95
'Nirvana', 75, **77,** 96
'Pretoria', **97**
Cape hyacinth. *See Galtonia*
Cardocrinum, xv
Cavanilles, Abbé, 93
Champlain, Samuel de, 72
Charlesworth, Geoffrey, 116
checkered lily. *See Fritillaria*
Chelsea Physic Garden, 89
Childanthus fragrans, 127
Childs, John Lewis, 102
Chincherinchee. *See Ornithogalum thyrsoides*
Chinese sacred lily. *See Narcissus tazetta*
Chionodoxa, xv, 19–20
luciliae, 19, 49
sardensis, 19, **21**
siehei, 19
x *Chionoscilla allenii,* 19
CITES, 5, 13
Clarina, Lord, 6, 8
Clark, William, 27
Claytonia virginica, 61
Clifford, H. Trevor, xv
Clint, Mrs. Morris, 146
Clintonia, xvi
Clivia, xvi, 119–120
miniata, 120
nobilis, 120
Clusius, Carolus, 9, 28, 44, 45, 46, 85, 146
Colchicum xv, xvi, 49, 110, 132–135
aggripinum, 134
autumnale, 134
bournmuelleri, 134
bowlesianum, 134
byzantinum, 134, **137**
cilicium, 134
giganteum, 134
luteum, 135

Colchicum (continued)
speciosum, 128, 134
'Album', **130,** 134
variegatum, 134
Colville, James, 99
Compositae, xv
Cooperia, 153
corms, defined, xiv
corn lily. *See Ixia*
Crinum, 116–117, 119, 127, 143
americanum, 119
angustifolium, 113
asiaticum, 119
bulbispermum, 117
campanulatum, 119
cruentum, 119
erubescens, 119
fimbriatulum, 117, **118**
macowani, 119
moorei, 117, 140, 141
obliquum, 113
pedunculatum, **118**
x *powellii*, 117
Crocosmia, xvi, 102, 103, 141
aurea, 103
x *crocosmiiflora*, 103
masonorum, 103
pottsii, 103
Crocus, xv, xvi, 4, 13–16, **21,** 110
autumn, 129–132, 136
cancellatus, 131
goulinyi, 131
kotschyanus, 131
longiflorus, 132
medius, 131
niveus, 132
ochroleucus, 131
pulchellus, 131
sativus, 131
speciosus, 129, **130,** 131
winter/spring, 13–16
biflorus, 14
chrysanthus, 14, 16
"Dutch," x, 16
flavus, xii, 16
korolkowii, 14
laevigatus fontenayi, 4, 129, 132
sieberi, xii, 4, 16
tomasianus, 11, 13, **15,** 25
vernus, x, 13, 16, **17,** 18
Crocus and Colchicum (Bowles), 16
Cyclamen, xiv, xv, 5, 11–13, 135–136
coum, **ix,** 4, 10, 11, **12,** 13
hederifolium, 135
neapolitanum. *See hederifolium, above*
Cyrtanthus, 111–114, 143
angustifolius, 113–114
carneus, 113
cooperi, 113
elatus, 114
hybridus, 114
mackenii, 113
macowani, 113
obliquus, 113
obrienii, 113
parviflorus, 113
purpureus, 114
sanguineus, 114

daffodil. *See Narcissus*
daffodil, summer or Peruvian. *See Hymenocallis*
Dahl, Andreas, 93
Dahlgren, Rolf, xv
Dahlia, xiv, xv, 90–93
coccinea, 92–93, **94**
merckii, 92
pinnata, 93
variabilis, 93
Darwin, Charles, 46
de Busbecq, Ogier Ghiselin, 29, 43–44
de Graaff, Jan, 80
De Hortus Germaniae Liber (Gesner), 44
Denver Botanic Garden, 79
Dicentra
canadensis, 57, 73
cucullaria, viii, 56, 57, **59,** 73
Dierama, 145
pendulum, 145
pulcherrimum, 127, **142,** 145
Dillenius, Johann Jakob, 63
Dioscorides, 28
Disporum, xvi
Dodecatheon, 11
Dodoens, Rembert, 8, 28
dogtooth violet. *See Erythronium*
Dutch East Indies Company, 111, 143
Dutchman's breeches. *See Dicentra cucullaria*

Eddison, Sydney, 25, 37
Eddleman, Edith, 4
Egger, Georg, 19
Elwes, Henry J., 6, 8
Endymion, 26
Eranthis, 22
cilicia, 11
hiemalis, **ix,** xiv, xv, 4, 5, **9,** 10–11, 151
tubergeni, 11
Erythronium, xv, 57–61
albidum, 58
americanum, 56, 57–58, 73
dens-canis, 61
grandiflorum, 58
montanum, **60,** 61
revolutum, 58
tuolumnense, 58
umbilicatum, 58, **59**
Eskimo potato. *See Fritillaria camschatcensis*
Eucomis, 120–121
autumnalis, 121
bicolor, 121, **122**
comosa, 121
pole-evansii, 121

fairy bells. *See Dierama*
false Solomon's seal. *See Smilacina*
Families of the Monocotyledons, The (Clifford and Yeo), xv
fertilization, 149–150
fire lily. *See Cyrtanthus*
Flora of Japan (Ohwi), 87
Florum et coronariarum odoratarumque . . . (Dodoens), 8
Forstius, Evrard, 46
Freesia, xvi, 104
alba, 104
corymbosa, 104
refracta, 104
sparmanii, 104
tubergenii, 104
Fritillaria, xiv, xv, 28–34, 57, 110
affinis, 31
camschatcensis, x, 31
imperialis, 29–30
japonica, 31
lanceolata, 31
meleagris, 28, **29,** 31, 34, 149
michailovskyi, 30–31
pallidiflora, 30, **32**
persica, 30
pontica, 33
purdyi, 31
pyrenaica, 33
thunbergii, 31
verticillata, 31
Fugger family, 44

Galanthus, xv, xvi, 4–10, 22, 36, 110, 146
caucasicus, 8
elwesii, 6, **7,** 8
ikariae, 8
imperati, 6
latifolius, 8
nivalis, **xi,** xiv, 4, 5, 6, 8, 57, 136
'Flore Pleno', 5, 6
'Magnet', **2,** 6
'Viridapicis', 5, 6
platyphyllus, 8
plicatus, 6, 8
Galton, Francis, 105
Galtonia, xv, 104–105
candicans, 104
princeps, 105
viridiflora, 105
Gama, Vasco da, 111
Gardener's Chronicle (journal), 63
geophyte(s)
climate and, x, xii
introduction and naming of, x
as term, viii, xv
Gesner, Konrad, 44
Gladiolus, xiv, xv, xvi, 43, 98–99, 101–102
blandus, 101
byzantinus, 98, 99, 102
callianthus. *See Acidanthera*
cardinalis, 99, 101
carneus, 99
childsii, 102
colvillei, 101
communis, 99
gandavensis, 98, 101
nanceianus, 101
nanus, 98, 101
purpureo-auratus, 101
ramosus, 101
saundersi, 101
tristis, 98, 99, 101, 102
Goldblatt, Peter, xii, 121
Goulimis, C. N., 131
Graeber, P. L., 49
grape hyacinth. *See Muscari*
Gray, Alec, 39
Greatorex, H. A., 6
grex, defined, 81
Griffiths, David, 66
Guernsey lily. See *Nerine sarniensis*
guinea hen flower. *See Fritillaria meleagris*

Haberhauer, Joseph, 50
Habranthus robustus, 146, 147
harebells. *See Dierama*
Heiser, Charles B., Jr., 72
Helianthus, 71–72
tuberosa, **70,** 71–72
Henry, Mary, 89
Herbal (Dodart), 89
Herbert, Dean, 13
Herbertia/Plant Life (journal), 146
Hippeastrum, xv, xvi, 106, 114
propagation of, 153
History of Inventions and Discoveries (Beckman), 44
Holden Arboretum (Ohio), 79
Hondius, Petrus, 72
Hoog, Johannes M. C., 6

Hoog, Michael, 75, 131
Hooker, Joseph Dalton, xv
Hortus Eystettenis (Bessler), 39
hurricane lily. See *Lycoris aurea*
Hyacinthella azurea. See Pseudomuscari azureum
Hyacinthoides, 26–27
  hispanicus, 27
  nonscriptus, 26–27
Hyacinthus, xiv, xv, 52, **53**, 55, 115
  orientalis, 52
  propagation of, 153
Hymenocallis, 105–107
  amamcaes, 106
  calathina, 105
  festalis, 107
  longipetala, 107
  narcissoflora, 105, 106–107, **108**
  occidentalis, 107
  propagation of, 153
  speciosa, 106
Hypoxidaceae, xv

Ifafa lily. *See Cyrtanthus mackenii*
Indian potato. See Apios americana
Ipheion, xv
Ipomoea batata, 98, 153
Ismene calathena, 105
Ixia, xii, 102, 104, 124–126
  bulbifera, 126
  columellaris, 126
  crocata, 103
  maculata, 125–126
  viridiflora, 126

jack-in-the-pulpit. *See Arisaema triphyllum*
Jefferson-Brown, Michael, 39
Jerusalem artichoke. *See Helianthus tuberosa*
Jones, Sam and Carleen, 107
jonquil. *See Narcissus*

Kaempfer, Engelbert, 87
Kaffir lily. *See Clivia miniata*
Keukenhof gardens (Holland), 25, 35, 47, 52, **53**
Kew Gardens (London), xv
Knysa lily. *See Cyrtanthus obliquus*
Korolkov, General, 14
Krelage, E. H., 46
Kronenburg, A., 49

la Chenal, Werner de, 115
Lachenalia, xv, 111, 115–116, 127
  aloides, 115
  bulbifera, 115
  mutabilis, 116
  orchoides var. *glaucina*, 116
  pearsonii, 115
  propagation of, 153
  violacea, 116
Lambert, Nina, 11
Leichtlin, Max, 101
Leiden Botanic Garden (Holland), 13, 30, 57, 107
Lemoine, Victor, 101, 103
Lenglart, M. (tulip grower), 46
Lent lily. See *Narcissus pseudonarcissus*
leopard's lily. *See Fritillaria meleagris*
Leopoldia comosa, 26
L'Ecluse, Charles de. *See* Clusius, Carolus
Leucojum, xvi, 22
  aestivum, 8, 27–28
  vernum, 4, 8, **9**, 10
Lewis, Meriwether, 27
Lilium, xv, xvi, 79–89, 105
  Asiatic hybrids, 80–81, 82, **83**
  auratum, 81, 82
  Aurelian hybrids, 81
  bulbiferum, 80
  canadense, **88**, 89, 152
  candidum, 80, 85, 86
  cernuum, 86
  chalcedonicum, 86
  concolor, 80
  x *dalhansonii*, 85
  hansonii, 85
  henryi, 81, 82
  japonicum, 81, 82
  lancifolium, xiv, 80, 86, 87
  leucanthum, 81
  longiflorum, 86, 152
  martagon, 85, 86
  Olympic hybrids, 82
  Oriental hybrids, 82
  Paisley hybrids, 85
  philadelphicum, 87
  propagation of, 152
  pumilum, 80, 81, 86
  regale, 87, **88**, 152
  rubellum, 81, 82
  sargentiae, 81
  speciosum, 81, 82, 87
  superbum, 89, 152
  x *testaceum*, 86
  tigrinum. See lancifolium, above
  Trumpet hybrids, 81–82
  tsingtauense, 80, 86
Lindley, John, 87, 120
Linnaeus, Carolus, 8, 28, 85, 93
Lobel, Matthias, 28, 39
Longwood Gardens (Pennsylvania), **97**
Lycoris, xvi, 138–139, 143
  albiflora, 140
  aurea, 140
  propagation of, 153
  radiata, **137**, 139, 144
  sanguinea, 140
  sprengeri, 139
  squamigera, 138, 139, 140

McGourty, Fred and Maryann, 75, 102
McRae, Judith Freeman, 81
Madonna lily. *See Lilium candidum*
magic lily. *See Lycoris*
Mathew, Brian, xv, 30
Maw, George, 19
Medeola, xvi
Merendera, xvi
merrybells. See *Uvularia grandiflora, U. perfoliata*
Mexico, Botanic Garden of the City of, 93
Miller, Philip, 89
Missouri Botanical Garden, 121
Modern Miniature Daffodils (Wells), 39
Monocotyledons, The (Dahlgren and Clifford), xv
Montbretia, 102
  pottsii, 103
Muhammad I, 85
Muhammad II, 43
Muscari, xv, 25–26, 55
  ambrosiacum, 26
  armeniacum, **23**, 25
  botryoides, 25
  comosa, 26
  latifolium, 25–26
  muscarini, 26
  propagation of, 153
  taxonomic changes, 26
Mussin-Pushkin, Count, 19

naked lady. *See Amaryllis belladonna*
Narcissus, xiv, xv, xvi, 36, 55, 110, 140
  asturiensis, 13, 43
  bulbocodium, 43
  cyclamineus, 39, 43
    'Jumblie', **40**, 41
  daffodils, xiii–xiv, 5, 18, 25, 35–43, 57
    classification of, 38–43
  eystettenis, 39
  jonquilla, 36, 41, 43
  poeticus recurvus, 41
    'Actaea', **40**, 42
  propagation of, 153
  pseudo-narcissus, 43
  tazetta, 41, 43
  telamonius plenus, 39
  triandus albus, 39
Narcissus (Jefferson-Brown), 39
Narrative of an Explorer in South Africa, A (Galton), 105
Nectaroscordum siculum, 79
Nelson, Rev. John G., 115
Nerine, xvi, 138, 143–145
  bowdenii, 144
  filifolia, 144
  flexuosa, 140
  propagation of, 153
  sarniensis, 111, 143, 144
  undulata, 145
New York Botanical Garden, 31, 47, **48**
Nichols, Beverly, 5
Nizhni Park (Russia), 44
Nomocharis, xv
Nothoscordum, xv

Ohwi, Jisaburo, 87
O'Keeffe, Georgia, 107
onions. *See Allium*
Ornithogalum, xv, 34
  arabicum, 34
  mutans, 34
  thyrsoides, 34
  umbellatum, **32**, 34
Oxalis regnellii, 98

Pancratium narcissiflorum, 105
peacock lily. *See Acidanthera*
Persian violet. *See Cyclamen coum*
pig lily. *See Zantedeschia*
pineapple lily. *See Eucomis*
planting techniques, 148–149
Plantsman, The (journal), xv
Pliny, 28
Polianthes tuberosa, xv, 146
Polygonatum, xvi, 69
  biflorum, 69, 73
  canaliculatum, 71, 73
Proctor, Rob, 55
propagation, 150–153
Pseudomuscari azureum, 26
Purdy, Carl, 66
Puschkinia, xv
  libanotica, 19

quamash. *See Camassia*

Ranunculaceae, xv, 151
Read, Mike, 51
Redfield, Richard, 65
reticulate, defined, xiv
rhizome tuber, defined, xiv

Rhodohypoxis, xv, **112,** 116
baurii, 116
Robinson, William, 28
Roderick, Wayne, 31
Rokku Mountain Alpine Botanic Garden (Japan), 31
root tuber, defined, xiv
Ross, Henry, 95
Royal General Bulbgrowers' Association (Holland), 104, 144

saffron crocus. *See Crocus sativus*
St. John's lily. *See Clivia miniata*
Salmon, Mike, 36
Sanguinaria canadensis, viii, 56, 57, 62–65, **67,** 71, 73
propagation of, 151
scales, defined, xiii
Scarborough lily. *See Vallota speciosa*
Scheepern, Dr. Johan van, xii
Scilla (squill), xv, 16–19, 26, 110, 115
bifolia, **15,** 18, 19
mischtschenkoana, 19
sibirica, 13, 16–18, **20,** 25, **64**
tubergeniana, 18–19
Shaw Arboretum (Missouri), 139
Siberian squill. *See Scilla sibirica*
Smilacina, xvi, 69
racemosa, 71, 73
stellata, 71
snake's head fritillary. *See Fritillaria meleagris*
snowdrop. *See Galanthus*
snowflake. *See Leucojum*
Snyder, Sandy, 52
Solomon's seal. *See Polygonatum*
Souchet, M., 101
Sparaxis, 125, 126–127
bulbifera, 126
grandiflora, 126
pulcherrima, 127
tricolor, 126
spider lily. *See Hymenocallis, Lycoris radiata*
spring beauty. *See Claytonia virginica*
squill. *See Scilla*
squirrel corn. *See Dicentra canadensis*
star of Bethlehem. *See Ornithogalum*
Sternbergia, 5
storm lilies. *See Zephyranthes*
Streptopus, xvi
Sunflower, The (Heiser), 72
Systema Naturae (Linnaeus), 8

Teune, Carla, xii, 13, 30, 57
Thunberg, Karl Peter, 87
Thuron, Sir John, 116
tiger lily. *See Lilium lancifolium*
Tomlinson, John and Helen, 30–31
Tommasini, Muzio de, 13
Trillium, viii, xv, xvi, 56, 57, 65–69, 71, 73, 110
apetalon, 69
cuneatum, 25, 26, 57, 65, **67,** 68, 69, 73
erectum, 65, 68
grandiflorum, 65, 66, **67,** 68, 69, **70**
kamtschaticum, 69
luteum, 65, 69, **70,** 73
propagation of, 151
sessile, 65, 66, 69
smallii, 69
undulatum, 69
Tritonia, 102–103, 125
aurea, 103
crocata, **100,** 103
hyalina, 103
pottsii, 103
tuber-corms, defined, xiv
tuberose. *See Polianthes tuberosa*
tubers (rhizome, root), defined, xiv
Tulbagh, Ryk, 143
Tulbaghia, xv
Tulipa, xiv, xv, 43–52, **54,** 55, 110
aucheriana, 52
Darwin, 46, 47
Double Early, Double Late, 46–47
eichlei, 50
Flemish, 46
fosteriana, 47, 50, 51
greigii, 18, 48, 49
hoogiana, 49
humilis, **50,** 52
kaufmanniana, 18, 19, **20,** 47, 48, 49, 51
korolkowii, 49
Lily Flowered (*retroflexa*), 47
linifolia, 52
Mendel, 46
Parrot, 47
praecox alba, **45**
Rembrandt, 47
Single Early, Single Late, 46, 47, **48**
tarda, 52
Triumph, 46, 47
tubergeniana, 49
viridiflora, 47
tulipomania, 44, 46
tunic, xiv
defined, xiii

University of California Botanic Garden, 31
Uvularia xvi, 71, 73
grandiflora, 71, 73
perfoliata, 71
sessifolia, 71

Vallota, 143
purpurea, 114
speciosa, 114
van der Zalm, Mevrouw, 26
van Sion, Vincent, 39
van Tubergen, C. G., 5, 50, 52, 141, 143
varieties introduced by, 6, 11, 18, 27, 49, 143, 144
Veltheimia, xv, 114, 153
bracteata, 114
capensis, 114
von Webern, Guido, 63, 65

wake-robin. *See Trillium*
wand flower. *See Dierama*
Watsonia, 123–124
aletroides, 123, 124, **125**
borbonica, 124
densiflora, 124
marginata, 124
pillansi, **122,** 124
water lily tulip. *See Tulipa kaufmanniana*
Wells, James S., 39
Wilder, Bob, 138
Wills, Philippa, 132
Wilson, E. H., 63, 87
windflower. *See Anemone*
winter aconite. *See Eranthis*
Wisley Award of Garden Merit, 13
wood lily. *See Lilium philadelphicum*
Wordsworth, William, 38

Yeo, P. F., xv

Zantedeschia, 107–109
aethiopica, 107, **108,** 109
albomarginata, 109
elliottiana, 109
rehmanni, 109
Zephyranthes, 146–147
atamasco, 146, 147
candida, 146
citrina, 147
grandiflora, 147
rosea, 147